TWENTIETH CENTURY VIEWS

The aim of this series is to present the best in contemporary critical opinion on major authors, providing a twentieth century perspective on their changing status in an era of profound revaluation.

Maynard Mack, *Series Editor*
Yale University

IMAMU AMIRI
BARAKA
(LEROI JONES)

A COLLECTION OF CRITICAL ESSAYS

Edited by
Kimberly W. Benston

Prentice-Hall, Inc. *Englewood Cliffs, N.J.*

Library of Congress Cataloging in Publication Data

Main entry under title:
IMAMU AMIRI BARAKA (LEROI JONES).

    (Twentieth century views)   (A Spectrum Book)
    Bibliography: p.
    1. Baraka, Imamu Amiri, 1934-   — Criticism and
interpretation. I. Benston, Kimberly W. II. Title.
PS3552.A583Z7   818'.5'409   78-8269
ISBN 0-13-451302-9
ISBN 0-13-451294-4 pbk.

To Charles T. Davis and Larry Neal,
godfathers and guides

10 9 8 7 6 5 4 3 2 1

PRENTICE-HALL INTERNATIONAL INC. *(London)*
PRENTICE-HALL OF AUSTRALIA, PTY., LTD. *(Sydney)*
PRENTICE-HALL OF CANADA, LTD. *(Toronto)*
PRENTICE-HALL OF INDIA PRIVATE LIMITED *(New Delhi)*
PRENTICE-HALL OF JAPAN, INC. *(Tokyo)*
PRENTICE-HALL OF SOUTHEAST ASIA PTE. LTD. *(Singapore)*
WHITEHALL BOOKS LIMITED, *(Wellington, New Zealand)*

Contents

I. *A Long Breath Singer:* General Assessment

II. *Being in the World:* Biography

III. *Testing the Notes:* Music Criticism

IV. *A Simple Muttering Elegance:* Prose

V. *Black Dada Nihilismus:* Poetry

VI. *Black Labs of the Heart:* Drama

Contents

Acknowledgment

Acknowledgment is gratefully made to those mentioned below for permission to quote:

The Bobbs-Merrill Company, Inc., Indianapolis, for excerpts from *Black Magic Poetry (1961-1967)*, copyright © 1969 by LeRoi Jones, reprinted by permission of the publisher, The Bobbs-Merrill Company, Inc.

Corinth Books, Inc., New Haven, for excerpts from *Preface to a Twenty Volume Suicide Note*, copyright © 1961 by LeRoi Jones. Reprinted by permission of Corinth Books.

The Sterling Lord Agency, Inc., New York, for excerpts from *Black Magic Poetry (1961-1967)*, copyright © 1969 by LeRoi Jones, used by permission of The Sterling Lord Agency, Inc.; and for excerpts from *The Dead Lecturer* © 1964 by LeRoi Jones, used by permission of The Sterling Lord Agency, Inc.

Preface

It is hardly an exaggeration to say that contemporary Afro-American literature and culture would not be what they are without the presence of Amiri Baraka. Name almost any black intellectual, poet, or dramatist who has written in the past fifteen years and attained to some stature and influence, and you name at the same time Baraka. He is to them all—whether or not they know and directly acknowledge it (and most of them do)—what Emerson was to the writers of the "American Renaissance": the categorical explicator of a world they contemplate poetically or philosphically without avoiding its Barakan interpretation.

Even the earliest commentators on Baraka's efforts sensed the emergence of a major force in modern American literature. Favorable or unfavorable, critics found the early work difficult, formless, and undisciplined, but also thought it sufficiently important to demand emphatic response. Richard Howard, for example, said of the poetry: "Nowhere do I recognize in these shattered phrases, in these abrupt releases of attention, the impulse to shape, to seek the containing form." And Bernard Bergonzi, reviewing *The System of Dante's Hell,* concluded bluntly: "It is not the business of art to use chaos to express chaos." Yet had Baraka's art been such and little more, one may doubt whether it would have been singled out for special notice. By 1961 (the date of Baraka's first volume of poetry, *Preface to a Twenty Volume Suicide Note),* there could scarcely have been anything remarkable about a writer whose works were "shapeless" or "chaotic." The spate of works produced by dadaists, surrealists, and "Beats" had already evoked such descriptions and was quite sufficient to drown a few dozen poems by another young "bohemian."

What was remarkable about Baraka's first productions was that they had their effect even before they were understood, and often even when they were misunderstood. The very minimum of the effect, moreover, left his audience with the impression that a poet with a notable sense of language and rhythm was saying something crucial about subjects of importance; at the very worst, he had somehow injured his statement by his violence and obscurity.

In the past decade, criticism of Baraka's works has vastly increased in quality and sophistication as well as in sheer mass. Although the intense nature of his compositions continues to elicit heady judgment, both friendly and hostile, a considerable body of careful, intelligent opinion has formed around Baraka's continuing achievement. This volume of critical essays, the first of its kind devoted exclusively to interpretations of Baraka's work, collects many of the best critiques produced to date. Every aspect of Baraka's literary pursuits has been attended to, for Baraka's accomplishment is finally felt in its totality rather than in any one of its many parts. Indeed, each phase, genre, and medium encompassed by his career modifies the others in mutual response and clarification.

Although I have chosen genre as this book's fundamental organizing principle, a few major themes are felt throughout the essays. Several critics—Lawrence Neal on Baraka's general "sensibility," Larry Coleman on *Tales,* and both Sherley Williams and John Lindberg on *Dutchman,* for example—emphasize the quest of the Barakan self for identity. Whether it be the sexual theme of "maleism" located in *The Toilet* by Robert Tener and in *Madheart* by Charles Peavy, or the more general "existential" concern with the ego's role in collective action that Esther Jackson and Nate Mackey disclose, the underlying topic of most Barakan pieces is seen to be (as Lula pointedly reminds Clay in *Dutchman)* manhood.

The Barakan pursuit of selfhood is typically framed in terms of a substitution of Afro-American for Western culture as one's nourishing influence. Thus many Baraka scholars have concentrated on the stance of his work before both comprehensive and specific aspects of these traditions. Lloyd Brown discovers a complex amalgam of Western literary archetypes in *The System of Dante's Hell,* which the novel's hero both renounces and clings to; Lee Jacobus and Clyde Taylor identify in the poetry a similar preoccupation with such figures as Eliot and Blake combined with a movement toward assumption of a distinctively black voice; and Cecil Brown and Ralph Ellison probe both the costs and the very possibility of this enterprise as reflected in Baraka's critiques of *Afro-American* tradition.

Lastly, most of Baraka's critics, regardless of the era or medium of the work they treat, stress the importance of two particular modes in both the structure and character of Baraka's thought: *myth* and *music*. From comic book heroes and demonic allegories to moral fables of black ascendancy, Baraka uses popular and esoteric myth as a containing framework for more unstable subject matter. And music—be it the dynamic hero of *Blues People* as interpreted by William Fischer, the jazz impulse educed from the poetry by Mackey, or the darkly ambiguous blues/minstrelsy delineated by Owen Brady in his analysis of *Great Goodness of Life*—is quite often a vehicle and manifestation of the disruptive force that myth attempts to enclose. In some sense, the prominent concern of self-search is expressed formally and thematically in Baraka's work as an endless dialectic between myth (with its security and confinement) and music (with its freedom and chaos).

The essays gathered here demonstrate the high level that criticism of Baraka has reached in explicating issues such as these. However, we are, with Baraka, in midcourse, and it would be rash to assert that any collection of such commentary had thoroughly unraveled the mastering design. Fortunately, the degree and range of interest excited by Baraka's work continues to expand as the design continues to unfold. It is hoped that the present volume will prove an impetus and aid to this ongoing study.

K.W.B.

Introduction

by Kimberly W. Benston

I

Amiri Baraka (formerly LeRoi Jones) is one of the most intriguing, controversial, and enigmatic figures in modern letters. However we choose to regard him, there is something compelling and elusive about the image he presents to our minds. In a career of encyclopedic, DuBoisean scope, he has written a novel, political and literary essays, stories, plays, several volumes of poetry, and aesthetic tractates, and he has come to be regarded variously as a teacher, an artist, a politician, a villain, and a prophet. Yet into none of these categories does he fit comfortably, and it is not until we grasp the fact that Baraka's works have been so many stages of self-revelation, an extended autobiography emanating from a peculiarly self-conscious sensibility, and that the significance of Baraka's works lies as much in the consciousness they graph as in the particularities they denote, that we are able to fully understand and measure his achievement.

Baraka entered the American consciousness not merely as a writer but as an event, a symbolic figure somehow combining the craft and insights of Euro-American radicalism with the rebellious energies of young Afro-America. The themes of initiation, renunciation, and reformation with which he is associated are reflected as much by Baraka's literal biography as by the spiritual autobiography that concerns us most. Indeed, the glamour and novelty of his own life of action have had a great share in creating his hold on our imagination. The ordinary contemporary artist of alienation rarely actually abandons his familiar environment for another more strange and uncharted, if also more promising; nor does the ordinary artist of revolution usually become physically embroiled in the violent outbursts his poetry celebrates. Certainly the sense of prodigy, the felt presence of a man wholly extraordinary and full of dangerous possibility had more at first to do with the immediate fame of Baraka's public activities than with the qualities of his early books. Indeed, Baraka's career as a whole is marked by radical and well-known departures of place and personal association as well as of ideology and aesthetic precept. And although the precise details of these matters of personal history are unclear and much debated, it is their resonance that counts. With all their shadow and controversy, they nevertheless suggest a purity of adventure appropriate to Baraka's avowed *ethos of commitment*.

Born to middle-class parents and a heritage of teachers and preachers, Baraka excelled in the institutions that structured his early life. Graduating from Howard University at a precocious nineteen, he endured two years in the Air Force and then, having contemplated such vocations as the ministry, medicine, and painting, left the service with a stack of miscellaneous writings under his arm. "Suddenly I said, 'Gee, I have all this stuff. I guess that makes me a writer.'" Settling in Greenwich Village in the late fifties, Baraka (then LeRoi Jones) quickly gained a formidable reputation as a poet among the more accomplished of America's avant-garde artists. The early poetry collected in *Preface to a Twenty Volume Suicide Note* (1961) reflects the modes of those "schools" with which the young LeRoi Jones had become intimately acquainted: the quasi-mystical emphasis on pure or "open" sound advocated by projectivists like Robert Creeley and Charles Olson; the sophisticated blend of irregular "elegance" and crafted "impurity" of the so-called New York Poets (Kenneth Koch, Frank O'Hara, and others); the bitter, vituperative stance before Western culture characteristic especially of Baraka's close friend Allen Ginsberg; and (less immediately apparent but ultimately more lasting) the aching lyricism inspired by Ornette Coleman, Sun Ra, John Coletrane, and other avant-garde jazz artists. Eloquently expressing the pathos and enervation of a generation dissatisfied by bland material pursuits and fearful of mass destruction, he achieved great personal success, winning recognition and awards from prestigious guardians of literary taste.

But Baraka obeyed his own pronouncements more thoroughly than we normally expect artists to do. If the West is, in fact, a "dying place," he reasoned, he could maintain his admired position within the "mainstream" and from there prophesy his own death; or, by identifying with the burgeoning aspirations of black culture (to which the "radical fringe" seems a mere extension of the dominant society), he could liberate his own seething desire, directing his energy enthusiastically toward a specific (thus precise and meaningful) aim: collective emancipation from a perceived tyranny. It is certainly true that even amidst the sad confusion of an early confession like "Notes for a Speech" (the last poem in *Preface*), Baraka sought an identity not only his but "my so-called people's" as well. But a vast psychological and political distance stretches between the muted yearning of "Notes for a Speech" and the fiery assertion that startled the American mind some half a decade later.

What was exceptional in this development was not so much the intellectual formulation—this had been shaping itself, however amorphously, in Baraka's mind since his Howard days—as the willingness, or rather insistence, on ex-pressing the formulation beyond the realm of metaphor, into the dominion of act. Thus Baraka's divorce from the "benevolent step/mother America" ("Hymn for Lanie Poo") was literalized by his moves from the Village to Harlem, from an inter- to an intraracial marriage, and (in a splendid blend of hermeneutics, symbolism, and performance) from the Western-Christian-"slave" name "LeRoi Jones" to the Pan-African-Islamic-warrior title "Imamu Amiri Baraka." Several events, both in America's life and in Baraka's own, impelled him toward this shift in allegiance from the alienated avant-garde of the American left to the angry vanguard of the Black Arts Movement. Robert F. Williams' 1959 call for armed self-defense by black Americans; violence against civil rights activists in the South and North alike; the assassination of Medgar Evers; the rise of liberated African countries; a prolonged series of impassioned debates on racial politics between Baraka and both Harlem-based black separatists and white Village liberals (capped by the 1964 Town Hall colloquy on "The Black Revolution and the White Backlash")—all these were major elements in Baraka's conversion to black nationalism. But two episodes stand out especially, framing that era of the early sixties: Baraka's trip to Cuba in 1960 and the assassination of Malcolm X in 1965.

In July 1960, Baraka accompanied several black intellectuals and activists (including Williams, Harold Cruse, Julian Mayfield, and John Henrik Clarke) to Cuba and discovered there a profound political rebellion successfully achieved by force of arms. "Revolutionary change through violence" could now be seen as more than fanciful jingoism; it was accomplished fact. "At first, I didn't understand that people could actually make a revolution," Baraka was to reflect later. "When I came back from Cuba I was turned completely around; I was never the same." The poet of violent defeat, of tragic impotence, now saw the means of avoiding the implications of tragedy, and the politically charged poetry that was to appear in *The Dead Lecturer* came into existence.

The years that intervened between the Cuban excursion and permanent abandonment of the mainstream left saw Baraka edging toward a nationalist aesthetic and politics. But, once again, the reality of violence shocked him into an intensified commitment to change: Malcolm X, who had increasingly become a symbol of black struggle and selfhood, was assassinated in early 1965. Whatever its actual circumstances, Malcolm's death signaled for Baraka an immediate and personal challenge:

> For Great Malcolm a prince of the earth, let nothing in us rest
> until we avenge ourselves for his death...
> let us never breathe a pure breath if
> we fail.   "A Poem for Black Hearts"

Baraka's life has continued to evolve in direct response to such subjectively focused perceptions of national and international affairs. He has developed a succession of organizations—The Black Arts Theatre and School (1965), Spirit House (1966), the Black Community Development and Defense Organization (BCD-1968), the Congress of African Peoples (1970)—which, as much as each of his identifiable artistic phases, emanate from a matrix of political and philosophical speculation. The terminal form of this evolution, as with all change, must be death, but Baraka ultimately wishes us to be as unconcerned with the final shape of his private life as with the permanence of any other institution. "When I die," he declares, "the consciousness I carry I will to black people" ("Leroy"). It is to that "consciousness," then, that we now turn our discussion.

II

Baraka's enterprise is the most general of which a contemporary artist-intellectual can conceive. Its themes are not only the dialectics of will and destiny; the discovery of self through recognition and creation of lineage; the ambiguities and necessities of history; and cultural values, but the rescue of all this through action: the restoration of energy and purpose to human activity, and the sense that this must be accomplished in an extreme situation, hence through a series of urgent (even violent) acts. His work thus presents an essential play between an action and its perspective, between the present and all known (historical) and foreseen (prophetic) time, between the loss of oneself in the moment and the recognition of oneself in terms of one's whole destiny. This duality endures, however radical the changes in ostensible subject matter or in genre. Or one might put it that the underlying subject matter itself never changes, and in his first works as in his latest the same issues dominate: there is an obsessive and consistent investigation of the place of the self in the "motion of history," of the private desire in an enveloping communal context, of the individual passion in the relentless rush of brute events.

The unity of Baraka's art—of his continuing spiritual autobiography—has been obscured in great measure by the frequency and violence of his conspicuous changes, political and artistic. Indeed, amid his dazzling array of statement, counterstatement, and innovation, Baraka's espousal of "change" as both act and maxim has been the singular distinct constant. Both the pain felt in his early poetry and drama and the celebration heard in his later works stem from the exertion of mind and body to win an expressive freedom from inherited structures, including those we have made and willed to ourselves. Clay's central speech in *Dutchman*, for example, is a major creative triumph precisely in its portrayal of the frightening yet liberating fluidity of self. His newly released imagination, exploring the life it might fully possess, fails to flow into the eagre of a collective consciousness and hence collides catastrophically with an intractable world that will not satisfy it. Clay, as embodiment of the ever-questing, ever-purifying self, was superseded in Baraka's drama by Walker, the purposeful revolutionary martyr, then by Black Man, the nationalist hero of the allegorical "morality play" *Madheart*, and, most recently, by the entire triumphant nation of *Slave Ship*. But we feel the metamorphic struggle everywhere in Baraka's poetry too, as his voice, now lyrical, now oratorical, now private, now public, searches for what Baraka, in his aesthetic manifestos, calls a "post-Western form," for what the old man of *The Slave* more suggestively terms a "meta-language"—a medium in which will and act, ideality and achievement, perception and expression can join in a unity beyond figuration, beyond the metaphors of art and the compromises of politics. It is a search fueled necessarily by ceaseless transformation, for Baraka, like his greatest direct progenitor, Dante, writes his autobiography within the tragic-comic order of

history, in proud defiance of the hell of fixity and in anxious preparation for his particular version of utopic vision. A "revolutionary
poet," he creates as a shaman of transition.

As a whole, Baraka's art charts the progress of a self or voice in its
agon of stasis against flux and its concomitant attempt to overcome
the dilemma of all natural energy (or "life," as Baraka would put it),
which has to seek its consummation in strife even though strife
threatens to consume and expend it. Nothing, no ego, no form, no
principle, is regarded as finally established; everything is in a process
of endless and progressive mutation. Baraka's beliefs, like the staccato explosiveness of the language that attempts to enclose them,
resist precise definition, not primarily because of intellectual incon-
sistency (a charge brought with some truth and more passion against
him) but principally because of an unshakable fear that delimitation
is only limitation, that minute description can only result in murderous circumscription. Such an attitude issues, in its negative aspect,
in a blind horror of anything that appears immutable, changeless,
or ultimate, and in a consequent fidelity to moods and passions that
retrospectively appear only momentary self-indulgences. But
Baraka's commitment to change is motivated by neither mental lazi-
ness nor love of undifferentiated vitality but by a fervent idealism
that equates passion with significance and consecrates no desire that
cannot be fully translated into act. For him, the question, "What is
tomorrow/that it cannot come/today?" ("Valery as Dictator"), is
solicitous and ravenous, not rhetorical.

Baraka's image as a restless experimenter devoted to disruptive
discovery is fixed in the public imagination by his political rhetoric
("the revolution-change" is a favorite Barakan formula), but his
iconoclastic temperament is evinced no less by his aesthetic specu-
lations. Whether speaking as a young practitioner of projectivist
verse, as revolutionary black artist, or as neo-Marxist theorist, Baraka
has championed the artistic *process* at the expense of its particular
products, elevating art as "energy" while denigrating it as formal
manifestation. Again, the assertion of inevitable metamorphosis,
expressed as opposition to received ("fossilized") traditions and their
artifacts, provides the continuity between the projectivist and Marxist
poet: the early "expressionistic" theory — an insistence that works of
art are significant insofar as they express human feeling and reveal
the particular qualities of a culture — and the later "historicist"
doctrine — a view of all experience, including cultural activity, as
time- and class-determined — are linked by an underlying relativism.

Baraka has always been fascinated by the dissolution and reshaping of artistic forms as they are subjected to the force of new social and emotional conditions. This concern is reflected most systematically in *Blues People,* a treatise on Afro-American music that treats the history of black expression as a ceaseless dialectical movement progressing from a "root" form of black inner life (such as blues, bebop, or modern jazz) through popular debasement to eventual reappearance of the essential energy in a new form. The detailing of this process is not primarily the record of a sustained tradition, or the tracing of similarities and continuities of styles; it is rather an essay of exceptional intensity on the effects of psychological crisis on a culture, and the possibilities of artistic response to such crisis. Baraka's imagination and critical sense are involved most by the outbreak of a new and spontaneous gesture in response to an altered spiritual condition (thus bebop is examined as a product of a particular quality of Afro-American urban alienation), or by the detection of the altered attitude behind the facade of traditional forms (thus rhythm and blues is viewed as exploiting a variety of preestablished techniques to effect a more subversive, "underground" expression). Some of the assertions of "energy's" triumph over "form" are less than subtle, and the actual historical conclusions are often as provocative as the manner that evokes them—hence Ralph Ellison's sharp critique of Baraka's study—but Baraka's dramatic sense catches with penetrating sympathy and great vividness the tension involved in that historical moment when an art form must choose between continuation or dissolution of canonical assumptions. It is such moments that Baraka's own art, following his theoretical pronouncements, seeks and, in the seeking, helps to create.

Baraka has never much cared whether his writing is judged "good" or "bad." This is not simply a rejection of the authority of traditional arbiters (although the issue of *authority* is indeed crucial, one which we must examine); he does not admit that sort of distinction, with its implication of a fixed standard, as a matter of general principle. Even artistic standards must flow as part of the enveloping material stream: "Masterpieces are for museums" *(Black Music).* The most famous (and to my mind, muddled) de-idealizing of art in the face of "external reality" occurs in the poem "Black Art," which asserts that "poems are bullshit unless they are/teeth or trees or lemons piled/on a step." The catalogue of random, seemingly unrelated objects that poems must *be* (and not simply be about) serves to emphasize the concreteness, the *object-ness* to which Baraka's aesthetic, at once utilitarian and incantatory, aspires. Baraka here uses the word to assualt the supposed priority of tropes over the natural objects they re-present. Of course, the status of the poem, "Black Art," as "pure," unrelieved mediation (and, more bluntly, as inert printed matter) belies its own exclamation of the natural world's authority over the word; nevertheless, the poem, in the very confusions of its literal declarations, cogently illustrates Baraka's essentially bifurcated view of art and accounts for his readers' consequent difficulty before the texts he has given them. For Baraka, literature is at once much less and much more than it is to the typical modern reader. It is less because he does not consider art an autonomous form existing as an object for detached contemplation; rather, it is indissolubly linked to the experience that gave rise to it and, in its pure state, is actually that experience itself. Yet literature is much more for Baraka than for a contemporary formalist because no appreciation of it can be purely linguistic; it is always affective ("im-pressive," Baraka would say) and hence profoundly social, "in the world." Representation for Baraka is intolerable insofar as it deviates from its referents, but it is necessary and even desirable insofar as it resists the oblivion of silence (a fate both suffered and courted by many of his Euro-American contemporaries) and marks a stance with authentic force against competing voices. The experience that Baraka's own writing chronicles may therefore be seen as a struggle to reconcile the self with language, to create at once a voice and a world worthy of expression.

Thus, for all his obvious iconoclasm, there remains in Baraka a longing for presence, a desire to recover and redress lost meanings that verges on a nostalgia for origins. It is at base a yearning for *power,* political in its particular emphases, poetic in its general resistance to the modern sense of entropy and impotence. Baraka's poetry, even before his appropriation of the myth of primordial African ethos (see especially *Blues People, A Black Mass,* and the verse of *Black Magic Poetry* and *Spirit Reach*), invents both the loss of power and the purpose for this "loss"—the temporal quest for origins or the recovery of power, the twofold struggle to re-imagine and then transcend the geneological source:

> I stare out
> at the horizon
> until it gets up
> and comes to embrace

> me. I
> make believe
> it is my father.
> This is known
> as genealogy.   "Hymn to Lanie Poo" (Part 4)

> ...We are in our hip terribleness so cool yet slow.
> A rocket bursts part our face killing our whole history.
> The spinx our father squats in the desert waiting to be caught
>   up with.
>   "Somebody's Slow is Another Body's Fast," in *Spirit Reach*

Baraka's art is forever rewriting a myth of lineage. Moreover, it exemplifies Wallace Stevens' adage, "Genealogy is the science of correcting other genealogists' mistakes"; its quest for power takes the form of measuring the difference between the genealogy he invents and those which his contemporaries and forebears have created. The authority that comes with canon-formation is both Baraka's foe and ambition, and he conceives this project as genealogical revisionism. Thus his new order would restore a subtending value structure, which the more apparent effort of deconstruction would dismantle. We see this not only in such masterful critiques of Western culture as the "Crow Jane" poems (in *The Dead Lecturer*), in which the poet's voice is transformed from a "teller" of the dominant tradition to an invocatory agent of its destruction; it also shapes Baraka's discussions of Afro-American tradition, such as "The Myth of a 'Negro Literature,'" in which the whole of black writing is displaced (and thereby dismissed) into "mainstream" literature. Perhaps the most striking instance of such revisionism occurs in *The System of Dante's Hell* where, as Lloyd Brown observes, various literary archetypes converge upon one another, competing for authority as guides to the hero's pilgrimage. By thus organizing his precursors, Baraka figuratively abrogates his obligations to them all, for his stationing crowds them between the visionary truth of his private journey and the actual (written) record of his experience.

Baraka's sundry innovations in artistic form and media are united by this intention of confronting, resituating, and ultimately displacing those literary authorities he discerns as threatening. As several of the essays collected here reveal, he loves to challenge the work of others. Much of the early poetry, especially that of *The Dead Lecturer,* is a direct challenge to both academic influences (especially Eliot, Pound, and Cummings) and the young poets associated with

Baraka's Village years (Creeley, Duncan, Olson, Ginsberg, and others).
Later volumes, such as *In Our Terribleness* and *It's Nation Time*, seek to arrest the formal power of Afro-American oral modes while supplanting their "universal" formulae with urgent political content. The drama, from the part-naturalistic, part-absurdist *Dutchman* to the archaically ceremonial *Slave Ship*, develops and diverges self-consciously from similar contemporary theatre, from Albee's *The Zoo Story* to *Dionysus in '69*. *Great Goodness of Life* is, in part, an answer to Genet's influential play, *The Blacks*, just as *Jello* and *Experimental Death Unit #1* are parodistic re-enactments of, respectively, popular entertainment (the Jack Benny Show) and esoteric experimentalism (Beckettean theatre). These agons of form and meaning evince the paradoxical insight to which Baraka's art (unlike his theoretical declarations) bears witness: in composing the desired "meta-language," a rebel poet must incorporate the language of an alien idiom in order to transcend it. This complex lesson lies at the heart of the noted essay, "Technology and Ethos," wherein Baraka expresses with almost self-mocking intensity his need to shape a new "kind of instrument," one that eclipses the standards and methods of his predecessors:

> A typewriter?—why shd it only make use of the tips of the fingers.
> ...If I invented a word placing machine, an "expression-scriber," *if you will*, then I would have a kind of instrument into which I could step & sit or sprawl or hang & use not only my fingers to make words express feelings but elbows, feet, head, behind, and all the sounds I wanted, screams, grunts, taps....

In their search for an "expression-scriber" as fresh and radical as the content of a "post-Western" revolutionary vision, Baraka's works variously engage the opening query of "Betancourt": "What are/ influences?" The lack of psychological subtlety and general "crudity" of structure evident in certain of his poems and plays (especially the poetry of *Black Magic Poetry* and in the agit-prop drama) reflect his most enraged attack upon inherited conventions. Yet in most of his writings the ideological rejection of traditional systems is held in dramatic tension with the poet's exorcistic rivalry with those systems. The protagonists of such plays as *Dutchman, The Slave,* and *A Black Mass* encounter within the plays and within themselves the very forms of consciousness they despise. Baraka, like every great revolutionary poet, has realized that he can begin to say what he is, or wishes to become, only by saying what he is not. And, like his self-limited and self-liberating heroes (for example, Clay of *Dutchman*, Walker of *The Slave*, or the titular hero of "A Poem for Willie Best"), he can create anew only with some recourse to the withering grammar of previous and pernicious generations. But by shocking that grammar sufficiently, by twisting it into unprecedented postures, he can make it generate new and living forms. It is only *with* the typewriter that, paradoxically, he can inscribe into his art the blueprint for a new instrument.

Baraka's poetry, in comparison with that of such Afro-American contemporaries as Hayden, Brooks, or Harper, is generally concerned with processes rather than moments: it is driven by a dialectical energy that pits idea against idea, image against image, voice against voice. In the effort to assert genealogical authority, the latter opposition is the crucial one. When Baraka effects a happy reconciliation of self with language, it is invariably "logocentric": even a casual perusal of the verse reveals a poet who distrusts writing and longs for the proximity of the self to its voice. This has always been so. Yet there is a discernible line of development in the poetry that leads from a willingness to interweave scenic and vocal details to an absolute privileging of the oral impulse. In such early poems as "The A.B.C.s," "One Night Stand," and "Duke Mantee," and in much of *The System of Dante's Hell*, the perceiving self emerges from the finely attentive rendering of visual detail. The process in which such personal revelation unfolds owes a good deal to the *paysage moralisé* of Cummings and Williams, and these early works are suffused with the unsentimental urban pastoral characteristic of imagist compositions. In some of the later works collected in *Preface*, however, the poet's dependence upon the visual leads to a despair of voicelessness:

> Can you hear this? Do you know
> who speaks to you? Do you
> know me?...
> these words
> are not music. They make no motions
> for a dance.   "The Death of Nick Charles"

By the time of *The Dead Lecturer*, we feel Baraka, under the influence of projectivist theory, successfully elevating sound above sight as the mark of apprehension:

> (Mama Death.
> For dawn, wind
> off the river.
> Wind
> and light, from
> the lady's hand. Cold
> stuff, placed against
> strong man's lips. Young gigolo's
> on the 3rd estate. Young ruffians
> without no homes.   "For Crow Jane"

The debt to imagism is clear here in the careful visual definition of the poem's context and in its compact, beautifully crafted simplicity. But the projectivist reach beyond imagist limits is apparent from the blues intonation of the first line and from the strategic little explosions of "gigolos" and "ruffians"—words that in their polysyllabic Italicism and colloquial tone break the sequence of imabic ponderosity, tumble the discourse from sight into sound, and, above all, by the slight surprise of their relation with "the 3rd estate," intimate a configuration of the ordering mind in what might otherwise seem a pure representation of sensory perception. In a poem that is on one level about the conflict between writing and voicing ("cold stuff" from the "lady's hand" set against "strong man's lips"), Baraka deliberately supersedes objective detail through the projectivist activity of "breathing through" the strict metrical enclosure.

Baraka's overt quarrel with projectivism and other contemporary poetic movements concerned the relation of politics and art, and it is openly waged throughout *The Dead Lecturer*. His conception of unfettered utterance aspired only secondarily to liberation of the particular thought or feeling; its primary ambition was eloquence in the Emersonian sense: prophetic speech. Art and politics were equally "in the world," and Baraka conceived it his duty to unite them. Anything less, he announces in his "Short Speech to My Friends," would be the "compromise" of "silence":

> A political art, let it be
> tenderness. ...
>   I address
>   / the society
>   the image, of
>   common utopia.

...Let the combination of morality
and inhumanity
begin.

Baraka found that, while his peers in the avant-garde were content to be "neutral" witnesses to cultural fragmentation, he was impelled as a black poet to be a chronicler of exile and an annunciator of nationhood. The need to break out of what seemed a privacy without authenticity into a large historical realm of collective experience moved him to anomalous poetic strategies and, at times, encouraged the expression of a second self cruder in sensibility, more resistant to the temptation of the aloofly elegant gesture. But in the exchange of muses whereby Baraka declares, "The poor have become our creators. The black. The thoroughly ignorant" ("Short Speech to My Friends"), black oral modes—the dozens, scatting, shouts, chants, blues and jazz rhythms—already evident in *Preface,* become the dominant poetic resource. The assumption of authority as a "long breath singer," the canonical mastery of "the crafted visions of the intellect" ("Green Lantern's Solo"), is signaled by an ability to people an expansive Afro-American landscape, to *name* in public invocation a lineage encompassing folk, personal, and racial heritage:

> For tambo, willie best, dubois, patrice, mantan, the
> bronze buckaroos.
> For Jack Johnson, asbestos, tonto, buckwheat,
> billie holiday.
> For tom russ, l'overture, vesey, beau jack...
> "Black Dada Nihilismus"

> My brother, Bigger Thomas, son of
> Poor Richard, father, of poor
> lost jimmy, locked together all
> of us...
> Bigger laughed...
> and his father, and brother, and the son's
> son, all rising, lord, to become the thing you told us.
> "That Mighty Flight"

Baraka thus creates for himself a voice that does not remain with the speaker but is collective, striving to make the communal audience speakers too, in an imaginative pattern of call-and-response. Where in the early poetry such visual notations as the open parenthe-

sis signify a turning inward that reduces the poet to an isolated observer who looks and marks but does not touch or speak, the spacing,
punctuation, lineation, and other typographical devices employed
in later verse guide the "reader's" hearing of the poem whether he
or she reads it silently or aloud. Indeed, Baraka has striven increasingly for a printed form that directs the poem's oral expression; that, in fact, negates the poem as written text, as memorial, and
affirms it as a score for performance, as act: "This poem has now
said/what it means, left off/life gone seconds ago" ("Ready or Not").
The wistful recognition in *Preface* and *The Dead Lecturer* that
"these words are not music" is replaced in *Black Art, In Our Terribleness,* and *Spirit Reach* by an exultant attention to the collective
spirit he hears "singing through my face...describing its own voice"
("Evil Nigger Waits for Lightnin'").

When we turn to Baraka's theatre, we find that for all the change
in medium the concerns are strikingly alike. Not only is there a continuity of subject matter, but of formal innovation as well. From the
ground-breaking manifesto "The Revolutionary Theatre" (1964)
to the post-nationalist notes on *The Motion of History,** Baraka has
insisted on a theatre that energetically seeks new forms, new intensity, and new language to present and be a part of our constantly
changing culture. And in the experimentalist modern Afro-American theatre that *Dutchman* symbolically initiated, no single body of
plays is more resolutely exploratory than Baraka's. The structural
metamorphoses displayed from *Dutchman* and *The Slave* (supra-
naturalistic) through *The Baptism* and *Madheart* (symbolic and allegorical) to *A Black Mass* and *Slave Ship* (mythic and ritualistic)
encompassed and, in great measure, accomplished the spectrum of
formal development demarcated by the contemporary black drama
movement. Every stage of innovation, however, is motivated by the
same urge: to expose the ferocious egocentricity upon which the
structures of material acquisition and power are erected and, further, to identify the social context of human action. Characters acting
and reacting upon each other, rather than the hero's inner life, comprise the basic unit of the Barakan theatre. (This may help explain
why his plays present a procession of interrelated types: drunken
matriarchs, destructive white seductresses, young black poets, old
slaves.) The singular consciousness in isolation is always the central
object of purgation and, whether it results from the tragic ambiv-

*See "Baraka: An Interview" by K. W. Benston, listed in the bibliography.

alence of a Walker, from the pathetic timidity of a Court Royal, or from the vicious rapacity of an Uncle Sam, isolation is ultimately in these dramas its own punishment, death no more than a symbol of irremediable self-estrangement.

Baraka's theatre is one of deliverance, inexorably oriented toward liberation through confrontation. At the same time, the very titles of several of his plays—*The Eighth Ditch, Dutchman, The Slave, The Toilet, Experimental Death Unit #1, Slave Ship*—betray metaphorically an obsession with images of entrapment and imprisonment. There persists throughout his plays an incredible hunger for hope, and yet his heroes are afraid. They often act like children when they are frightened: they laugh and swagger...a rather creaky laugh and nervous swagger, which force the audience to confront a weakness too evident to be disguised that is yet an energy too formidable to be insignificant. Baraka's universe, like those of his ancestors "Poor Richard" (Wright) and "lost jimmy" (Baldwin), derives partly from childhood, as is evident in plays such as *The Toilet* and *The Baptism* as well as in the quasi-autobiographical prose of *The System of Dante's Hell* and *Tales*. With consummate skill and accuracy, he has seized upon the poetic truth of the language of childhood—of speech directed as a shower of stones, a nakedness of diction with no shadows, no ambiguity, no false mystery behind it—and crafted it into a vehicle of sudden illumination and unqualified anger. Such is the language of the awakened Clay, the defiant Walker, the bitter Karolis, the aroused Black Man, and countless lesser figures.

Language itself, as in the poetry, is a major protagonist throughout Baraka's drama. A struggle for control of the available syntax lies at the very heart of the early plays. From the opening dumbshow of *Dutchman*, in which Clay stares innocently after a "face" designated in the text as "it," Lula is metonymically reduced to an inhuman talking body, a *voix fatale* more magpie than muse. Soon they are engaged in linguistic rivalry, including an agon of naming (*Lula.* "Are you talking to my name? *Clay.* "What is it, a secret?"). Clay's attempt at self-assertion through rhetorical resistance is cut short by his own recognition that a dependence on borrowed words, on the "metaphors" of Lula's "bastard literature," separates him from the cleansing language of violent acts. Walker, too, laments that "I learned so many words...but almost none of them are mine." Their entrapment in alien idioms involves a loss of cultural continuity, a divorce from the language of their shared past. As Baraka's theatre progresses, leaving these tragic victims at the threshold of an

immense discovery, the oppressive force represented by Lula is
further abstracted (and thus distanced) as the Voice in *Great Goodness of Life,* the inarticulate beast-devils in *Madheart* and *A Black
Mass,* and finally as the howling "Voice" of Uncle Sam in *Slave
Ship,* which, after waging a prolonged war of sound against the
captive black nation, suffers a death-by-uproar inflicted by the collective exclamations of the "old slave ship." In his dramatic chronicles, as in his more personal poetic annals, Baraka fashions a voice
for himself and for his people as a tool of self-liberation, only to discover that this voice and the liberated self are one and the same.

III

Baraka, the poet of process and dramatist of consciousness-in-
transition, concentrates his imagination with unbridled verve and
exquisite poise on the present moment—without, like other modern
writers, seeking to arrest it as a haven in the flux of time. Yet he
also has been fascinated and bedeviled by the past, and he often
seems uncertain as to whether he should be exorcising it (as in *Slave
Ship*), integrating it into his vision (as in *In Our Terribleness*), celebrating it (as in *Blues People*), or perhaps perpetuating it as a kind
of warning (as in *A Black Mass*). From the beginning of his career,
Baraka has been aware that history as creation and as action is never
separable from that various spectacle that stretches backward in
time: "A culturally aware black politics would use all the symbols of
the culture, all the keys and images out of the black past, out of the
black present, to gather the people to it" ("The Need for a Cultural
Base," in *Raise Race Rays Raze*). In the same moment he would
plunge us forward into the flow of life and point us backward to
the assembled testimony of the past, to the plantation and the slave
ship and the flickering shadows of African ceremony.

Like many Afro-American writers, then, Baraka acknowledges
that to know who you are implies awareness of where you've come
from: genealogical revision and self-definition are more generous,
less impetuous, when they proceed from a sense of continuity. But
Baraka rarely privileges history as knowledge, as archaeological
recollection that assesses but does not alter. It would, in fact, be fee-

ble to say Baraka treats "the problem of history." His works assert
that history is human destiny; that revolution is the authentic and
"real" form of the historical process; that the individual will must
come to terms with the logical necessities of change. History for
Baraka is, again, process: a dynamic dialectic of opposing forces. It
is more an avenging than a recording angel; indeed, Baraka's re-
ifications of history—in *Blues People*, in *Dutchman*, in *Slave Ship*—
transform it from a category of human understanding to the substance of life itself. In his writing (as in his own life), history becomes
radical reality.

Baraka's secular gospel proclaims but one commandment: man's
salvation is to move with history. For his heroes there is a fatality
prior to individual fate; they cannot accept a world independent of
their acts, and so endeavor to identify themselves with forces greater
than their being, even at the risk of losing part of their humanity.
Walker's declaration in *The Slave* stands as a Barakan credo: "Right
is in the act! And the act itself has some place in the world...it makes
a place for itself." The early characters suffer from an inability to
enact what they perceive, to write in blood the revolutionary equa-
tion of deed and intelligence. Clay dreams on history, remaining
powerless to destroy what he fears and abhors. He is a witness who
interprets the world but cannot transform it, a prophet who speculates on the "simple act" of revolt but does not participate in the
event. Similarly, Walker nearly dies from paralytic indetermination
(the assertion just quoted is followed by the confused query,
"Right?").

Yet Clay and Walker represent not so much Baraka's own hesita-
tions as his current views of the events in which his protagonists
were actors as well as victims. Doubt, petty bickering, and projective fantasy, he was telling us, would be violently terminated by the
overpowering "motion of history." Increasingly, Baraka's heroes
find the power and resolve to seize history by the throat and engage
the world in deadly encounter. They see history embodied in rebellion and struggle; their dream intertwines the fragmented past and
the *hic et nunc* of present realities, but focuses most clearly on a
future that promises a society released from the humiliations of
denial, deceit, and subjugation. They conspire with history to forge
particles of selfhood into a communal whole, to realize in fact as in
vision that "the nation is like our selves":

get up rastus for real to be rasta farari
   ras jua
   get up got here bow
     It's Nation
     Time!

                                     "It's Nation Time"

    Baraka's poetic exhortation to collective greatness gains from the contrary extremities of a philosophy devoted at once to the exaltation of the individual and the search for a perfect community. As much as for any of his characters, the aim of Baraka's pursuit of identity, of what I've presumed to term an extended quest for oracular speech, is a fusion of autobiography and history aligned with the evolving spiritual biography of his people. Whatever his ideological position, he has attempted to mold a rhetoric that enables him to dissolve the differences between history and self—as well as between the different functions of the self (political, natural, artistic)—and so to overcome political disenchantment by revealing himself (in a manner paralleled in our history only by Emerson and DuBois) as the representative citizen. Much of the specific political action in Baraka's life may be subsumed under this general notion; simply put, he seeks a role in living history to advance and sustain his idea of man.

    Baraka's recent rejection of cultural nationalism and embracement of Marxism is understandable in light of the view of history embedded in his work. For cultural nationalism, with its Arcadian vision of great civilizations that flourished before the blue-eyed devil sowed strife in the garden (a utopic idealization party fostered by such Barakan works as *Blues People* and *Slave Ship*), is ultimately a philosophy *against* history. Baraka willingly accepts his onetime advocacy of this vision as a necessary stage in the struggle for decolonialization. I would go further in seeing the former and present positions as equally of a piece with both the struggle for genealogical authority and the search for a corporate self, which together compose the basic enabling myth of Baraka's entire *oeuvre*. Marxism, more fully than cultural nationalism, lends him the fundamental sense of belonging to a definite time, a definite place, and a specific milieu, without which authentic pronouncements, even a true understanding of the self, cannot be born. This is for Baraka a deeply felt need. Its psychological roots extend at least as far back as "Notes for a Speech":

                    Those
            heads, I call
            my "people."
                    (And who are they. People. To concern
            myself, ugly man. ...
            They shy away. My own
            dead souls, my, so called
            people.

"Fraternal liberation," the current watchword of the Barakan enterprise, means a type of relationship cleansed of both sentimentality
and suspicion, in which the individual can feel trusted, hence encouraged: "concerned." Marxism appears to Baraka at this moment
the best available means of attaining the ever-desired end: to break
through the barriers of personality and establish a binding relation
with the world of others.

Baraka needs a norm for his action, an indication about the future,
a principle of structure and vigor. There may be no more connection
between his eclectic Marxism and actual international revolution
than there previously was between cultural nationalism and the
"last days of the American empire." At present, the two orders of fact
are related (as they were before) primarily by Baraka's decision that
they be so. Eventually, Marxism will likely prove for him the latest
development of the implacable need to act "in the world" by which
he is possessed. We may look forward to the progress of his continuing adventure from no better perspective than that afforded by
the final "summit" reached by the young poet-hero of *The System of
Dante's Hell:*

> Stars were out. And there were no fists just dull distant jolts that spun
> my head. It was in a cave this went on. With music and whores danced
> on the tables. I sat reading from a book aloud and they danced to my
> reading.

This last vision comes at the novel's quintessential Barakan moment:
the point of transition between the wretched man who *was* and the
wiser visionary who *is,* at once the point of departure and the point
of arrival of the work we have before us. The chaotic conjunction of
book and dance is a perfect emblem of the polarities that charge Baraka's art: the *logos,* the principle of intelligibility that expresses his

vision yet (de)limits the aspirations of his voice; and the ecstatic *ritual*, the mode of the body that unifies act and desire but only momentarily interrupts analytic perception and only illusorily suspends the flux of history. Their combination produces a delirium and a vertigo for him who would seek the necessary "meta-language," the master form. When, and only when, this is achieved, he may cease the task of genealogical revision and declare himself (with all who "sing through [his] face") the father's true successor. Until then, the adventure must continue, prodded by a haunting but never answerable question:

> Though I am a man
> who is loud
> on the birth
> of his ways. Publicly redefining
> each change in my soul, as if I had predicted
> them,
>   and profited, biblically, even tho
>   their chanting weight,
>   erased familiarity
>   from my face.
>   A question I think
> an answer; whatever sits
> counting the minutes
> till you die.
>   When they say, "It is Roi
>   who is dead?" I wonder
>   who will they mean?
>   "The Liar"

PART ONE

A Long Breath Singer: General Assessment

That Boy LeRoi

by Langston Hughes

...In a talk I made in Paris concerning American Negro poetry, I said that I am glad Negro poets are doing everything other American poets are doing, and that their styles range from Harlemese to Villagese, from the conventional to the beatnik, from Pulitzer Prize winning Gwendolyn Brooks to Obie Award winner LeRoi Jones. Mr. Jones is currently the white-haired black boy of American poetry. Talented in other forms of writing as well, particularly theatre, Mr. Jones might become America's new Eugene O'Neill — provided he does not knock himself out with pure manure. His current offering, "The Toilet," is full of verbal excrement.

I remember that much vaunted realism of David Belasco in my youth. None of the Belasco productions I saw on Broadway can hold a candle to "The Toilet," scenic or acting-wise. The set for "The Toilet" consists largely of a series of urinals, and the first thing the first actor does when he comes onstage is to use one. All the facilities of a high school toilet are used by the other performers, too, at various times. The bold and brilliant bunch of young Negro actors look as if they all come directly from Shirley Clark's roughneck film, "The Cool World," whose leading man now plays, as if to the manner born, the leading role in "The Toilet." So realistic is both acting and direction in this play that the leading white boy, beaten to his knees by a gang of Negroes, drools spittle upon the stage as he tries to rise. The triumphant black boys end up sticking the white student's head into a urinal. What all this does for race relations (as if it mattered at this late date), I do not know.

Both "The Toilet" and "The Slave" may be taken as serious exercises in masochism and sadism, full of bloody kicks, and better than "The Brig" for thrills. Certainly the whites at the St. Marks Playhouse are well beaten up in both plays before the evening ends. In "The Slave," Al Freeman, Jr., as a black nationalist violently opposed to white liberals, slaps, kicks, punches, shoots, and physically does in all the whites on stage. At one point in the proceedings, he pointed his pistol dead at Nat Hentoff in the first row of the auditorium. Long ago, the bully boy of Southern folklore, Stackolee, used to boast, "I'm the baddest Negro God's got." But Stackolee grew up in the good old days before the era of James Baldwin and LeRoi Jones, so Stackolee never laid eyes on Al Freeman, Jr. in a New York theater. I think that Stackolee, as a Negro of the old school, although of the sporting world, might be horrified, especially at the language used before ladies.

Therefore, for the sake of today's sensitive Negroes and battered white liberals, I would like to offer the producers at St. Mark's Playhouse a suggestion—double cast both plays, and alternate performances racially. Every other night let all the present Negro characters be played by white actors, and vice versa. Four times a week I would like to see *white* school boys in "The Toilet" beating up a *colored* boy and sticking his head into a urinal. In "The Slave," let a bullying *white* man kick, curse, browbeat, and shoot a nice liberal *black* professor and his wife in their suburban living room. To reverse the complexions on stage every other night by alternating casts would make for a very intriguing theatrical evening. Black would then be white—and white, black—which alternately would cancel out each other—since some critics (like the able Michael Smith in *The Village Voice*) claim that LeRoi Jones may not really be writing about color at all, but instead is concerned with no group "smaller than mankind." God help us all!

The Development of LeRoi Jones

by Lawrence P. Neal

...In order to ensure his salvation and to escape from the
supremacy of the white man's culture the native [intellec-
tual] feels the need to turn backwards towards his unknown
roots.... Because he feels he is becoming estranged...[he]
decides to take all for granted and confirms everything
even though he may lose body and soul....

FRANTZ FANON—THE WRETCHED OF THE EARTH

I

LeRoi Jones is Black, is thirty-one years old, is a man dedicated
to the liberation of his people by any means necessary. In this latter,
he is not unique. There are many others like him. A significant part
of the generation born in the mid-thirties feels the same way. That is,
they have almost a cosmic desire to tear out of the value system that
their parents had so much faith in. Large numbers of this generation
have had the "benefits" of a college education. Like Jones, they
were sent off to obtain an education which would insure them more
freedom and success, more security than their parents, and a greater
share of the American pie. But for the Negro, education is full of
interesting paradoxes. While the system exposes its good face, its
ugly one also comes into view. For those who refuse to accept illusions, there is rebellion.

All of this is not to say that Jones is involved simply in some kind
of youthful rebellion against the established order. There is more to
it than that. What we would like to suggest is that Jones has been involved in a search for a unified identity, an identity that is in tune

The development of LeRoi Jones" by Lawrence P. Neal. From *Liberator,* January
1966, 4-5., and February 1966, 18-19. Reprinted by permission of the author.

with the following exigencies: the spiritual demands of Black people, revolutionary tendencies in the social order, the Black community, the Third world; and a necessity to bring aesthetics in line with ethics. Jones is somewhat of a public figure. Almost everyone, especially his former friends on the lower East Side, has had their opinions on what they consider to be a sudden change in Jones's personality. But changes seldom suddenly occur.

LeRoi Jones is the product of a generation which promises to be especially militant. This is the generation that was subjected to the same illusions as their partents, but managed to recognize, in the midst of it all, that they were involved in a gigantic hoax. This was especially true of the students who went to Negro colleges like Central State, Fisk, Lincoln and Howard University, where Jones studied. He must have seen the Negroes at Howard trying to escape from their Blackness, trying to merge and assimilate into a culture that had no place for them, a culture that is spiritually bankrupt. Jones is a poet. A man of soul, sensitive to the world around him; and merely the simple desire for a poet's truth must have made that world a rather bizarre place in which to live. He speaks of Howard often with a strange kind of irony. For even though it is apparent that the situation at Howard was not consistent with the development of a Black frame-of-reference, he was able to cultivate some real strong friendships there. And much of the social life was Black in a way that it could never have been had he gone to a predominately white university.

He began writing poetry while at Howard, a place where creativity challenges inimical pursuits. Jones has a special place in his work for the black bourgeoisie. In *Blues People,* for example, he devotes considerable discussion to their impact on American culture, and their attempts to whiten Black culture. Again in his play, *The Slave,* the bourgeoisie is alluded to. This time the allusion is more sinister and grave, much in keeping with the revolutionary LeRoi Jones of the white man's press and news media.

This latter brings me to another aspect of the development of LeRoi Jones. That is, his public image. For about a year now, and especially since Malcolm's death, Jones has been projected by the news media as a venom-filled monster oozing with hate of the white man. The *Village Voice's* "expert" on the Negro question, Jack Newfield, has done his share in distorting Jones's public image. Next, in chronological order, are the *Herald Tribune, World-Telegram,* and a myriad of television stations. LeRoi has himself not been especially tactful in these instances. This, I find highly disconcerting. He has not decided, in a tactical sense, what he hopes to accomplish by speaking to Black people via white media. Actually, many militants feel, he has just begun to talk to Black people. Herein lies an extraordinary power on Jones's part, if he is able to direct it. He speaks with a conviction and an ironical sense of wit that young Blacks identify as being related to their situation. But until he understands the nature and limitations of his power, he will make the same mistakes all others before him have made. And the mistakes will be made with eyes wide open, in the light of day.

The task, as Jones sees it, is to develop "Black consciousness," a Black spiritual frame-of-reference based on the humanism of the Bandung (non-white) world. The coming into being of such a spirit implies a revolutionary dynamic. Hence, Jones and the Black Arts advocate a revolutionary aesthetics that "moves to reshape the world, using as its force the natural force and perpetual vibrations of the mind in the world."[1]

Jones comes to these "nationalistic" ideas in a rather indirect fashion. Previously, he had started out as a writer closely identified with the literati of the Village. Many "beat" writers were included in an anthology edited by Jones entitled *The Moderns.* I don't think that it is inaccurate to say that, in terms of writers, Jones' closest associates were mostly white. This was probably, however, not by design on the part of Jones; rather it was bound up with the nature of the literary scene in the Village, and the particular orientation that he had brought to bear on his work. The only Black literary magazine of any importance in downtown literary movements was *Umbra.* Nothing of Jones' appears there.

Small literary magazines are always cropping up in the Village. Jones published a great deal of poetry in many of them. He himself published many of his contemporaries in *Yugen,* which he edited along with his former wife, Hettie Cohen. There were also numerous poetry readings. LeRoi was becoming a well-known figure in East Village artistic circles. His audience, mostly whites, saw him as one of the most creative spirits on the literary scene. And Jones was steadily producing a great deal of carefully written poetry—poetry which had its technical roots in the works of William Carlos Williams and Charles Olsen, and which had a particular kind of intensity and irony belonging to LeRoi Jones alone. Some of his early

[1]See Jones's essay, "The Revolutionary Theatre" *LIBERATOR,* 1965.

poems published in *Yugen,* and *Preface to a Twenty Volume Suicide Note,* indicate an underlying conflict in the writer, the source of which appears to be the absence of a unifying dynamic between the "I" of the poems and the world.

In later work, the conflict appears to be based on an attempt to transcend the political ineptness of the West. Some of the poems in *The Dead Lecturer* are very decidedly political. For example, here are a few lines from a poem entitled, *Short Speech to My Friends:*

> The perversity
> of separation, isolation,
> after so many years of trying to enter their kingdoms,
> now they suffer in tears, these others, saxophones whining
> through the wooden doors of their less than gracious homes.
> The poor have become our creators. The black. The thoroughly ignorant.
> Let the combination of morality
> and inhumanity
> begin.

And in *"The Politics of Rich Painters"* the decadence of Western art is examined; Jones finds that, "The source of their art crumbles into legitimate history." What soon begins to emerge is what we discover in the poem *Black Dada Nihilismus:* the white arts of the West are displaced for the "blacker arts." The poem concludes:

> For tambo, willie best, dubois, patrice, mantan, the
> bronze buckaroos.
> For Jack Johnson, asbestos, tonto, buckwheat,
> billie holiday.
> For tom russ, l'overture, beau jack,
> (may a lost god damballah, rest or save us
> against the murders we intend
> against his lost white children
> black dada nihilismus.

All of the figures mentioned are, somehow, clues to his understanding of the Black man's social and historical reality in the Western world.

As a Black man, and a poet, the particular kind of insight and wry humour found in Jones's later work have always been there, lurking to leap out at some time or another. He could never be simply another "Negro" writer either. He felt then, and feels even more so now, that Black literature must disengage itself from the "heinous elements of the culture."

II

As long as Jones remained *literary* he was a welcomed member of the white literary world—a world which, of course, likes a little controversy every now and then, a little "excitement" to make the decadent nature of their lives more bearable. The "excitement" they have in mind is, of course, mostly verbal; or an occasional fight over a literary technicality. They can't conceive of it going any further. The white producer of Jones's play *The Slave* was asked by a young poet-writer, a friend of Jones', if he didn't feel somewhat threatened by the play's implications. The producer replied calmly: *Oh he's not serious. It's only a play.*

For the world of *The Slave* is one of Black revolution, the establishment of a new order. To whites, art is an object somewhat removed from the real world. What occurs in art is never intended to be. Therefore, it is possible for a white writer to hold and live by ideas and values radically different from those advocated in his works. Or at least *to act* as if there was no organic relationship between the aesthetics of his art and the ethics of his life. He somehow sees these as separate acts. The white man hears the blues poeple wailing in a deep night of agony and pain, but hears only a part of it all. The other part is some kind of truth unbearable that condemns the white man to a state of beastliness. When Lula in *The Dutchman*, a play that won LeRoi an Obie award, is forced to see the truth of the following words by Clay, she murders him:

> If Bessie Smith had killed some white people she wouldn't have needed that music. She could have talked very straight and plain about the world. No metaphors. No grunts. No wriggles in the dark of her soul. Just straight two and two are four. Money. Power. Luxury. Like that. All of them. Crazy niggers turning their backs on sanity. What it all needs is that simple act. Murder. Just Murder! Would make us all sane.

It is a ritual murder, standing for the collective murder and castration of Black manhood. Lula's murder of Clay is an exercise in the

ritual release of guilt. At the end of the play another "victim" gets
on the subway. And then we understand that Lula is the bitch-
goddess who occurs and reoccurs in world literature and who will
go on committing murder until she herself is killed and the cycle
stopped.

Afro-American music, its personality and development, has also
occupied much of Jones's attention. His work, *Blues People: Negro
Music in White America,* is the most important study to date on the
subject. One thesis in *Blues People* is that Afro-American music
("jazz") is moving outside of the Western forms; that, however much
the music is related to the socio-historical development of American
culture, it has a tendency to seek an existence *outside* of that development in a world of its own, with its own sense of style and value.
Coltrane, Ornette Coleman, and many others are evaluated as the
forerunners of a "new" musical aesthetic; and its very existence
testified to the presence of a new revolutionary Afro-American personality. In this connection, Jones published several significant
articles in *Revolution,* a magazine devoted to revolutionary nationalist developments in the Third World. These articles testified to a
new revolutionary spirit among Afro-American artists, and Jones
was the most articulate spokesman of that spirit.

It is too soon to predict where all of this is going. The Black Arts
is a long way from being the organization it has promised to be. But
hopes are high. Jones has managed to direct his tremendous talents
towards meaningful activities in the Black community. However,
he will not find this a simple task. For America infects Black intellectuals often with a peculiar kind of estrangement—an estrangement that makes reconciliation between the community and her "intellectuals" a difficult affair. Jones has not been unaffected by this
estrangement. Neither has the Black Arts. And what we have tried
to suggest here is that acting upon Jones have been forces from both
within and without. As a creative person, he has been driven by a
desire to evolve a unifying philosophy of art, one suited to his needs
and to his people's. The other forces are historical. They involve
the destruction of an epoch. The West is dying and no man of soul
wants to be identified with that death. No Black man of soul wants
it said that his art supports that which is inhumane and beastly. No,
we are not noble: we turn inward on our Blackness because we fear
the spiritlessness of the deaths that we would die if we did not.

Black Literature and LeRoi Jones

By Cecil M. Brown

As a "young black writer," I am indebted to American and English literature, but I hold my most personal allegiance to Black Literature, and to most recent writers, like LeRoi Jones. No one, I suppose, has been more influenced than I have by Jones' work. In recent months, however, I have sensed in the air a schism between Jones' art and Negro Literary tradition, and I am thinking of his indictment of Negro writers like Arna Bontemps, Richard Wright, and James Baldwin, and I am also thinking, more specifically, of his essay, "Myth of A Negro Literature." I am aware of the tradition of literary manifestos, which is to deny in traditional literature whatever it is it proposes to supply; Jones, however denies the existence of a "negro literature," and offers to instruct us on how to go about creating one. It seems all too easy to dismiss the works of established Black writers with so quick a stroke; there must be something, a line, a phrase—in the whole of centuries of writings by Blacks worth saving. Another important and related question is: Assuming we do give up traditional Black literature, where would Jones, as a manifesto poet, lead us?

Jones' journey·from where he was to where he is, is more important to me than any other journey in literature. It is the authentic modern-day descent from purgatory into hell; it is essentially a poetic manifesto, as is witnessed by the swelling number of young Black literary followers. It says, as all poetic manifestos say, e.g., preface to the Lyrical Ballads, "Let's get back to the original source, baby." Only indirectly is it literary criticism, in the sense that a new poem is critical of old poems. But most of what he has to say in *Home* about Black Literature and Black authors cannot be taken, even at its best, as anything approaching literary criticism.

"Black Literature and LeRoi Jones" by Cecil M. Brown. From *Black World*, June, 1970, 24-31. Reprinted by permission of the author.

In that essay, "Myth of A Negro Literature,"[1] Jones argues that there is nothing in Black Literature comparable to blues (and jazz), which we have all agreed is the high water-mark of Afro-American genius; he implies in the title of his essay, and further on explicitly states, that there is no such thing as a "negro literature." This assumed lack of development in the literary sphere is due solely to the fact that middle-class Blacks (who are, for Jones, preoccupied with "striving for respectability") have dominated the literary scene so long.

Even James Baldwin, Richard Wright, Jean Toomer and Ralph Ellison have fallen shy the mark, for by imitating "white models" they have succeeded in writing serious works only in the sense that Somerset Maugham is "serious writing." "That is, serious, if one has never read Herman Melville or James Joyce. And it is part of the tragic *naivete* of the middle-class (brow) writer, that he has not."

What strikes one about this assessment of "negro literature" is that it is too facile; at a first glance, it seems credulous; but on a second reading, one finds one's self being asked to swallow something quite unnatural. And as is true with all smooth surfaces, there is more to a facile explanation of "negro literature" than meets the eye.

A literature of a people is not something whose existence is dependent on somebody's definitions; it exists if the people exist; if there is a people, there is a literature. A people can have a magnificent literature, a frivolous literature, a supernatural literature, but they cannot *not* have a literature, for a people's literature is nothing more than their own repertory of myths, myths being the manner in which they decide to organize their experience in and about nature. Jones would have "negro literature" be something like the blues and jazz—a distinct thing which one could dangle before the eyes of his white friends or foes in order to say, "Look we're just as good as you." (As if there is some reason to doubt it!)

To say, then, that the Afro-American has failed to create a literature comparable to the blues is, I think, erroneous for this reason: the lyrics of the blues is literature; furthermore, this influence of the blues has given a distinct flavor to the works of Arna Bontemps, Richard Wright, Jean Toomer, James Baldwin, and so forth. This can be demonstrated easily enough, but we must first understand that

[1] The LeRoi Jones essay, "Myth of A Negro Literature," appeared originally in *The Saturday Review* (April 20, 1963). It was collected in *Home,* a volume of essays by Jones published by William Morrow in 1966.

blues is music only when it begins to use the techniques of white popular song; what distinguished blues was its lyrics, the story these lyrics told. (And it was this story that inspired jazz.)

The words in blues are notoriously lacking in either lyricism or delicacy of sentiment, and it is only in the rhythm, melody, and musical accompaniment that it approaches popular song. Blues without music (*i.e.*, blues without the candy-coating) is true literature, and it is literature not because it was produced by Blacks—though it seems unlikely it would have ever come to be if Blacks had never existed—but because it confronts life with a positive and realistic attitude.

There is in blues, as in the popular songs, disappointment, but the attitude toward this disappointment is what distinguishes blues as being art. The most vivid account of disappointment involves desertion and heartbreak as in "Young Woman's blues," by Bessie Smith:

> Woke up this morning when the chickens were crowin' for day,
> Looked on the right side of my pillow, my man had gone away.
> By the pillow he left a note,
> Reading, "I'm sorry, Jane, you got my goat"...

Unlike the girl in the popular song who pines away with self-pity, and demoralization, Jane's reaction is realistic; the song continues:

> I'm a young woman, and I ain't done running around.

In blues, the failure of a love affair is by no means the end of life; the failure of the love affair—or anything else—is included in, is a part of life. Understanding blues in the positive sense clarifies what James Baldwin meant when he said that whites won't begin to understand Blacks until they accept Death.

In its attitude toward life, its philosophy, and the story it tells, blues is important art, and not because of its "music," not in its being sung but in what it has to say. And I do not mean it is didactic, but only that it asserts a "reality."

In *Dutchman*, Clay's attitude towards blues ("If Bessie Smith had killed some white people she wouldn't have needed that music"), in confusing blues with popular song, sees blues as a by-product, an otherwise unnecessary antidote; such an attitude would further imply that the importance in blues lies in its ability to soothe, as popular songs soothe. But, blues is high art, and popular songs are not.

Blues is, moreover, a verbal art, which is another way of saying it is literature. The men who wrote blues—like Langston Hughes, for example—were not popular song writers, but poets. One would have to be very prejudiced, indeed, not to see the strain of blues in the works of, for instance, James Weldon Johnson, Langston Hughes, James Baldwin.

The best works produced by Blacks have been thematic. (There are two broad divisions of literary works, the fictional and the thematic; the former comprises works of literature with internal characters, and includes novels, plays, narrative poetry, *etc.*, everything that tells a story; in thematic literature the author and the reader are the only characters involved; this division includes lyrics, essays, didactic poetry and oratory.)[2] The oratory of Frederick Douglass, the autobiographies of Douglass, Malcolm X, Eldridge Cleaver, Ralph Ellison, James Baldwin (in his essays), James Weldon Johnson, Richard Wright—all of these are works in which the central character (the author) is talking directly to his audience (the white world), and in such works it is not necessary to create scenery or characters, or place of location, etc., as in fictional literature, simply because we see it around us everyday—i.e., the scene is America, the time is Now, and the characters are forever me and you and Charles.

Jones' plays follow closely this Black literary tradition. The most valuable part of *Dutchman,* for instance, is Clay's speech to Lula (i.e., to the white world); and Walker's power in *The Slave* is derived from his brutal confrontation with the white world, although he himself is flesh and blood of that world, too. In neither of these plays is there a single thread of relationship between Black and Black; rather it is Black confronting white. The same is true of, say, *The Toilet,* where the important relationship is between the black gang leader and the sensitive white boy. This is fine, precisely as we would have it.

In *The Slave,* Jones has carried the thematic tradition as far as anyone could hope to carry it. If we say that in this tradition the author, as presented in the work, is the most important character, the next step is for the author to present his personal life as the sub-

[2]For this division, I am indebted to Northrop Frye, *Fables of Identity* (New York, 1963).

ject of his art. The white writer may have to fabricate, but the Black writer only has to reveal himself, reveal his "personal" self. LeRoi Jones' best and most memorable character is LeRoi Jones himself; in this, he is very much like Charlie Parker who, when asked what his best piece was, said "Me." When Jones says, "Wittgenstein said ethics and aesthetics are one, I believe this," we had better take him seriously. The relationship between Jones and Walker is the natural, logical extension of the thematic tradition in Black literature; one need not go to Wittgenstein for that.

But in denying the existence of "negro literature," in castigating established Black writers, Jones is saying, in effect, that his plays are different from that literary tradition. I think there are more similarities than differences between Clay and Bigger Thomas, or Clay and Paul in Baldwin's "This Mornin, This Evening, So Soon." Jones has said he hoped Black writers would produce art that did not conform to the white man's "deceitful 'acceptance' of *buy and sell* America." And he points to the work of famous Black writers ("the false prestige of the Black *bourgeoisie*") as examples. We turn to Jones' own work, expecting, naturally, a difference. Both *The Slave* and *Dutchman* conform to the white man's definition of protest. White critics, the enemy, have called the plays "shocking," "fierce" and "honest." *Dutchman* has been so successful—i.e., has conformed so well to what white liberals want to see—that it has been produced into a movie so the whole family, not just the esoteric few, can enjoy it.

Dutchman and *The Slave* conform to the white man's definition of protest, not because they were not violent enough (it is really the other way around), not because they were not Black enough, or *didn't tell it like it is,* but because they are *theater!*

Jones' attack on the Black *bourgeoisie* is mis-directed; his frustration results from the unwillingness of literary form to be used as a social and political weapon, as propaganda. Literature is, in fact, notoriously *bourgeoisie, middle-class,* conservative, backward-looking, in its nature. Literature looks backward to its own conventions, and those conventions look back to original myths. Literature is backwards in this sense: poets are still writing poems in which the sun rises and sets, after science has said long ago, that this is illusory. As an art, as Northrop Frye says, literature deals "not with the world that man contemplates, but with the world man creates"—and these two worlds can be miles apart.

It is propaganda, which is in the world of science, not art, that

Jones is speaking of when he chides James Baldwin for escaping into "the sanctity of his FEELINGS." Jones continues: "If one has nothing to SAY but, 'I can feel,' or, 'I am intelligent,' there is really no need saying it. These things in themselves are very boring...Unless a man will tell you something, pass on some piece of information about the world" (*Home*, p. 118). It is not information about the real world, but one's personal feelings, that go into the making of literature. The difficulty in distinguishing between literature and propaganda is that they both use the same medium: words. But these words, although they may be the same, are referring to two entirely different worlds.

Jones wants a revolutionary literature, a literature that will change the outside world, a literature that will make white men "tremble, curse, and go mad, because they will be drenched with the filth of their evil." But revolutionary literature is a contradiction in terms, for the moment anything revolutionary hits the stage, or the printing press, it is magically transformed into literary *tradition;* it then looks back into *literary history* for its predecessors, and it ceases to find its referent in the outside world, i.e., the world of science and politics. If there is nothing in the literary tradition of which this new "revolutionary" element may be said to be the offspring, then we call it "original" and pretend it is going to change the outside world; but it cannot, because its very nature is centripetal.

It is unnecessary for Jones to ignore the whole of Black Literature, simply because the nature of literary form is what it is. It is not necessary to conclude, as he does, that Black Literature is mediocre; but then, this is a white critic's judgment, for it implies a comparison between the literatures of Black Americans and white Americans, and such a comparison is not possible since we are dealing with two completely different things. In arguing for the mediocrity of Black Literature, Jones stacks the cards with such examples as Phillis Wheatley and Charles Chesnutt. Poor Miss Wheatley, she has been used by everybody as an example to prove any and everything about the Afro-American and literature (and it is surprising to find Jones dwelling on such a *cliche;* couldn't he have given us something more original?). We know a lot about Miss Wheatley's life as a slave, not by what she said, but by what she did not say. In her poetry, she followed the poetic conventions of her day, and to ask why she didn't break with those conventions and write about slave life around her (if there was any) is to ask why she was a conformist and not a literary innovator. An impossible question.

Young Black writers should write whatever they feel impelled to write and let the labels fall where they may; at the same time, it is not necessary to condemn the whole tradition of Afro-American literature because it does not conform to what one happens to be writing. No Black writer can write anything worthwhile without being influenced by writers—essentially blues writers—like Richard Wright, James Baldwin and James Weldon Johnson. And they need not go around saying they can.

LeRoi Jones (Imamu Amiri Baraka):
Form and the Progression of Consciousness

By Esther M. Jackson

My own mode of conscience. ...
The act so
far beyond
itself, meaning all forms, all
modes, all voices...[1]

I

The sixties saw the beginning of a fourth phase of the growth of the American drama as an indigenous kind. By the mid-fifties, the innovative developments initiated in the theatrical experiments of Eugene O'Neill had come to a point of rest. In the early sixties a reverse motion became evident. The interest in *synthesis* which had characterized the creative activity of playwrights of the thirties and forties was to be superseded by a preoccupation with *disassociative processes* — with analytic forms.[2]

One of the most important of the interpreters of these disassociative forms was to be the poet-playwright-theorist LeRoi Jones (Imamu Amiri Baraka).[3] By the end of the sixties, Jones-Baraka would

"LeRoi Jones (Imamu Amiri Baraka): Form and the Progression of Consciousness" by Esther M. Jackson. Reprinted from the *CLA Journal,* 17 (September 1973), 33-56, by permission of the College Language Association and the author.

[1]LeRoi Jones, "Rhythm & Blues (3)," in *The Dead Lecturer* (New York: Grove Press, 1964), p. 47.

[2]For a discussion of disassociative forms in the arts, see Erich Kahler, *The Disintegration of Form in the Arts* (New York: Braziller, 1968), p. 27.

Some of Kahler's theories of form can be traced to Georg W. F. Hegel. See "Lectures on Aesthetics," trans. Bernard Bosanquet and William Bryant, in *The Philosophy of Hegel,* ed. Carl J. Friedrich (New York: Modern Library Edition, 1953), pp. 373-395.

[3]Jones appears to have taken the name "Imamu Amiri (or Ameer) Baraka" gradually, assuming it totally in the early seventies. For biographical data, see "Jones, (Everett) LeRoi," in *Current Biography* (1970), pp. 204-207.

join the ranks of a select group of American dramatists whose visions of reality have not only influenced the course of modern theatre but have altered the Western imagination. Like Eugene O'Neill, he would become both interpreter and creator of a new consciousness, the maker of symbolic forms expressive of critical events taking place in the collective imagination.

Jones would share with the mainstream of American dramatists of the sixties this preoccupation with consciousness in crisis. But the basis of his singular significance in world theatre would be his vision of reality. For he would find in the Black ghetto the contemporary form of an ancient archetype. In his dream-haunted poet, seeking to compose the disordered realities of his world, Jones would project the universal condition of contemporary man. His drama, like his poetry and his essays, records a search for meaning. The body of his work would trace a progression of consciousness, a poetic passage from despair to the tranquility of ethical totality. The central motive of his progression of consciousness would derive from his perception of racial conflict in American life.

The use of race as a dramatic theme is not new. Racial consciousness is a recurrent motif in Western theatre, motivating actions in Euripides' *Medea* and Shakespeare's *Othello,* no less than in Edward Albee's *The Death of Bessie Smith.* Blackness as an icon of estrangement is a theme in the works of Paul Green, Tennessee Williams, Thornton Wilder, and William Saroyan, and appears with frequency in the plays of Eugene O'Neill. That which distinguishes LeRoi Jones' treatment of racial consciousness from earlier interpretations in Western arts and letters is the comprehensive nature of its reference. For in the world of Jones, racial consciousness is not merely an aspect of social and/or psychological truths; it is the totality of an agonizing reality.

Jones has given some credit for his metaphysics of color to the symbolic forms of Melville. In an essay in the volume *Home,*[4] he has written of Melville's racial symbolism:

> My faith in Melville, for instance, and the faith I give his language is completely passed through the world into my own references of mind and spirit. They cannot be got at.[5]

Jones' progress beyond Melville's metaphysics of color relates to his

[4] LeRoi Jones, *Home: Social Essays* (New York: William Morrow, 1966).
[5] LeRoi Jones, "Brief Reflections on Two Hot Shots," in *Home,* p. 119.

primary creative motive. His "referent for moral disorder"[6] has led him to reverse the system of meanings assigned by the mainstream of American writers to "Blackness" and "Whiteness." The importance of his aesthetic experiments relates to his revaluation of the symbolism of color; not only to the impact of his imagery on the forms and contents of the American arts but on the idea of race in Western consciousness.

II

I am inside someone who hates me.[7]

It is perhaps appropriate to interpret LeRoi Jones' career as an artist in terms of his attempts to give sensuous concreteness to a dynamic consciousness. For Jones, the search for form would be symbolic of a continuing effort to mediate between warring factions within the perceiving mind. In an essay in the volume *Home*, he has written of art as a creative transaction between experience and understanding:

> Form is simply *how* a thing exists (or what a thing exists as). When we speak of man, we ask, "How does he make it?" Content is *why* a thing exists. Everything has both these qualities; otherwise it could not (does not) exist. The art object has a special relationship between these two qualities, but they are not separable in any object.[8]

Jones shares with romantic artists from Dante to Edward Albee this commitment to form as the symbolization of consciousness.[9] If his concept of form is in this sense traditional, it has a distinguishing characteristic in its prescriptive content. For the body of his work — poetry, drama, and non-dramatic prose — is devoted to the interpretation of the reality which he defines as "Black." About this determining characteristic, he has written:

> Let the world be a Black Poem
> And Let All Black People Speak This Poem
> Silently
> or LOUD[10]

[6] The phrase is adapted from *"The end of man is his beauty,"* in *The Dead Lecturer*, p. 31.

[7] LeRoi Jones, *"An Agony. As Now."* in *The Dead Lecuter*, p. 15.

[8] LeRoi Jones, "Hunting Is Not Those Heads on the Wall," in *Home*, p. 176.

[9] Hegel, "Lectures on Aesthetics," pp. 351-367.

[10] LeRoi Jones, "Black Art," in *Black Fire: An Anthology of Afro-American Writing*, eds. LeRoi Jones and Larry Neal (New York: William Morrow, 1968), p. 303.

Jones' commitment to a concept of form as the concretion of consciousness recalls a critical question raised by Hegel. If art is indeed the representation of consciousness, what are the appropriate modes of its expression? A student of Hegel, Jones has sought to redefine the expressive conditions outlined by the romantic theorist.[11] On some occasions, he has followed Hegel's definition of romantic art, describing form as the symbolization of inner subjectivity:[12]

> The Black Artist must draw out of his soul the correct image of the world. He must use this image to band his brothers and sisters together in common understanding of the nature of the world (and the nature of America) and the nature of the human soul.[13]

At other times, he has defined form as the concretion of ideas. About this classical motive, Jones has commented, "I do believe, desperately, in a 'poetry of ideas.'"[14]

Like romantic theorists, particularly Hegel, Jones has sought to mediate between mind and soul—idea and image.[15] The body of his work traces the passage of a poetic consciousness from a state of crisis to a sense of ethical totality. Jones' essential romanticism seems to have been reinforced by his early schooling in the tradition of the American transcendentalists. Some aspects of his theories reflect the neo-Hegelian formulations of Ralph Waldo Emerson, Walt Whitman, and Henry David Thoreau. Like the transcendentalists, Jones on occasion has interpreted art as an expression of a spiritual harmony—or disharmony—extending to the natural world. In an introduction to an anthology called *The Moderns,* he wrote in Emersonian terms of the "landscape" of American consciousness:

> Environment, in these uses, becomes *total,* i.e., social, cultural, and physical, and not merely scenery. Though it is landscape, in the way the poet Charles Olson has used the word: what one can see from where

[11] Jones, a philosophy minor at Howard University, was a student of Hegel's ideas. He was also winner of John Hay Whitney and Guggenheim awards; and a lecturer in literature at Columbia University and the New School for Social Research. See Stephen Schneck, "LeRoi Jones or, Poetics and Policemen or, Trying Heart, Bleeding Heart," in *Five Black Writers,* ed. Donald B. Gibson (New York: New York University Press, 1970), pp. 193-205.
[12] Hegel, "Lectures on Aesthetics," pp. 351-395.
[13] Jones, "State/meant," in *Home,* pp. 251-252.
[14] Jones, "A Dark Bag," in *Home,* p. 123.
[15] Hegel, "The Phenomenology of the Spirit," trans. James B. Baillie and Carl J. Friedrich, in *The Philosophy of Hegel,* pp. 411-414.

one is standing. The common concern of each of these writers is local, and in a broader though vaguer sense, American.

The exact reasons for Jones' rejection in the mid-sixties of this early faith in transcendental harmony are difficult to verify. Whatever the causes, his withdrawal from the "Concords" and "Waldens" of early sensibility to the "Harlems," "Newarks," and "Lower East Sides" of later perception was to be decisive. For the young philosopher of transcendental harmony would in the middle sixties become the poet of a rapidly disassociating sensibility. Like that of another major American dramatist, the spiritual life of Jones would appear to have been "rent asunder."[16] If religious and sexual crises appear to have been the instrument of estrangement in the experience of Eugene O'Neill, the principal factor motivating the fragmentation of Jones' consciousness would seem to have been racial conflict, and its assualt on his sense of male identity....

The poems in the volume *The Dead Lecturer* are important both for their lyric beauty and their symbolization of those despairing states of consciousness which characterized Jones' progressive estrangement from himself and the world as he then knew it.They trace a double progression. Clearly, they portend that annihilation of the superficial personality which Hegel thought prerequisite to the achievement of genuine selfhood.[17] But they also record another destruction. For never again in the years which followed would Jones the poet create works of such beauty and compressed meaning. The poetic Jones, envisioning the sacrifice of his lyrical powers to the dream of spiritual tranquility, interpreted the coming change as death. A poignant comment on the death of this "lyrical Jones" is embodied in the first stanza of the poem *"The end of man is his beauty"*:

> And silence
> which proves/ but
> a referent
> to my disorder.[18]

But if this lyrical Jones seemed dead, another persona was about to emerge. The "dead lecturer," self-categorized aesthete of the New

[16]Hegel's language in "The Phenomenology of the Spirit," in *The Philosophy of Hegel*, pp. 455-457.

[17]Hegel, "The Phenomenology of the Spirit," p. 405.

[18]Jones, *The Dead Lecturer*, p. 31.

School and Columbia University, would be replaced by a new kind of poet—a singer of new songs.

The metamorphosis of the poet LeRoi Jones into the moralist Imamu Amiri Baraka is evident in the ego-dissolving language of *The Dead Lecturer.* This renunciation of the lyrical self by Jones would serve to deny the control of Western literary traditions over his art. It would—at least, theoretically—render his consciousness a *tabula rasa* on which new images and ideas could be given shape. In "SHORT SPEECH TO MY FRIENDS," he envisioned arrangements of verbal forms which he might now project in the deepening silence:

> A compromise
> would be silence. To shut up, even such risk
> as the proper placement
> of verbs and nouns. To freeze the spit
> in mid-air, as it aims itself
> at some valiant intellectual's face.
>
> There would be someone
> who would understand, for whatever
> fancy reason.[19]

III

> The time of thought. The space of actual move-
> ment.[20]
> Where the God is a self, after all.[21]

Jones' career as an artist and thinker can be read then as a progression from lyrical to moral consciousness. A critical transition in this development is a work of the middle sixties, *The System of Dante's Hell* (1965).[22] Like its Renaissance progenitor, *The System of Dante's Hell* is a symbolization of a major event in the consciousness of the poet and in that of his age. Challenged by the complexity of his simultaneous visions, Jones created an urban epic; that is, he recorded simultaneous and conflicting progressions within created images. His "hip" epic superimposes the structural form of Dante's narrative over the violent progress of a Black poet's night journey through a modern city.

[19]*Ibid.,* p. 30.
[20]*Ibid.,* p. 71.
[21]*Ibid.,* p. 16.
[22]LeRoi Jones, *The System of Dante's Hell* (New York: Grove Press, 1965).

In *The System of Dante's Hell,* Jones moved from the intense
subjectivity of his lyric forms to more objective explication. In this
middle work, he sought to extract from—or project into—the flow
of angry images ideas about the universal meaning of his experience.
Here, he has superimposed on the unfolding spectacle a series of
legends interpreting actual and symbolic events. *The System of
Dante's Hell* juxtaposes warring images—visions of the past usurp-
ing the present; sensuality pervading abstraction; individuality dis-
solving into universality; "Whiteness" deepening into "Blackness."
Like Dante's protagonist, Jones' contemporary poet-hero begins
his journey in the world of external events; he descends into a Hell
of inner conflicts; and comes ultimately to the portals of salvation.
Jones' Hell—like his Heaven—is a state of consciousness. He describes this "Inferno" of mind, soul, and spirit:

> Hell in the head. ...
> Hell is actual, and people with hell in their heads. ... The struggles
> away or towards this peace in Hell's function. (Wars of consciousness.
> Antithetical definitions of feeling(s).[23]

The organizing theme of this work, like that of Jones' lyric poetry,
is race. The poet describes the anguish which he endures, as the figures of his consciousness—the "White ideas" and "Black images"—
collide. The development of Jones' epic form over his lyric verse
appears to have involved the introduction of ethical ideas into the
texture of his imagery. The resulting montage of sensuous images
and ethical ideas would be characteristic of both his epic and dramatic forms.

IV

> As Dialogues with the soul, with the self, Selves,
> screaming furiously to each other.[24]

It was to be expected that Jones' search for form would lead to the
drama. For drama alone undertakes to interpret the psychological-
social-rational-aesthetical-ethical universe which emerged in his
middle work. His experiments with a theatre of consciousness have
involved a wide range of expressive modes. *The Toilet* (1964), *The*

[23]*Ibid.,* pp. 153-154.
[24]Jones, *The Dead Lecturer,* p. 69.

Baptism (1964) and *Madheart* (1968) are dreamplays, surrealistic visions of a disassociating consciousness. *Slaveship* (1967, produced 1969) has a more objective reference. It is a "soul-epic," adapting dramatic narrative to the interpretation of historic consciousness. *Jello* (produced 1964-65) is a dramatic pamphlet, a satire on racial attitudes in public life. A work of strong autobiographical significance is *Great Goodness of Life* (1969), a surrealistic treatment of racial strife in an urban ghetto of the sixties. The protagonist in this Kafkaesque work is not an artist but a middle-aged Black civil servant who is experiencing the crisis of consciousness which afflicted Jones' poets in earlier works.

Jones' method in these experimental works is familiar. He renders in theatrical form acute crises of consciousness. His dramas attempt, with varying degrees of verisimilitude, to set inner conflicts in actual settings. The problem for most of these works is their unremitting didacticism. It is the explicit moralizing which diminishes the dramatic value of these experimental plays. Jones' relentless manipulation of the thoughts and actions of his characters tends to deprive them of that freedom which is a condition of effective drama.

... Jones' most effective dramatization of a consciousness in crisis is *Dutchman* (1964).[25] The superiority of this play over other examples of Jones' theatre is its cohesive union of image and idea within an effective dramatic action. The freedom of its characters provides this play with a quality of suspense seldom maintained in others of Jones' dramatic works.

Dutchman is set in an environment reminiscent of the theological universe of *The System of Dante's Hell:*

> In the flying underbelly of the city. Steaming hot, and summer on top, outside. Underground. The subway heaped in modern myth.[26]

This subway train connotes a complex reality. A symbol of actual events, it mirrors the violence of the modern city. This speeding train symbolizes the urgency of desire, the motive force of the life process. The title refers explicitly to the journey of the mythological "Dutchman," condemned to wander until the Day of Judgment. There is yet another use of the term which is significant. In theatre, a "dutchman" is a canvas patch, masking the divisibility of two scenic units—two flats. Thus, the dark train, rushing underground, is

---

[25]LeRoi Jones, *Dutchman and The Slave* (New York: William Morrow, 1964).
[26]Jones, Stage Directions, *Dutchman*, p. 3.

Jones' icon of the reality of race.[27] The seer—the observing "I" in
this journey—is a poet; this time younger and more innocent than
he appeared in *The Dead Lecturer, The System of Dante's Hell*, or
The Slave. The pliable "Clay" (Adam) is both actor and observer in
this progression; sharing a moment of guilty knowledge with a
modern "Eve," offering an eternal apple.

The complexity of the symbolism in *Dutchman* allows Jones to
trace a number of interrelated actions. The first of these is objective.
The drama reports a common event in the modern city, a murder.
Its exposition seeks to reveal the causes of this act, through the ex-
ploration of secondary actions. The most evident of the secondary
actions is psychological. Clay and Lula attempt to divest themselves
of their conventional personalities in order to discover their true
"selves." A significant action is linguistic. Jones' characters probe
the complex relationship between symbol and reality at individual
and social levels of meaning. All actions finally converge in a spasm
of violence; the situation returns to normalcy; and the train moves
into the dark, carrying a new victim.

If the action in *Dutchman* is potentially tragic, the drama does
not reach a conclusion appropriate to tragic form. Although he perceives the nature of his crisis, Jones' poet stops short of ethical en-
lightenment (the *Aufklaerung*),[28] of Hegel's description.

V

He had got, finally, to the forest of motives.[29]

Throughout the careers of Jones the poet and Jones the playwright, there has existed a shadow-figure, Jones the theorist.[30] If
in the early phases of his career, Jones spoke primarily as artist, he
was in the late sixties to turn to analysis and commentary as his
primary modes of expression.

[27] Hugh Nelson, "LeRoi Jones' *Dutchman:* A Brief Ride on a Doomed Ship," in
Educational Theatre Journal (March, 1968), pp. 53-58.

[28] Hegel, "The Phenomenology of the Spirit," p. 432.

[29] Jones, "A Poem For Speculative Hipsters," in *The Dead Lecturer*, p. 76.

[30] In the essays in *Home*, Jones adapted a number of themes appearing in the writings of romantic philosophers such as Hegel to the interpretation of the experience
of Black Americans. See, for example, his use of Hegel's concept of the relationship
between culture, consciousness, and language in "The Phenomenology of the
Spirit," pp. 443-453.

If Jones' poetry and drama are in the romantic tradition, so is his prose. His social, political, aesthetic, and ethical ideas have their roots in the theories of Friedrich Schiller, Johann Wolfgang Goethe, Georg Hegel, and Richard Wagner. Like these romantic theorists, Jones interprets art not only as personal salvation, but as the primary instrument of culture, the index of history. Jones' contribution to social, political, aesthetic, and moral thought follows, both in form and content, romantic examples. That which distinguishes his theory, like his art, from the tradition of high romanticism is its specific intent. As theorist, Jones has sought to reconstitute the ideational structures consolidated by the major romantic thinkers; extending their perceptual, interpretive, and evaluative apparati to include new forms and contents. Jones' theories are designed to extend Western aesthetic and ethical systems. Ironically, his theorizing began by adapting restrictive patterns to new uses. The body of his thought seeks to transvalue dominant racial doctrines by positing "Blackness" as transcendent meaning. It is, in context of this critical motive, interesting to examine the early essays in the volume *Blues People*.[31] For here, the basic tenets of a philosophy of art and culture are expressed in relatively simple form. Jones' theories are given fuller explication in the essays in the volume *Home*. The discussions in this series comprise a more or less formal poetics, relating original and traditional concepts of character, action, language, thought, spectacle, and lyric to the problem of contemporary form.

Jones follows the stylistic example of the Romantics — particularly Nietzsche — couching intricate ideas in a densely symbolic language, translating sophisticated concepts into a syntax combining formal expression with the obscure imagery of the public mind. Language is perhaps the major theme of Jones' major theoretical works. Like Hegel, he interprets language as the primary instrument of consciousness. His essays are concerned specifically with the problem of developing verbal forms appropriate to the interpretation of the experiences of Black men in contemporary settings.

In an essay entitled "Expressive Language,"[32] Jones offers a prop-

[31]Jones' poetics is outlined in two major works: *Blues People: Negro Music in White America* (New York: William Morrow, 1963); and *Home: Social Essays* (New York: William Morrow, 1966).

Less formal application of his developing ideas of art is evident in *Black Music* (New York: William Morrow Paperbacks, 1968).

[32]Jones, "Expressive Language," *Home*, pp. 166-172.

osition which has become a tenet of his "school" of art and criticism.
Here, he claims that the language of the ghetto is the receptacle of a
complex historic consciousness. As such, it is a dynamic form suffused with profound and subtle meanings. In an ironic comment on
the linguistic games of Ludwig Wittgenstein, Jones celebrates the
subtleties of language used by an old Harlem preacher:

> I heard an old Negro street singer last week, Reverend Pearly Brown,
> singing, "God don't never change!" This is a precise thing he is sing-
> ing. He does not mean "God does not ever change!" He means "God
> don't never change!" The difference, and I said it was crucial, is in the
> final human reference...the form of passage through the world. A
> man who is rich and famous who sings, "God don't never change," is
> confirming his hegemony and good fortune...or merely calling the
> bank. A blind hopeless black American is saying something very dif-
> ferent. He is telling you about the extraordinary order of the world.
>
> ...As no Blues person can really believe emotionally in Pascal's God,
> or Wittgenstein's question, "Can the concept of God exist in a per-
> fectly logical language?" Answer: "God don't never change."[33]

Jones' essays treat problems of content as well as questions of form.
Like other American dramatists, he has been challenged by the need
for myths and legends appropriate and accessible to popular au-
diences. He has attempted to compose heroic myths particularly
appropriate to the interpretation of the experiences of Black Americans; to shape contents capable of interpreting humanistic ideals in
a contemporary-minded public language.

VI

In 1966, Jones joined with other participants in a conference on
culture from which a manifesto on "Black Aesthetics" issued. With
its demand for the submission of art to historical purpose, this manifesto completed the progression of consciousness which had become
evident in Jones' work in the early sixties:

> The embracing of a total Black Aesthetic, which has *always,* naturally,
> informed our lives in our freest consciousness, and the abandonment
> of the oppressive, *unnatural* European aesthetic. The *reassertion* of
> Black Tradition, which is the totality and total complementarity of all
> arts and the artists as fellow priest-physician craftsmen, together.[34]

[33]*Ibid.,* pp. 171-172.
[34]See "The 3rd Annual Black Power Conference: Creativity Workshop Report
and Resolution," in *Black Theatre,* No. 2 (1969), 7.

The publication of this manifesto marked the emergence of Imamu Amiri Baraka. While Jones-Baraka has sought to free himself from Western aesthetic traditions, the quality of his mind has made that cultural innocence which he covets difficult. Jones-Baraka has seemed to find a mediating agent for the continuing conflict between soul and mind in the principle of spirituality. In the late sixties he was to posit the existence of a Divine Power:

> [T]hings are being manifested that we don't have doctrines to explain. In the total scope of things, there is no such thing as the supernatural, except the Divinity, because everything flows out of the Divinity.[35]

Since 1968, Jones-Baraka seems to have reversed the order of his concern, tending to devote himself more to reality than to its imitation.[36] Today, he is more important for the influence of his examples on form and content in the American arts than for his own creative contribution.[37] At this moment in the early seventies, no conclusive interpretation about the final meaning of his career can be made. If, however, the sum of his achievement were to rest on his present accomplishments, his contribution to the American theatre would be of major significance.[38] For he has revitalized the form and content of the drama, translating into accessible public forms major perspectives drawn from the history of ideas. He has given life to a new dramatic protagonist, the Black poet-intellectual seeking meaning in the hostile environment of the modern city. He has re-established the roots of stage language in the public imagination. Most significantly, he has emerged as a major interpreter of the crisis of meaning which haunts contemporary man.[39] Like Eugene O'Neill, LeRoi Jones (Imamu Amiri Baraka) is an innovator whose vision of critical realities hitherto unexpressed has served to revitalize the American drama. His ingenious forms will undoubtedly find interpretation and development in world theatre of the seventies, eighties, and nineties.

[35]"Islam and Black Art: LeRoi Jones Talks with Marvin X and Faruk," in *Black Theatre*, No. 2 (1969), 17.

[36]See Hegel, "The Philosophy of History," in "Selections from *The Philosophy of Hegel*," trans. Carl J. and Paul W. Friedrich (New York: Modern Library Edition, 1953), pp. 11-42.

[37]See Jones-Baraka's comment on "Technology & Ethos," in *Raise, Race, Rays, Raze: Essays Since* 1965 (New York: Random House, 1971), pp. 155-157.

[38]Kathryn Jackson, "LeRoi Jones and the New Black Writers of the Sixties," in *Freedomways*, 9 (Fall, 1969), 232-247.

[39]LeRoi Jones, *It's Nation Time* (Chicago: Third World Press, 1970).

Being in the World: Biography

The Trial of LeRoi Jones

by Theodore R. Hudson

During the summer of 1967, serious civic disorders (or a citizen uprising, a consumer demonstration, a revolt, or riots, as you please) broke out in Newark.[1] Groups and individuals roamed the streets smashing windows, looting, setting fires, destroying property, attacking people. City and state law and military personnel and citizens struggled to contain the violence, using tear gas, firearms, physical force, and appeals. Shots were fired—by the police, the military, and citizens. Scores of people, mainly blacks, were injured; a number were killed, some from gunfire. In an essay which was to appear later in *Raise* as "From: The Book of Life" Jones describes the events as a sort of messianic phenomenon:

> The city is burning! The Devil's city is in flame! And because evil beings have tortured our people by worshipping dumb objects more than human life, our people run through the streets with these objects. Sometimes they are murdered. But also they run with what they need smashing and destroying the temples of the UnGodly. Temples where evil beings sell our people things and keep them chained to illusions of Desire. [pp. 53-54]

The essay ends with the inscription: "—Essex County Jail/Summer 1967/Year of Rebellion."

During the height of the confusion and violence, LeRoi Jones, accountant Charles McCray, and actor Barry Wynn, riding in Jones' Volkswagen bus, were stopped and arrested by police officers at

[1]For Jones' version of events and forces which led up to this outbreak and for his description of incidents during the outbreak, see "Newark: Before Black Men Conquered" and "From: The Book of Life," both in *Raise, Race, Rays, Raze* (New York: Random House, 1971).

South Seventh Street and South Orange Avenue in Newark's west side. The charges were unlawfully carrying firearms—two revolvers and a box of ammunition—and resisting arrest. Somehow Jones suffered a head injury that required sutures and a loosened tooth that had to be pulled the next day or so. The police attributed Jones' wounds to his having been hit on the head by a bottle thrown by some unknown person. Jones accused the police of premeditated brutality. As to the guns, Jones claimed he did not know where they had come from but suspected that the police had "planted" them.

At the arraignment, the bail was set at $25,000, an amount Jones described as "ransom, not bail." The bail was made—$2,500 in cash and the rest covered by two homes posted by friends of Jones' parents. The trial came up before Judge Leon W. Kapp sitting in Essex County Court. The jury was all-white. The verdict was guilty.

Between his arrest and the trial, *Evergreen Review* published in its December, 1967, issue Jones' poem "Black People!," which reads in part:

BLACK PEOPLE!

What about that bad short you saw last week
on Frelinghuysen, or those stoves and refrigerators, record
     players, shotguns,
in Sears, Bambergers, Klein's, Hahnes', Chase and the smaller
     joosh
enterprises? What about that bad jewelry, on Washington Street,
     and
those couple of shops on Springfield? You know how to get it,
     you can
get it, no money down, no money never, money dont grow on
     trees no
way, only whitey's got it, makes it with a machine, to control you
you cant steal nothin from a white man, he's already stole it he
     owes
you anything you want, even his life. All the stores will open if
     you
will say the magic words. The magic words are: Up against the
     wall mother
fucker this is a stick up!...

During the sentencing proceedings, Judge Kapp read this poem aloud in court, omitting what he considered "obscenities" and substituting for them the word "blank." Then followed dialogue between Kapp and Jones:

DEFENDANT JONES: Are you offering that in evidence?

THE COURT: Just a minute.

DEFENDANT JONES: It should be read wholly, if you are.

THE COURT: "The Author: LeRoi Jones, Evergreen Publications, December, 1967."

DEFENDENT JONES: Let me read it.

THE COURT: Just a minute. This diabolical prescription to commit murder and to steal and plunder and other similar evidences—

DEFENDANT JONES: I'm being sentenced for the poem, is that what you are saying?

THE COURT: —causes one to suspect that you were a participant in formulating a plot to ignite the spark on the night of July 13, 1967 to burn the City of Newark and that—

DEFENDANT JONES: You mean, you don't like the poem, in other words.

THE COURT: ...Another shocking excerpt from a speech which you delivered on September 15, 1967 at Muhlenberg College has been brought to my attention.

DEFENDANT JONES: Did I have the guns then too?

THE COURT: Which reads—

DEFENDANT JONES: Is that what I'm being tried for, Muhlenberg College?

THE COURT: "Unless we black people can come into peaceful power and begin the benevolent rule of the just, the next stage of our rebellion will burn Newark to the ground. This time City Hall and the rest of the greco Romans will go down, including the last of these greco Romans themselves."
It is my considered opinion that you are sick and require medical attention.

DEFENDANT JONES: Not as sick as you.

THE COURT: It has been suggested by some of your literary friends that you are a gifted writer, which I am willing to concede, except that I abhor the use of obscenities and your foul language. It is most unfortunate that your talents have been misdirected. You have the ability to make a wholesome contribution to ameliorate existing tensions and the resolution of the social and economic problems of our community by the introduction of constructive measures. Instead we find that you are in the vanguard of a group of extreme radicals who advocate the destruction of our democratic way of life by means of criminal anarchy.

DEFENDANT JONES: The destruction of unrighteousness.

THE COURT: ...If the philosopher can make his own law, so can the fool.

DEFENDANT JONES: We see that.

THE COURT: If the virtuous man can make his own law, so can those who spring from the gutter.

DEFENDANT JONES: Yes, we see that again.

THE COURT: There can be no substitute for freedom, but there can be no freedom where anarchy prevails. There can be no substitute for justice, but there can exist no justice where law and order have perished. Your behavior, both past and present, constitutes a threat and a menace to our society.

DEFENDANT JONES: And you all are a threat to the world.

THE COURT: The sentence of this Court, on the basis of your conviction for the unlawful possession of two revolvers—

DEFENDANT JONES: And two poems.

THE COURT: —in violation of *New Jersey Statute 2A: 151—41,* a misdemeanor, on Indictment No. 2220—66, is that you be confined to the New Jersey State Prison to serve a term of not less than 2 years and 6 months and not more than 3 years and that you pay a fine of $1000.

DEFENDANT JONES: Sir, black people will judge me, brother Kapp. Don't worry about that.

THE COURT: You are excused. Take him upstairs.[2]

The New York Times' headline read, "The Magic Word was 'Prison.'" *Time* magazine of the same week intoned, "Curtains for LeRoi." The judge's introduction of the poem and of the excerpt from Jones' Muhlenberg College speech and the relatively severe sentence (the average sentence for similar riot-connected convictions was six

[2]Sentencing proceedings, *State of New Jersey* v. *Everett LeRoi Jones, Charles McCray, & Barry Wynn, Essex County Court, Law Division, Criminal Indictment* No. 2220—66, January 4, 1968, pp. 19-24, passim.

months, some of this time suspended or on probation) caused some professional and lay disrespect for Judge Kapp. Among those showing concern was the American Civil Liberties Union, which issued a statement which read, in part, "This is clearly a violation of Jones' right to free speech. ... Actions of this kind tend only to exacerbate an already tense Negro community and do not serve the cause of justice."[3] Another was a "Committee on Poetry" in support of Jones, which issued a broadside bearing the names of supporters, including Corso, Creeley, and Ginsberg.

Jones appealed and eventually the conviction was reversed in a retrial.

[3]Quoted in "Poetic Justice," *Newsweek*, January 15, 1968, p. 24.

Blues People

by Ralph Ellison

In his Introduction to *Blues People* LeRoi Jones advises us to approach the work as

> ...a strictly theoretical endeavor. Theoretical, in that none of the questions it poses can be said to have been answered definitely or for all time (sic!), etc. In fact, the whole book proposes more questions than it will answer. The only questions it will properly move to answer have, I think, been answered already within the patterns of American life. We need only give these patterns serious scrutiny and draw certain permissible conclusions.

It is a useful warning and one hopes that it will be regarded by those jazz publicists who have the quite irresponsible habit of sweeping up any novel pronouncement written about jazz and slapping it upon the first available record liner as the latest insight into the mysteries of American Negro expression.

Jones would take his subject seriously—as the best of jazz critics have always done—and he himself should be so taken. He has attempted to place the blues within the context of a total culture and to see this native art form through the disciplines of sociology, anthropology and (though he seriously underrates its importance in the creating of a viable theory) history, and he spells out explicitly his assumptions concerning the relation between the blues, the people who created them and the larger American culture. Although I find several of his assumptions questionable, this is valuable in itself. It would be well if all jazz critics did likewise; not only would it expose those who have no business in the field, but it would sharpen the thinking of the few who have something enlightening to contribute. *Blues People,* like much that is written by Negro Americans at the present moment, takes on an inevitable resonance from the Freedom

Movement, but it is in itself characterized by a straining for a note of militancy which is, to say the least,distracting. Its introductory mood of scholarly analysis frequently shatters into a dissonance of accusation, and one gets the impression that while Jones wants to perform a crucial task which he feels *someone* should take on—as indeed someone should—he is frustrated by the restraint demanded of the critical pen and would like to pick up a club.

Perhaps this explains why Jones, who is also a poet and editor of a poetry magazine, gives little attention to the blues as lyric, as a form of poetry. He appears to be attracted to the blues for what he believes they tell us of the sociology of Negro American identity and attitude. Thus, after beginning with the circumstances in which he sees their origin, he considers the ultimate values of American society:

> The Negro as slave is one thing. The Negro as American is quite another. But the *path* the slave took to "citizenship" is what I want to look at. And I make my analogy through the slave citizen's music—through the music that is most closely associated with him: blues and a later, but parallel, development, jazz. And it seems to me that if the Negro represents, or is symbolic of, something in and about the nature of American culture, this certainly should be revealed by his characteristic music. ... I am saying that if the music of the Negro in America, in all its permutations, is subjected to a socio-anthropological as well as musical scrutiny, something about the essential nature of the Negro's existence in this country ought to be revealed, as well as something about the essential nature of this country, i.e., society as a whole. ...

The tremendous burden of sociology which Jones would place upon this body of music is enough to give even the blues the blues. At one point he tells us that "the one peculiar reference to the drastic change in the Negro from slavery to 'citizenship' is in his music." And later with more precision, he states:

> ...The point I want to make most evident here is that I cite the beginning of the blues as one beginning of American Negroes. Or, let me say, the reaction and subsequent relation of the Negro's experience in this country in *his* English is one beginning of the Negro's conscious appearance on the American scene.

No one could quarrel with Mr. Jones' stress upon beginnings. In 1833, two hundred and fourteen years after the first Africans were brought to these shores as slaves, a certain Mrs. Lydia Maria Child, a leading member of the American Anti-Slavery Society, published a paper entitled: *An Appeal in Favor of that Class of Americans Called Africans.* I am uncertain to what extent it actually reveals Mrs. Child's idea concerning the complex relationship between time, place, cultural and/or national identity and race, but her title sounds like a fine bit of contemporary ironic *signifying*—"signifying" here meaning, in the unwritten dictionary of American Negro usage, "rhetorical understatements." It tells us much of the thinking of her opposition, and it reminds us that as late as the 1890s, a time when Negro composers, singers, dancers and comedians dominated the American musical stage, popular Negro songs (including James Weldon Johnson's "Under the Bamboo Tree," now immortalized by T. S. Eliot) were commonly referred to as "Ethiopian Airs."

Perhaps more than any other people, Americans have been locked in a deadly struggle with time, with history. We've fled the past and trained ourselves to suppress, if not forget, troublesome details of the national memory, and a great part of our optimism, like our progress, has been bought at the cost of ignoring the processes through which we've arrived at any given moment in our national existence. We've fought continuously with one another over who and what we are, and, with the exception of the Negro, over who and what is American. Jones is aware of this and, although he embarrasses his own argument, his emphasis is to the point.

For it would seem that while Negroes have been undergoing a process of "Americanization" from a time preceding the birth of this nation—including the fusing of their blood lines with other non-African strains, there has persisted a stubborn confusion as to their American identity. Somehow it was assumed that the Negroes, of all the diverse American peoples, would remain unaffected by the climate, the weather, the political circumstances—from which not even slaves were exempt—the social structures, the national manners, the modes of production and the tides of the market, the national ideals, the conflicts of values, the rising and falling of national morale, or the complex give and take of acculturalization which was undergone by all others who found their existence within the American democracy. This confusion still persists and it is Mr. Jones' concern with it which gives *Blues People* a claim upon our attention.

Mr. Jones sees the American Negro as the product of a series of transformations, starting with the enslaved African, who became Afro-American slave, who became the American slave, who became, in turn, the highly qualified "citizen" whom we know today. The slave began by regarding himself as enslaved African, during the time when he still spoke his native language, or remembered it, practiced such aspects of his native religion as were possible and expressed himself musically in modes which were essentially African. These cultural traits became transmuted as the African lost consciousness of his African background, and his music, his religion, his language and his speech gradually became that of the American Negro. His sacred music became the spirituals, his work songs and dance music became the blues and primitive jazz, and his religion became a form of Afro-American Christianity. With the end of slavery Jones sees the development of jazz and the blues as results of the more varied forms of experience made available to the freedman. By the twentieth century the blues divided and became, on the one hand, a professionalized form of entertainment, while remaining, on the other, a form of folklore.

By which I suppose he means that some Negroes remained in the country and sang a crude form of the blues, while others went to the city, became more sophisticated, and paid to hear Ma Rainey, Bessie, or some of the other Smith girls sing them in night clubs or theatres. Jones gets this mixed up with ideas of social class—middle-class Negroes, whatever that term actually means, and light-skinned Negroes, or those Negroes corrupted by what Jones calls "White" culture—preferring the "classic" blues, and black, uncorrupted, country Negroes preferring "country blues."

For as with his music, so with the Negro. As Negroes became "middle-class" they rejected their tradition and themselves. "...they wanted any self which the mainstream dictated, and the mainstream *always* dictated. And this black middle-class, in turn, tried always to dictate that self, or this image of a whiter Negro, to the poorer, blacker Negroes."

One would get the impression that there was a rigid correlation between color, education, income and the Negro's preference in music. But what are we to say of a white-skinned Negro with brown freckles who owns sixteen oil wells sunk in a piece of Texas land once farmed by his ex-slave parents who were a blue-eyed, white-skinned, red-headed (kinky) Negro woman from Virginia and a blue-gummed, black-skinned, curly-haired Negro male from Mississippi, and who not only sang bass in a Holy Roller church, played the market and voted Republican but collected blues recordings and was a walking depository of blues tradition? Jones' theory no more allows for the existence of such a Negro than it allows for himself; but that "concord of sensibilities" which has been defined as the meaning of culture, allows for much more variety than Jones would admit.

Much the same could be said of Jones' treatment of the jazz during the thirties, when he claims its broader acceptance (i.e., its economic "success" as entertainment) led to a dilution, to the loss of much of its "black" character which caused a certain group of rebellious Negro musicians to create the "anti-mainstream" jazz style called bebop.

Jones sees bop as a conscious gesture of separatism, ignoring the fact that the creators of the style were seeking, whatever their musical intentions—and they were the least political of men—a fresh form of entertainment which would allow them their fair share of the entertainment market, which had been dominated by whites during the swing era. And although the boppers were reacting, at least in part, to the high artistic achievement of Armstrong, Hawkins, Basie and Ellington (all Negroes, all masters of the blues-jazz tradition), Jones sees their music as a recognition of his contention "that when you are black in a society where black is an extreme liability [it] is one thing, but to understand that it is the society which is lacking and is impossibly deformed because of this lack, and not *yourself*, isolates you even more from that society."

Perhaps. But today nothing succeeds like rebellion (which Jones as a "beat" poet should know) and while a few boppers went to Europe to escape, or became Muslims, others took the usual tours for the State Department. Whether this makes *them* "middle-class" in Jones' eyes I can't say, but his assertions—which are fine as personal statement—are not in keeping with the facts; his theory flounders before that complex of human motives which makes human history, and which is so characteristic of the American Negro.

Read as a record of an earnest young man's attempt to come to grips with his predicament as Negro American during a most turbulent period of our history, *Blues People* may be worth the reader's time. Taken as a theory of American Negro culture, it can only contribute more confusion than clarity. For Jones has stumbled over that ironic obstacle which lies in the path of any who would fashion a theory of American Negro culture while ignoring the intricate network of connections which binds Negroes to the larger society. To do so is to attempt a delicate brain surgery with a switch-blade. And it is possible that any viable theory of Negro American culture obligates us to fashion a more adequate theory of American culture as a whole. The heel bone is, after all, connected, through its various linkages, to the head bone. Attempt a serious evaluation of our national morality and up jumps the so-called Negro problem. Attempt to discuss jazz as a hermetic expression of Negro sensibility and immediately we must consider what the "mainstream" of American music really is.

Here political categories are apt to confuse, for while Negro slaves were socially, politically and economically separate (but only in a special sense even here), they were, in a cultural sense, much closer than Jones' theory allows him to admit.

"A slave," writes Jones, "cannot be a man." But what, one might ask, of those moments when he feels his metabolism aroused by the rising of the sap in spring? What of his identity among other slaves? With his wife? And isn't it closer to the truth that far from considering themselves only in terms of that abstraction, "a slave," the enslaved really thought of themselves as *men* who had been unjustly enslaved? And isn't the true answer to Mr. Jones' question, "What are you going to be when you grow up?" not, as he gives it, "a slave" but most probably a coachman, a teamster, a cook, the best damned steward on the Mississippi, the best jockey in Kentucky, a butler, a farmer, a stud, or, hopefully, a free man! Slavery was a most vicious system and those who endured and survived it a tough people, but it was *not* (and this is important for Negroes to remember for the sake of their own sense of who and what their grandparents were) a state of absolute repression.

A slave was, to the extent that he was a *musician,* one who expressed himself in music, a man who realized himself in the world of sound. Thus, while he might stand in awe before the superior technical ability of a white musician, and while he was forced to recognize a superior social status, he would never feel awed before the music which the technique of the white musician made available. His attitude as "musician" would lead him to seek to possess the music expressed through the technique, but until he could do so he would hum, whistle, sing or play the tunes to the best of his ability on any available instrument. And it was, indeed, out of the tension between desire and ability that the techniques of jazz emerged. This was likewise true of American Negro choral singing. For this, no literary explanation, no cultural analyses, no political slogans—indeed, not even a high degree of social or political freedom—was required. For the art—the blues, the spirituals, the jazz, the dance—was what we had in place of freedom.

Technique was then, as today, the key to creative freedom, but before this came a will toward expression. Thus, Jones' theory to the contrary, Negro musicians have never, as a group, felt alienated from any music sounded within their hearing, and it is my theory that it would be impossible to pinpoint the time when they were not shaping what Jones calls the mainstream of American music. Indeed, what group of musicians has made more of the sound of the American experience? Nor am I confining my statement to the sound of the slave experience, but am saying that the most authoritative rendering of America in music is that of American Negroes.

For as I see it, from the days of their introduction into the colonies, Negroes have taken, with the ruthlessness of those without articulate investments in cultural styles, whatever they could of European music, making of it that which would, when blended with the cultural tendencies inherited from Africa, express their own sense of life—while rejecting the rest. Perhaps this is only another way of saying that whatever the degree of injustice and inequality sustained by the slaves, American culture was, even before the official founding of the nation, pluralistic; and it was the African's origin in cultures in which art was highly functional which gave him an edge in shaping the music and dance of this nation.

The question of social and cultural snobbery is important here. The effectiveness of Negro music and dance is first recorded in the journals and letters of travelers but it is important to remember that they saw and understood only that which they were prepared to accept. Thus a Negro dancing a courtly dance appeared comic from the outside simply because the dancer was a slave. But to the Negro dancing it—and there is ample evidence that he danced it well—burlesque or satire might have been the point, which might have been difficult for a white observer to even imagine. During the 1870s Lafcadio Hearn reports that the best singers of Irish songs, in Irish dialect, were Negro dock workers in Cincinnati, and advertisements from slavery days described escaped slaves who spoke in Scottish dialect. The master artisans of the South were slaves, and white Americans have been walking Negro walks, talking Negro flavored talk (and prizing it when spoken by Southern belles), dancing Negro dances and singing Negro melodies far too long to talk of a "mainstream" of American culture to which they're alien.

Jones attempts to impose an ideology upon this cultural complexity, and this might be useful if he knew enough of the related subjects to make it interesting. But his version of the blues lacks a sense of the excitement and surprise of men living in the world—of enslaved and politically weak men successfully imposing their values upon a powerful society through song and dance.

The blues speak to us simultaneously of the tragic and the comic aspects of the human condition and they express a profound sense of life shared by many Negro Americans precisely because their lives combined these modes. This has been the heritage of a people who for hundreds of years could not celebrate birth or dignify death and whose need to live despite the dehumanizing pressures of slavery developed an endless capacity for laughing at their painful experiences. This is a group experience shared by many Negroes, and any effective study of the blues would treat them first as poetry and as ritual. Jones makes a distinction between classic and country blues, the one being entertainment and the other folklore. But the distinction is false. Classic blues were both entertainment *and* a form of folklore. When they were sung professionally in theatres, they were entertainment; when danced to in the form of recordings or used as a means of transmitting the traditional verses and their wisdom, they were folklore. There are levels of time and function involved here, and the blues which might be used in one place as entertainment (as gospel music is now being used in night clubs and on theatre stages) might be put to a ritual use in another. Bessie Smith might have been a "blues queen" to the society at large, but within the tighter Negro community where the blues were part of a total way of life, and a major expression of an attitude toward life, she was a priestess, a celebrant who affirmed the values of the group and man's ability to deal with chaos.

It is unfortunate that Jones thought it necessary to ignore the aesthetic nature of the blues in order to make his ideological point, for he might have come much closer had he considered the blues not as politics but as art. This would have still required the disciplines of anthropology and sociology—but as practiced by Constance Rourke, who was well aware of how much of American cultural expression is Negro. And he could learn much from the Cambridge School's discoveries of the connection between poetry, drama and ritual as a means of analyzing how the blues function in their proper environment. Simple taste should have led Jones to Stanley Edgar Hyman's work on the blues instead of Paul Oliver's sadly misdirected effort.

For the blues are not primarily concerned with civil rights or obvious political protest; they are an art form and thus a transcendence of those conditions created within the Negro community by the denial of social justice. As such they are one of the techniques through which Negroes have survived and kept their courage during that long period when many whites assumed, as some still assume, they were afraid.

Much has been made of the fact that *Blues People* is one of the few books by a Negro to treat the subject. Unfortunately for those who expect that Negroes would have a special insight into this mysterious art, this is not enough. Here, too, the critical intelligence must perform the difficult task which only it can perform.

The Aesthetic of *Blues People*

by William C. Fischer

The last pieces in LeRoi Jones' *Preface to a Twenty Volume Suicide Note* (1961) pursue the poet's growing rejection of old and borrowed expressive modes, poetry representative of the white-dominated Beat literary movement of which he was a part when he first started writing poetry. Jones begins to see that the "new" poets were, from a black point of view, writing in "old" ways inhospitable to his creative needs as a black artist. He begins to reach for a possible conception of a new self and a workable poetic alternative in the poems at the end of *Preface,* but without any intrusion at this point of political perspectives. He is still a Europeanized man, "Don Juan in Hell," but with a hint of possible rebirth, "like a new man/ or my old self...." The last poem of *Preface,* "Notes for a Speech," is inconclusive as a statement of a new genealogy, but does point in the direction of a new cultural consciousness. It is undefined as yet— "African blues/ does not know me...," he laments—but his non-Western origins will become increasingly apparent through the effort that results in *Blues People* two years later.

In many respects *Blues People* (1963) is the working out of the uncertainty expressed in "Notes for a Speech." Jones' subsequent research materializes in the anticipated speech, one that interprets "the essential nature of the Negro's existence in this country," by tracing the developing styles of black American music. It is Jones' attempt to define for himself the social and emotional implications of what he comes to see as the fundamentally different nature of his black American culture *vis-a-vis* what he calls the American mainstream. Jones' stance is not one of traditional scholarly "objectivity." The tone of his argument is energized by a growing ideological com-

"The Aesthetics of *Blues People*" by William C. Fischer. From "The Pre-Revolutionary Writings of Imamu Amiri Baraka," *The Massachusetts Review* 14, no. 2 (1973), 259-305. Reprinted from *The Massachusetts Review,* copyright © 1973 by permission of The Massachusetts Review, Inc.

mitment to a new cultural frame of reference, a new genealogy, one
that is African in its origins and Afro-American in terms of his own
specific placement in the world (to use his phrase again) as a United
States "citizen." The modes of speech and communication within this
new cultural perspective, as Jones shows, refer basically to a resilient
non-Western musical tradition, as set off against the prevailing
literary and media modes of the American culture satirized in *Preface.*

The basic ideological premise of *Blues People* is the delimitation
of a sharp dichotomy between the African/ Afro-American and the
Western/ European-American culture families. The inherently different values, styles, and world views on each side of the dichotomy
have significant political implications when forced into a tenuous
state of co-existence as they were under the New World system of
African enslavement. Slavery itself, debilitating as the practice is
under any circumstances, is not the sole issue. The cultural despot-
ism imposed upon the newly arrived African accounts for the basest
effects of the American version of the institution: "...to be brought
to a country, a culture, a society, that was, and is, in terms of purely
philosophical correlatives, the complete antithesis of one's own
version of man's life on earth—that is the cruelest aspect of this
particular enslavement."[1] Jones stresses than an African enslaved
by another African (as often happened) would at least still be recog-
nized by his vanquisher, because of the thread of cultural acquain-
tance that connected them, as another man, another human being,
however much exploited and abused. The New World slave "was
not even accorded membership in the human race." All the sustaining forms of African culture—those institutions and systems of
thought which had tangible political, economic, and artistic manifestations—were obliterated by the non-African slave-holders. The
only Africanisms that survived, Jones emphasizes, were those that
did "not have *artifacts* as their end products." Such "nonmaterial
aspects of the African's culture" as religion, music, and dance "were
almost impossible to eradicate."

This focus on cultural dislocation has elicited some sharp criticism.
Ralph Ellison, who categorically rejects any racial ideology in favor
of an aesthetic cultivation of the ambivalences and intricacies at
work in the interaction of black and white experience, sees Jones'

---

[1]*Blues People* (New York, 1963), p. 1; further page references in parentheses in
my text.

account as oversimplified and lacking in attention to artistic considerations: "It is unfortunate that Jones thought it necessary to ignore the aesthetic nature of the blues in order to make his ideological point, for he might have come much closer had he considered the blues not as politics but as art."[2] As indicated by the circumstances surrounding the poem "Betancourt" (written in Havana in 1960 during a visit to Cuba with a group of black writers invited by Fidel Castro), Jones had already resolved this issue in favor of politics.[3] *Blues People* was not written primarily with an eye toward intellectual objectivity and academic nicety of taste. What might be construed as Jones' tendency toward mythicizing[4] is meant to reflect an independent style and value system in black music that are ideologically consistent with his increasingly nationalist point of view.

In his own way, in fact, Jones is very much concerned with art, especially in the comparative way that African and Western music function in their respective cultures. African music, like all African art, grows out of specific social and religious experiences of the people who actually participate in the making of that music. Western music—and all "serious" creative art since the humanist Renaissance, Jones would insist—exists as a fine arts tradition in which most people do not participate directly but instead passively stand by to appreciate the artifacts produced by a select few. Functionalism is the key concept in the distinction:

> If we think of African music as regards its intent, we must see that it differed from Western music in that it was a purely *functional* music. Borneman lists some basic types of songs common to West African cultures: songs used by young men to influence young women (courtship, challenge, scorn); songs used by workers to make their tasks easier; songs used by older men to prepare the adolescent boys for manhood, and so on. "Serious" Western music, except for early religious music, has been strictly an "art" music. One would not think of any particular *use* for Haydn's symphonies, except perhaps the "cultivation of the soul." ... It was, and is, inconceivable in the African culture to make a separation between music, dancing, song, the artifact, and a man's life or his worship of his gods. (pp. 28-29.)

[2]Review of *Blues People* in *Shadow and Act* (New York, 1964), p. 250. Included in this collection, pp. 55-63.

[3]See the author's "The Pre-Revolutionary Writings of Imamu Amiri Baraka," *The Massachusetts Review* 14, no. 2 (1973), 272-73—Ed.

[4]Charles Keil, *Urban Blues* (Chicago, 1966), p. 39. Keil objects mildly to Jones' mythicizing, likening the emphasis on traditional blues to the moldy fig attitude of jazz buffs, but praises the precision and insight of most of Jones' musical analyses.

This conception of an art which issues directly out of the experience of the people — as having a social function, a use — is germane to the cultural and political intentions of Jones' later poetry and drama as Imamu Amiri Baraka, and is the African/Afro-American basis for rejecting the notion that a poet's work should not deal with politics.

Having established the cultural premise of his study, Jones then sets about to examine in detail the styles and implications of Afro-American music. He begins with a discussion of the important features of African music that determine the development of Afro-American blues and jazz, especially in terms of the rhythms and of the tonal and timbral flexibility in African vocal music. He identifies such non-Western stylistic elements as communal antiphony and improvisation, interpreting their social significance as they are acted upon by the tensions of Afro-American experience. Consistent with his cultural ideology, Jones characterizes as the blues those surviving Africanisms in music that have remained most resistant to the incursions of Western musical styles and conceptions. The closer Afro-American music stays to the marrow of the blues tradition the closer it is to the people; and thus is it a faithful and accurate representation of their black perspective on the American experience.

Although the ostensible focus is on the music, one of Jones' persistent and inevitable concerns is the development of Afro-American speech, uses of language whose morphology and inflection are viable evidence of surviving Africanisms,[5] and many of whose stylistic aspects are often deeply embedded in musical experiences — much more so than is the case in Western culture where the relationship has developed essentially into one between spoken language and the dictates imposed upon it by the forms of written language. The reciprocity between African speech and music is signally dramatized by the talking drums: they not only reproduce speech rhythms but also the tonal and timbral qualities of the human voice. (p. 26.) This reciprocity is carried over into Afro-American experience, so that to talk about Afro-American forms of music is necessarily to talk about Afro-American uses of language as well. Where the artistic impulses of Western culture tend to channel speech energy into written forms, into literature, the creative thrust of Afro-American

[5] Jones frequently refers to Melville Herskovits' *The Myth of the Negro Past* (New York, 1941) as the source for several of his discussions on Afro-American speech. Herskovits' important study is essentially concerned with demonstrating the extensive survival of Africanisms in Afro-American culture, thus belying the myth that black Americans have no line of connection with their African past.

culture directs the dynamics of language into musical forms. Jones points out that early patterns in Afro-American music like the "shouts" and "field hollers" were mainly stylized formulations of speech, "little more than highly rhythmical lyrics," and that such vocalizations essentially determine the style in which black musicians play their instruments: "Even the purely instrumental music of the American Negro contains constant reference to vocal music. Blues-playing is the closest imitation of the human voice of any music I've heard; the vocal effects that jazz musicians have delighted in from Bunk Johnson to Ornette Coleman are evidence of this." (p. 28.) A. B. Spellman speaks pointedly of the long-term historical function of Afro-American music as a vocabulary, a surrogate form of language, so to speak: "The frenetic religiosity of Afro-American slave music was clearly an attempt at establishing a vocabulary of release by a people whose languages were conscientiously taken from them by slave owners, who even went so far as to destroy their drums, a major means of communication. It is from this perspective that the development of Afro-American music must be viewed: as the progressive refinement of a sublimated vocabulary...."[6]

Finally, Jones must deal with the implication of all of this for himself as a writer, as a black poet initially working with the literary forms of written English. On the basis of his analysis of spoken language in a musical context, his assessment is inevitable. With a cursory glance over the comparatively brief tradition of black American writers, he concludes that their work has been "essentially undistinguished." (pp. 130-131.) Quite simply, music, not literature, is the primary expressive mode in Afro-American culture, and music-related uses of language are able to convey most accurately the quality—"the essential nature"—of the existence of the black American. Having renounced the "old" literary way, Jones is discovering that the pure African-derived alternatives may not be literary at all, but rather exist outside of literature. Or, as will turn out to be the case, short of abandoning writing altogether, he will be forced to adapt the written word to extra-literary influences, to innovate radical techniques that will move literary expression as close as possible to spoken language and music. For the moment, however, Jones sees the issue less as a matter of the need for new techniques of writing, and more a question of simply identifying which forms of

[6]"Not Just Whistling Dixie," in *Black Fire: An Anthology of Afro-American Writing*, eds. LeRoi Jones and Larry Neal (New York, 1969), p. 160.

expression represent "a legitimacy of emotional concern" with black experience. The writing of *Blues People* brings him to validate intellectually his emotional rejection of himself as a traditional poet as expressed in the self-lacerating lyrics of *Preface.* Speaking in general of the extent to which American culture has modified the styles of black music, he says: "Of course, that mainstream wrought very definite and very constant changes upon the *form* of the American Negro's music, but the emotional significance and vitality at its core remain, to this day, unaltered." (p. 131.) His faith had not been so certain in the earlier poetry. Black music is a loose point of reference for several of the poems in *Preface,* especially blues-related poems like "LOOK FOR YOU YESTERDAY..." and "Roi's New Blues," although these constitute more a rejection of the tradition than a recognition of its sustaining qualities and functional forms. "The Bridge" makes abundant use of musical terminology transformed into metaphors of personal disorientation, but on the whole music exists in that collection as a matter of vague referral, as in the writings of Ginsberg and Kerouac, not as an aesthetic model. Some poems toward the end do make intermittent reference to a viable black music, but this motif is relatively non-specific.

The main thrust of Jones' downgrading of a so-called Negro literature in *Blues People*—a thesis appearing in its earliest version as a lecture in 1962 and then subsequently as an essay entitled "The Myth of a Negro Literature"[7]—is a class analysis of the function of literature for the black writer. Under the chapter rubric "Enter the Middle Class," Jones claims that the literary tradition is not only incapable of representing the emotional concerns of black people, but as an art it serves the more practical social purpose for a black man of paving the way into middle-class America. The price, needless to say, is an emotional uprooting from one's black experience. For an Afro-American to utilize the most potent art form of the West is necessarily to identify with the middle-class experiences and values that shape the conventions of that art, resulting in the sort of dissipation and self-deprecation represented by the poetry in *Preface.* Referring particularly to turn-of-the-century writers like Charles Chesnutt and Sutton Griggs, although no doubt speaking also out of the emotional tangle of his own black middle-class origins and recent literary experience, Jones reveals the hoax:

[7]An address delivered at the Society for African Culture, 14 March 1962; published in *Saturday Review* (April 20, 1963); reprinted in *Home,* pp. 105-115.

Literature, for most Negro writers, for instance, was always an example of "culture," in the narrow sense of "cultivation" or "sophistication" in an individual within their own group. The Negro artist, because of his middle-class background, carried an artificial social burden as the "best and most intelligent" of Negroes, and usually entered into the "serious" arts to exhibit his social graces—as a method, or means, of displaying his participation in the serious aspects of Western culture. To be a writer was to be "cultivated," in the stunted bourgeois sense of the word. (p. 132.

With the coming into prominence of the Nation of Islam (especially through the preachings of Malcolm X) along with the culturally modified Marxist orientation of Third World revolutionary politics (as represented closest to home by the example of Cuba and Jones' experience there), it is not surprising to find Jones' cultural-political views reflecting the changes as well. *Blues People* represents the working out of some of these changes in Jones' mind without the related complication, as in *Preface,* of having to draw out the strands of his personal and domestic life at the same time.

A Simple Muttering Elegance: Prose

Jones (Baraka) and His Literary Heritage in *The System of Dante's Hell*

by Lloyd W. Brown

After a long period of political invective, critical studies of LeRoi Jones now appear to be shifting from mere name-calling to the reasoned criticism that seeks to understand the difficult complexities of his art. This recent shift has been most evident in studies of his poetry, especially with regard to the literary antecedents as well as philosophical heritage of Jones' poetic art.[1] As some of these recent studies have shown, the allusory texture of Jones' style seems to demand an analysis that demonstrates the connections between his art and earlier writers. This demand is the more pressing at this time because, name-callers aside, most students of Jones' work have been concentrating on his socio-literary background almost exclusively in relation to the idioms of Black American music and language. These idioms are, of course, vital in Jones' art, but his achievements as a writer cannot be fully measured in isolation from that Western heritage which is so evident in his allusory structures and which require rather careful examination at this time precisely because so many of Jones' own statements, in his art and in his political essays, *seem* to repudiate that heritage in its entirety.[2] However, it would be misleading to assume that such a repudiation automatical-

"Jones (Baraka) and His Literary Heritage in *The System of Dante's Hell*" by Lloyd W. Brown. From *Obsidian* 1, no. 1 (Spring 1975), 5-17. Reprinted by permission of the author.

[1]Esther M. Jackson, "LeRoi Jones (Imamu Amiri Baraka): Form and the Progression of Consciousness," *College Language Association Journal,* 17, No. 1 (September 1973), 33-56; Lee A. Jacobus, "Imamu Amiri Baraka: The Quest for Moral Order," in *Modern Black Poets,* ed. Donald B. Gibson (Englewood Cliffs: Prentice-Hall, 1973), pp. 112-126. These essays are included in this volume on pp. 36-47 and 97-111, respectively.

[2]See, for example, the Jones' preface to *Black Magic: Collected Poetry 1961-67* (Indianapolis: Bobbs-Merrill, 1969).

ly negates the importance of Western literature and philosophy in
his work—including those very works which appear to reject the
Western heritage. For in the first place even the rhetoric of outright
rejection may have the effect of confirming the ultimate importance
of the "rejected" tradition in Jones' art—and this frequently happens
even in a collection like *Black Magic* (1969) where a stringently anti-
Western poem functions within and appeals to a *Western* mode of
contemporary poetic appreciation (a literate as well as oral medium,
allusive, compacted, and accessible to the literary cognoscenti rather
than to the masses at whom it is, allegedly, aimed). And, secondly,
when the act of repudiation becomes the burden of a given work
then, willy-nilly, the repudiated tradition remains crucial, not only
in the immediate contextual sense of its thematic role, but also in the
long-term and more fundamental sense of its continuing influence
(negative or otherwise) on the artist himself. In other words, and at
the risk of belaboring the obvious, the rejected tradition continues
to function in the artist's work for the simple reason that a conscious
act of repudiation does not necessarily constitute an expunging: the
philosophical habits and technical skills which Jones developed during the early phases of his art have not disappeared merely because
he questions aspects of Western culture and certain traditions in
Western literature. And as long as these habits and skills which have
been shaped by his Western heritage remain, then there will always
be a tension between the artist's proclaimed repudiation and the
continuing role of that heritage in his work. In brief, what is at issue
here is not simply the direct contributions of Western literature and
philosophy to Jones' art, but also the ambiguous relationship between the writer and that Western tradition—that is, the main issue is
one of Jones *and* his literary legacy.

Jones' only novel is very appropriate here because quite apart
from the obvious reference to Dante Alighieri's *Divine Comedy*,
The System of Dante's Hell is saturated with allusions to the major
writers of Western literature, from Homer to Eliot. Moreover, the
novel is a sustained dramatization of the continuing ambiguities
that are inherent in the relationship between Jones and his literary
heritage.[3] The richly allusive texture of the narrative is amply il-
lustrated by Roi's initial impressions upon entering a brothel in the
Bottom, a Southern Black ghetto: "He pointed like Odysseus and

---

[3]References to Jones' novel are based on *The System of Dante's Hell*, Evergreen
edition (New York: Grove, 1966).

like Virgil, the weary shade, at some circle. For Dante, me, the yng wild virgin of the universe to look. To see what terror. What illusion. What sudden shame, the world is made. Of what death and lust I fondled and thot to make beautiful or escape, at least, into some other light, where each death was abstract and intimate" (p. 126). This brief, almost casual, introduction to the brothel scene juxtaposes allusions to the Ulysses archetype in Homer *(The Odyssey)* and Dante (*The Inferno*, in which Virgil guides the poet to hell), Tennyson's "The Lotus-Eaters" where Ulysses is "pointing" the way to his travel-worn crew, and James Joyce's *Ulysses* (the entry of the "virginal" young poet into a brothel — a parallel that is subsequently reinforced by Roi's self-identification as Stephen Dedalus).[4] Finally, the literary allusions are interwoven with the mythic reference in that the echoes of the Joycean Dedalus recall the legend of another artist-creator, the mythical Daedalus. The remarkably compact nature of these multiple allusions has an important perspectival effect. The form and structure of these compacted allusions create a telescoping effect — the kind of historical perspective which enables us to perceive the Ulysses archetype, simultaneously, in a succession of epochs in literature, from Homer to Joyce. In effect, the passage offers an archetypal perspective on the literary tradition with which Jones interacts throughout the novel.

This interaction is based on Jones' ambivalence towards that Western heritage. Thus it is significant that in perceiving the literary tradition behind the Ulysses archetype Roi identifies himself with Dante and with Joyce's Dedalus; for there is a clear distinction between Dante and Joyce in their treatment of the archetype. In Dante's *Inferno* Ulysses' passionate quest for knowledge and for the complete experience of life itself demands our admiration, in much the same way that Tennyson's Ulysses (in both "The Lotus-Eaters" and "Ulysses") commands our respect. But Dante's Ulysses is predominantly a figure of sin, the sin of pursuing knowledge egotistically, to the neglect of family and social responsibilities. On the other hand, James Joyce's Ulysses archetype, Leopold Bloom, is a predominantly sympathetic figure of compassion and humanity, but Stephen Dedalus, the young poet, is his antithesis, a cold-blooded artist-intellectual who offers a dry, abstract detachment where Bloom offers a warm involvement. So that in identifying Roi with Dedalus *and* Dante, Jones evokes a sense of detachment from the Ulysses

[4]Compare A. Walton Litz, *James Joyce* (New York: Twayne, 1966), pp. 78-79.

archetype insofar as it represents the (Western) mind in its quest for knowledge. Moreover, this detachment emphasizes Roi's inadequacy in the kind of humanity that the Joycean Ulysses symbolizes — and in specifically ethnic terms this underscores the limitations of Roi's self-acceptance as a Black. But in another sense Roi *is* Ulysses, for as a symbol of the quest for knowledge and for an expanded consciousness the Ulysses figure represents Roi's odyssey for human and ethnic wholeness in the novel; and as such, the archetype promises a capacity for growth even in Roi's most limited moments in the novel. Moreover, in the final analysis, this kind of ambivalence towards the Ulysses archetype is developed on an ironic basis. Since the Ulysses archetype represents not merely growth and knowledge as such, but also those *Western* traditions, in literature and philosophy, which have shaped Roi's early development, then the maturing of Roi's ethnic humanity has to result in an increasing detachment from the archetype's cultural sources — in proportion to Roi's growing uneasiness with his acquired middle-class values. In other words, Roi's association with the Ulysses archetype and its literary interpreters underscores both his involvement in, and emergent rebellion against, the Western heritage that is embodied by the archetype. Moreover, the irony of developing a (Black) odyssey motif in order to disengage himself from Ulysses and his West is complemented by the ironic strategy of identifying himself with *Western* literary symbols (Dante and Dedalus) in order to express his growing detachment from the literary and philosophical traditions of the West. And, by extension, Roi's ambivalence towards the White West reflects LeRoi Jones' general treatment of the Western "fact" in the novel as a whole. The Western heritage is deeply suspect but its influence is pervasive, precisely because it is the source of so many of the referents that are available to the Black artist who is attempting to define his own sense of identity and tradition. And this is so because any honest attempt by the artist to define the present nature of his art and to project his sense of artistic growth requires him to recount and assess the past (which is indelibly Western in a case like LeRoi Jones') as well as the present and future. In effect, the Western traditions of history and of the novelist's own past embody ethno-cultural values which not only subvert or threaten Black self-acceptance but are also intertwined with the roots of his art. Consequently, the very act of attempting to counter that subversiveness attests to the pervasiveness of the Western influence on his art. That influence is implied in the large number of references to Western writers, but especially by the allusions to the three writers with whom we are primarily concerned here—Dante, T.S. Eliot, and Joyce.[5]

Of these three, Dante's relationship with Jones' novel is the most immediate. The parallels between *The Inferno* and the thematic structure of *The System of Dante's Hell* are accessible enough.[6] The localized symbol of hell which Dante derives from Christian eschatology offers his readers a moral hierarchy that is represented by the progressively degenerate sinners of the nine circles. In Jones' work the novelist dispenses with Dante's Christian schema in order to concentrate wholly on hell as a socio-cultural experience which is defined in localized terms by the Black ghetto and a hostile White society, and in psychological terms, by the protagonist's racial self-hatred. Altogether, the nine circles of Dante's *Inferno* have been transformed from an objectified entity into a subjective experience —the experience of Roi's degeneration throughout the novel. For as he progresses, in a material sense, from the harshness of the ghetto to the relative security of mainstream America, his ethnic and human values degenerate; and that degeneration is measured by the inverted hierarchy of the nine-circle structure, from the vestibule to the circle of the heretics. Or, in the words of Jones' epilogue:

> I am and was and will be a social animal.
> Hell is definable only in those terms. I can get no place else; it wdn't exist. ...
> Hell in the head.
> The torture of being the unseen object, and, the constantly observed subject.
> The flame of social dichotomy. Split open down the center, which is the early legacy of the black man unfocused on blackness (p. 153).

Accordingly, the autobiographical themes of *The System of Dante's Hell* project Roi's development as a continuing descent into the psychological hell of racial self-hatred, of being "unfocused on blackness." And in order to modify Dante's conventional eschatology for the purposes of this psycho-ethnic emphasis, Jones "put The Heretics

---

[5] Major writers named or cited in the novel also include Pound (pp. 31, 119), Cummings (p. 31), Proust and Yeats (p. 58), Kierkegaard (p. 86), Kafka (p. 87), Dylan Thomas (p. 119), Homer and Tennyson (p. 126).

[6] See Lloyd W. Brown, "LeRoi Jones (Imamu Amiri Baraka) as Novelist: Theme and Structure in *The System of Dante's Hell*," *Negro American Literature Forum*, 7, No. 4 (Winter 1973), 132-142.

in the deepest part of hell, though Dante had them spared, on higher ground. It is heresy, against one's own sources, running in terror, from one's deepest responses and insights...the denial of feeling... that I see as basest evil" (p. 7).

However, these parallels or adaptations do not reflect Jones' complete interest in Dante. That fundamental ambivalence which we have remarked earlier in his view of Western traditions in general is particularly strong in relation to Dante. At the same time that the eschatological system of Dante's nine circles provides Jones with a symbolic structure for his own ethnic themes, those themes are also based on a concept of hell and morality ("hell in the head") which rejects Dante's highly systematized image of the Christian hell. Moreover, this rejection includes the general tradition of abstract systems in Western culture, and those socio-economic systems that are based on the Western mystique of scientific rationalism: "IN THIS CONCEPTION OF THE ENTIRE WORLD OF TECHNOLOGY WE TRACE EVERYTHING BACK TO MAN AND FINALLY DEMAND AN ETHICS SUITABLE TO THE WORLD OF TECHNOLOGY" (p. 98). And, of course, this culture has also evolved the racial and socio-economic systems which have encouraged the existence of the ghetto-system in Black America. And in turn, Jones' scepticism about Dante's Western Christianity and the Western abstractionism of *The Inferno* is counterbalanced by the fact that he shares with Dante a strong attraction to the vitalism of the Ulysses archetype—a vitalism that Dante's Ulysses describes as a passion "to experience the far-flung world/ and the failings and felicities of mankind. ...to press on toward manhood and recognition."[7] But, to complete Jones' ambiguous relationship with Dante, the creative possibilities of the Ulysses archetype are undermined, in Roi's character, by the distinctively Western ethos which, as we have already seen, is represented in the figure. Interestingly enough, Jones' ambivalence towards Dante and his Ulysses re-enacts Dante's own ambevalence towards Ulysses and his pagan sources: in the ethnic context of Jones' American hell and in the social experience of the Black Ulysses-Dante-Roi, Dante's Christianity is the real paganism, and the narrowly systematizing modes of Western epistemology are the real heresy. Consequently, Roi's experiences in the Bottom amount to a kind of conversion, or at the very least, the prelude to conversion. He recognizes the self-destructiveness of his "imitation

[7]*The Inferno*, trans. John Ciardi, Mentor edition (New York: New American Library, 1954). Canto XXVI, ll. 92, 93, 111.

white" identity as a "young pharaoh," a young "White": "Young pharaoh, romantic, liar. . . . My soul is white, pure white, and soars" (pp. 128, 140). This confession is prompted by his encounter with Peaches, the Black prostitute, whose crude self-acceptance is superior to his racial self-hatred. Consequently, on looking at Peaches Roi "felt the world grow together as I hadn't known it. All lies before, I thought. All fraud and sickness. This was the world. It leaned under its own suns, and people moved on it. A real world of flesh, of smells, of soft black harmonies and color. The dead maelstrom of my head, a sickness. The sun so warm and lovely on my face, the melon sweet going down. Peaches' music and her radio's" (p. 148).

The duality that is inherent in Jones' relationship with Dante and the traditions represented by *The Inferno* brings us to the issue of the artist's place in time and tradition. More specifically, this brings up the subject of Jones' awareness of the place of *his* art in time and tradition—that is, the relationship between (Western) tradition and his individual/ethnic talent. And in this regard there are clear analogies between Jones' novel and T.S. Eliot's description of the artist and tradition. Hence, to return to that ubiquitous Ulysses archetype, the sense of simultaneity which Jones derives from the archetypal mode is similar in kind to that historical mode of perception which Eliot describes in *Tradition and the Individual Talent:*

> [Tradition] involves, in the first place, the historical sense, which we may call nearly indispensable to anyone who would continue to be a poet beyond his twenty-fifth year; and the historical sense involves a perception, not only of the pastness of the past, but of its presence; the historical sense compels a man to write not only with his own generation in his bones, but with a feeling that the whole of the literature of Europe from Homer and within it the whole of the literature of his own country has a simultaneous existence and composes a simultaneous order. This historical sense, which is the sense of the timeless as well as of the temporal and of the timeless and of the temporal together, is what makes a writer traditional. And it is at the same time what makes a writer most acutely conscious of his place in time, of his own contemporaneity.[8]

The Ulysses archetype in *The System of Dante's Hell* exemplifies the workings of Eliot's historical sense in that the archetypal mode readily accommodates Jones' simultaneous perception of the past

[8]T.S. Eliot, *Selected Essays 1917-1932* (London: Faber & Faber, 1932), p. 14.

and present, and his awareness of his own relationship with literary tradition—in this case, with the long heritage represented by the successive roles of the archetype in "the literature of Europe since Homer." Moreover, as we have seen, Roi's intellectual growth entails an identification with Dante and with Joyce's Dedalus; thus it is reasonable to conclude that his maturation is modelled in part on the kind of relationship which Eliot sees 'between youthful talent and established tradition. In other words, Roi is "acutely conscious" of his ethnic and cultural "contemporaneity" in American society, first in terms of his imitation whiteness, and second in terms of his emerging racial conscience. Moreover, he perceives the "presence" and the "pastness" of cultural traditions in the West when he identifies with some of the major representatives of that tradition and when he becomes aware of the Ulysses archetype as a Western mode in his past and as an emotional catalyst for his future ethnicity.

If Eliot's essay sheds light on the significance of tradition and individuality in *The System of Dante's Hell,* his other critical works also provide the key to a specific area of Jones' reaction to Western tradition. Hence there are significant parallels between Jones' ambivalence towards Dante, on the one hand, and on the other hand, T.S. Eliot's qualified acceptance of Dante's *Inferno.* For while Jones adapts Dante's thematic structure and rejects its underlying eschatology, Eliot is constrained to account for his positive response to Dante's poetic imagination in the absence of any real enthusiasm for Dante's dogma: "I deny that the reader must share the beliefs of the poet in order to enjoy the poetry fully" (*Selected Essays,* p. 255). Thus, in the final analysis, the significance of Dante in Jones' novel is similar to those ties which contemporary critics have traced between the *Divine Comedy* and Eliot's contemporaries. According to Erich Auerbach, for example, "although the Christian eschatology that had given birth to this new vision of man was to lose its unity and vitality, the European mind was so permeated with the idea of human destiny that even in very un-Christian artists it preserved the Christian force and tension which were Dante's gift to posterity."[9] Auerbach's observations deserve to be noted in some detail here not only because they are an apt summary of Dante's significance for the Anglo-Catholic Eliot and the decidedly *anti*-Christian Jones, but also because Auerbach's comments can also be applied to the char-

---

[9]Erich Auerbach, "The Survival and Transformation of Dante's View of Reality," in *Dante: A Collection of Critical Essays,* ed. John Freccero (Englewood Cliffs: Prentice-Hall, 1965), p. 12.

acteristic ambivalence with which Jones views Eliot himself in *The System of Dante's Hell.*

His sense of tradition and his double-edged reaction to Dante's dogma and Dante's poetic imagination suggest that Jones' themes have been shaped by Eliot's work or, at the very least, by the *kind* of criteria which Eliot contributed to modern criticism. On this basis Jones' fictive vision complements the close affinities which his protagonist, Roi, feels for Eliot, among others: "Eliot, Pound, Cummings, Apollinaire were living across from Kresge's. I was erudite and talked to light-skinned women" (p. 31). But even here the sense of identification with Eliot and *his* erudite tradition (including Ezra Pound and E.E. Cummings) is counterbalanced by the immediate context. The reference to his sexual preference for light-skinned women implies Roi's racial self-hatred. And this sexual motif and its ethnic implications establish an ambiguous context for his tribute to the Western heritage: Eliot and the others are crucial to his intellectual growth, but they are also seen, in retrospect, as part of those Western values which he has perverted into a "light-skinned" denial of his racial identity. This implied detachment from Eliot is more explicit as Roi is subsequently forced to come to terms with the heresy of his racial self-denial. As an heretic, in the final circle, Roi now sees his intellectual heritage from the West in terms of beauty and agony: "And I turned away & doubled up like rubber or black figure sliding at the bottom of any ocean. Thomas, Joyce, Eliot, Pound, all gone by & I thot agony at how beautiful I was" (p. 119). And in that self-revealing encounter with Peaches and the world of the Bottom, Eliot and *his* world are an alien, even subversive, irrelevance: "The world? Literate? Brown-skinned. Stuck in the ass. Suffering from what? Can you read? Who is T.S. Eliot? So what? A cross. You've got to like girls. Weirdo. Break, Roi, break" (p. 134).

Roi's self-admonition is crucial here, for we need to determine whether Jones' ambivalence towards Eliot and the West evolves into a complete break with the Western heritage. Altogether, Jones' relationship with both Dante and Eliot establishes his duality as an artist. The close identification with Dante's art and with Eliot's intellectuality acknowledges the extent to which Roi and Jones are logically the creatures of their Western environment. But, as we have already noted in the treatment of Dante and in the growing detachment from Eliot, Jones is simultaneously a creator in that he is searching out, and giving expression to, modes of ethnic selfhood which question, even break away from, Eliot's West. Having been molded by the Western traditions represented by the Ulysses archetype, Jones is now on a new odyssey that starts with a deep-seated scepticism about the Western roots of his identity. But does this scepticism amount to a complete "break" in the novel? Does Jones' Black odyssey imply a complete negation of the West? The answer is obviously important in any final assessment of Jones' relationship with the Western heritage, and that answer lies largely in the significance of James Joyce in *The System of Dante's Hell.*

In identifying Roi as Stephen Dedalus, Jones links the ethnic development of his protagonist with James Joyce's insights into the growth of the artistic imagination, in both *A Portrait of the Artist as a Young Man* and *Ulysses.* Hence Roi's odyssey for ethnic self-awareness is intensified by the artist's simultaneous search for a sense of moral purpose. In *Ulysses* Joyce draws upon the Ulysses myth to project that image of a complete and sympathetic humanity which Leopold Bloom embodies and against which we measure the cold virginity of Roi's personality. And the brothel scene in which Roi admits that cold virginity obviously recalls the brothel episode, in *Ulysses,* in which Leopold Bloom encounters Stephen. In Jones' brothel scene the Ulysses archetype appears fleetingly as Roi's companion, but later it appears in the person of Peaches whose "warm" world under "real" suns melts Roi's cold intellectuality. And appropriately it is to her that he (wordlessly) confesses the limitations of the Dedalus mentality: "Hot hot tears and trying to sing. Or say to Peaches, 'Please, you don't know me. Not what's in my head. I'm beautiful. Stephen Dedalus. A mind, here where there is only steel. Nothing else'" (p. 140). And throughout all of this the implication is that Roi's development as a whole human being, and his maturity as an artist, depend on the acquisition of the sympathetic warmth of the Joycean Ulysses.

But here we are brought once again to the characteristic ethnocultural ambivalence of the novel. Roi-Dedalus' crisis of identity is based on his allegiance (as a "young pharaoh") to a Western heritage that *includes* Joyce. Thus, in one sense, Stephen Dedalus' Anglo-Irish tensions are analogous to the Black-White double-consciousness of Jones' Roi-Dante-Dedalus, in much the same way that the incomplete humanity of Joyce's Stephen is echoed in the coldness of Jones' Roi. But, in another sense, the *completion* of Roi's humanity and, with it, the maturation of his art, depend on a "break" (to borrow his own self-admonitory phrase) from Joyce and his tradition. Paradoxically, Roi-Dedalus can only become Roi-Ulysses— he can only realize the *kind* of completeness that is symbolized by Bloom-Ulysses—by breaking away from the heritage that is the source of Joyce's Ulysses archetype. And by extension, Roi-Jones can only mature as an artist through the destruction of Ulysses-Joyce. Ironically, Joyce himself has perfected the kind of characterization that is recalled by the development of Jones' protagonist. In both *A Portrait of the Artist* and *Ulysses,* Stephen Dedalus' growth as an artist is based on a deep ambivalence towards sources (Roman Catholic, Irish, paternalistic) that are at once formative and restrictive. In *A Portrait of the Artist* Stephen seeks an intellectual wholeness by fleeing family and Ireland. The flight obviously recalls Stephen's mythic namesake, Daedalus. But it is also based on Joyce's well known theory of symbolic fatherhood—especially in *Ulysses* where Dedalus speculates on the manner in which the child figure is really a projected image of the father-artist.[10] In effect, the self-realization of the artist-son requires the negation of the father-artist image; Stephen Dedalus' intellectual and artistic maturity depends on some negation of his family sources and cultural roots. Consequently, Roi's growth, in *The System of Dante's Hell,* follows the Joycean pattern of symbolic fatherhood insofar as that growth requires the destruction of Roi's (symbolic) Western parentage. In effect, Jones' Roi-Dante-Dedalus reinforces the paradoxical nature of his relationship with Joyce and the Western heritage in the very process of "breaking" away from that heritage—precisely because the break is so closely modelled on the Joycean artist's growth-as-rebellion.

Moreover, to conclude this paradox, the very real limits of this break-away are also modelled on the qualified nature of Stephen Dédalus' repudiation of his own heritage. It is appropriate, and significant, that in each author the ambiguous heritage is symbolized by hell. In Jones' novel hell, of course, represents the ethno-cultural

---

[10]James Joyce, *Ulysses* (New York: Modern Library, 1934), pp. 195, 206-208. Compare A. Walton Litz, *James Joyce* (p. 18); Edmund L. Epstein, *The Ordeal of Stephen Dedalus: The Conflict of the Generations in James Joyce's "A Portrait of the Artist as a Young Man"* (Carbondale & Edwardsville: Southern Illinois University Press, 1971), pp. 5-11.

and rationalistic roots of his Western roots. In *A Portrait of the Artist* the priest's horrific vision of hell confirms Stephen's strong Roman Catholic sensibilities through the sheer force of its impact on his sense of (carnal) guilt: "Every word for him!... Flames burst forth from his skull like a corolla, shrieking like voices: Hell! Hell! Hell! Hell! Hell!"[11] As students of Joyce have agreed, Stephen's rebellion against his Irish-Catholic heritage does not constitute a complete break. The intellectual alienation from his religious background cannot completely expunge the kind of deep impressions which Catholicism and its symbols (including hell) have left on his imagination and moral sense. And ironically enough, Stephen's adult acts of intellectual repudiation confirm the depth of those impressions.[12] In a similar vein, the Joycean modes through which Jones projects his disenchantment with Joyce's West demonstrate the extent to which the evolution of the Black artist's aesthetic and moral wholeness confirms strong ties with the Western heritage, even in the act of repudiation. Hence Jones' Roi-Dante-Dedalus experiences the kind of intellectual growth and ethnic self-realization that demands a rejection of self-destructive Western criteria, but his artistic imagination bears the indelible marks of the Western influence which he inherits through Dante's moral vision, Eliot's critical insights, and the self-conscious imaginativeness of Joyce's art.

The System of Dante's Hell ends on this note of tension between intellectual repudiation of Western values, on the one hand, and on the other hand, the continuing imaginative links with the literary traditions of Western culture. Thus when Roi is attacked and driven from the Bottom by a gang of young Blacks, who see him only as "Mr Half-white muthafucka" (p. 151), he eventually wakes up "with white men, screaming for God to help me" (p. 152). His screams for help are the logical outcome of the painful self-discoveries in the Bottom, the new awareness of the incompleteness that has resulted from his "imitation" ethnicity and from his racial apostasy. And insofar as his scream for God is prompted by this awareness, then the novel ends on a note of new beginnings. Roi *has* started the odyssey for his lost humanity. But the epilogue emphasizes immediately thereafter that God "is simply a white man, a white 'idea' in this society, unless we have made some other image which is stronger,

---

[11]James Joyce, *A Portrait of the Artist as a Young Man*, Definitive Text (New York: Viking Press, 1964), pp. 119-125.

[12]See, for example, A. Walton Litz, *James Joyce*, p. 78.

and can deliver us from the salvation of our enemies" (p. 153). Consequently, the concluding scream for God's help heralds a Black odyssey for "some other image," but the fact that that scream is addressed to God the white man/ idea, underscores the degree to which Roi's imagination and rhetoric are still linked with the cultural heritage which that godhead represents.

Altogether, Jones' novel evokes the art and intellectual criteria of Dante, Eliot and Joyce in order to reject the philosophical and literary heritage which they represent, and as a fitting conclusion, calls upon the God of the West in the final act of repudiating the West. In the final analysis this unresolved tension has the effect of projecting the art and symbols of Jones' cultural revolution in qualified rather than in unequivocally un-Western terms. And in this regard the paradoxes of his relationship with the West make for a far more complex conclusion that the straightforward and unqualified transformations ("into the spiritual, knowledgeable Black writer/ artist") which some critics have found at the end of the novel.[13] Moreover, the kind of relationship which unfolds in the novel has important implications for the precise significance of the Western heritage in Jones' more recent works. For while the themes and rhetoric of repudiation have obviously been more fully developed in the poems and plays published since the novel, we still need to demonstrate, rather than only assume, that the imaginative modes and symbolic structures have been *entirely* cleansed, if that is the appropriate word, of their Western sources. The paradoxes which surround these sources in *The System of Dante's Hell* should be proof enough of the need for such a demonstration.

[13]See Paulette Pennington-Jones, "From Brother LeRoi Jones through *The System of Dante's Hell* to Imamu Ameer Baraka," *Journal of Black Studies,* 4, No. 2 (December 1973), 198.

LeRoi Jones' *Tales:* Sketches of the Artist as a Young Man Moving Toward a Blacker Art

by Larry G. Coleman

> I wanted something want it now. But don't know what it is
> except words. I could say anything. But what would be
> left, what would I have made? Who would love me for it?
>
> LEROI JONES, TALES

"Who will love me for the things I say?" This is perhaps the perennial question the artist asks. Even as he demands love and acceptance for the work he is doing, the artist is continually seeking a more suitable style and reality for himself. Perhaps more than anyone else he is painfully aware of the changes he must experience. He must investigate new forms and he must discover if the forms he accepts suit his own individual identity. A quest like this is most noticeable in a writer's autobiographical pieces.

LeRoi Jones is a Black artist, and an investigation of his art will illustrate his own peculiar method of combining experience as an artist along with his own racial identity. One might ask why it was necessary for Jones to delineate a meaningful identity and unity of direction for himself; that is, why does he find it necessary to question the nature, reality and depth of his words as evidenced in the quote at the beginning of this paper. A possible answer is that there was some problem about Jones' identity as a Black artist, a problem which permeated much of his writing.

It is most natural for a developing literary talent to explore different literary forms and traditions in order to achieve an artistic quality which is most suited to himself. Like Pound, Joyce and Eliot, LeRoi Jones found that the literary and cultural tradition influencing his writing presented a problem for him. The problematic ele-

"LeRoi Jones' *Tales:* Sketches of the Artist as a Young Man Moving Toward a Blacker Art" by Larry G. Coleman. From *Black Lines* 1, no. 2 (Winter 1970), 17-26. Reprinted by permission of the author.

ments in his art made it necessary for him to discard that tradition and many of its characteristics for a more viable one. Jones' reasons, however, for changing or adjusting his style, structure and artistic form were, unlike the others', intricately interwoven into his cultural and racial experience in America.

An attempt on his behalf to resolve some personal artistic complications is clearly evidenced in *Tales*. Except for a few instances these tales are arranged chronologically showing the development of experience and ideas in the life of a single individual. "The Chase," "Uncle Tom's Cabin: *Alternate Ending,*" and "The Death of Horatio Alger" are childhood stories. "The Alternative" and "The Largest Ocean in the World" are about late adolescence. "Going Down Slow," "The Screamers," and "Salute" tell of the varied experiences of a young developing artist in bohemia, the derelicts ward of a hospital, the Newark black ghetto and the Air Force. This paper shall attempt to analyze the style and content of several of these autobiographical stories. I will show how these stories structurally present a conflict between two cultural and artistic worlds, one Black and one white—a conflict which resided in the mind of their author—and how they chart a movement toward the resolution of that conflict.

There is a definite thematic and structural continuity in *Tales*. Each story has a central figure, a narrating persona, whose consciousness and personality bring all the stories together in the form of a loosely constructed novel. The style of writing is somewhat varied. One story, "The Alternative," juxtaposes the archaic diction of Cavalier poetry with the melodious rhythms of ghetto slang. This mixture of British and Afro-American literary and cultural strains informs the underlying tension and problematic tone of *Tales*.

On the thematic level, alienation from one's environment is the unifying element in the following stories: "A Chase," "The Alternative," "Uncle Tom's Cabin: *Alternate Ending,*" "The Death of Horatio Alger," "Going Down Slow," "Heroes Are Gang Leaders," "Salute" and "Words." The persona of these autobiographical sketches experiences intense loneliness whether in the streets of Newark, on the campus of Howard University, in the streets of Greenwich Village or in the derelicts ward of a New York hospital. Not until midway in the tales beginning with "Screamers" and "Words" does this persona even begin to feel at ease with his surroundings.

The main structure in the first half of the tales involves a conflict which occurs between the central figure and one or more of the other characters in the story. Here the conflict which alienated the character from those around him is resolved only in terms of a further alienation of the persona manifest in actual physical separation, defeat, intimidation and drugs.

The first story, "A Chase (Alighieri's Dream)," in a series of short flashing telegraphic images, imposes a dreamlike atmosphere over the Newark ghetto where Jones grew up. The extreme sensitivity of the young persona-dreamer emerges from beneath a frenetic rapid cataloguing of scenes and people in these New Jersey streets. The narrative itself moves like the rapid shifts in the musical phrasing of an intricate piece of improvisation. Midway in the story the persona is being pursued:

> Duck down, behind the car. Let apple pass; a few others. Now take off back down Court, the small guys couldn't run. Cross high, near Graychun's, The Alumni House, donald the fags, the jews, to kinney...
>
> Tales., 2.

The central character in "A Chase" is in some kind of conflict with the people around him. A clue to the reason why the nameless persona in Jones' story is being pursued is only suggested in the following lines:

> You should be ashamed. Your fingers are trembling. You lied in the garage. You lied yesterday. Get out of the dance, down the back stairs.
>
> Tales., 1.

This dream is not unlike all others. Thus the reader must be satisfied with the events presented in this eclectic narrative piece, and with the story they tell.

Much like a symbolist poem, this story merely "suggests" while never explicitly "stating" very much. It suggests a strong division between its persona and others in the story. This division is enhanced by the central metaphor of the sketch: an elusive fake football move which allows the persona to escape his opponents:

> A hip, change speeds, head fake, stop, cut back, a hip, head fake... then only one man coming from the side...I watched him all my life close in...I stopped still the ball held almost like a basketball, wheeled and moved to score untouched.   Tales., 3.

The metaphor of deception, the fake football fantasy move, and the fact that the persona is heading uphill at one point while everyone else is travelling downward—that he finishes atop the hill in a suit of black wool (in Jones' symbolism the material of bondage and imprisonment) overlooking the area he ran away from—all reveal separation and alienation imposed upon the nameless dreamer in "A Chase."

The dreamer's alienation, along with its causes, assumes sharper focus in the second more lengthy story "The Alternative." The main character of this story is named Ray McGhee and is called the "leader." The location is not Newark, New Jersey but a dormitory on the Howard University campus where Jones was an exceptional student for three years. Most of the action occurs in young McGhee's dormitory room. He works in the leadership capacity of resident advisor and dormitory counselor.

Like the persona of the first story Ray is a very sensitive and highly introspective individual; he exhibits the stereotyped characteristics of the artistic individual and all the action of the story is filtered through his artistic consciousness. The tension of this narrative piece arises from a conflict between McGhee and several young students under his jurisdiction. A source of this conflict springs from the idea of "higher education" as an "alternative" to lower class Negro culture. To the students, Ray symbolized the product of "higher learning." This identity, however, causes Ray to have mixed feelings about education. That is, the "leader" does not favor the kind of education that will destroy the Black students' culture, cutting them off from a "world of feeling":

> These same who loved me all my life. These same I find my senses in. Their flesh a wagon of dust, a mind conceived from all minds... "Is this my mind my feeling. Is this voice something heavy in the locked streets of the universe. Dead ends. Where their talk is bitter vegetable." That is, the suitable question rings out against the walls. Higher learning. That is...the leader in seersucker, reading his books.   *Tales.,* 7.

The symbolism of the "wool suit" (identifying the wearer with imprisonment and alienation from his environment) in "A Chase" is continued in the leader's seersucker suit. He is later described as "happy to die in a new grey suit," perhaps the grey flannel of Madison Avenue and Wall Street, personifications of the business establishment which is far removed from the culture and quotidian experience of members of the Black community.

Thus the devaluation of the "establishments" of "higher learning," "art" and "literature" must be viewed as complex manifestations of the problems and conflict embodied in some of these tales
and their author.

The position of Ray McGhee in relation to the students—a position like that of the Black literary artist educated in a literary tradition utterly alien and uninteresting to the majority of Black people
—is an amphibious one. He straddles both the worlds of "higher
learning" (in the ways of white western culture) and the world of
the Black students Pud, Jimmy Jones, and Everett whose life styles
at this point are identical with those of the lower class Black ghetto
dweller.

The leader's vocabulary incorporates the verbal nuances and
styles of the Black community as well as "words no one understands"
because of their syllabic lengthiness. This duality of expression is
exemplified when in one and the same breath the leader can quote
lines from Yeats' "Second Coming" ("Hardly are those words out
when a vast image out of *Spiritus Mundi*/Troubles my sight...")
and can verbalize a Black poetic form, *the dozens* ("F--- you cats and
your funny looking families too"). (Tales., 18, 19.)

The dissimilarities between Ray (a name given to the character
who is sympathetic to homosexuals in both the "Alternative" and
in Jones' play *The Toilet*) and some of the students result from the
leader's extreme sensitivity. It is a measure of Jones' concern in
Tales that he stresses these differences between the leader and the
students, between the poet and the race of people that poet comes
from, and between young LeRoi Jones as he was represented in his
fiction and the people he and his poetic sensibility had to confront.

Thus, in "The Alternative," Jones depicts the central conflict
within many of the *Tales*—that art and education in the *mainstream
cultural tradition* can often hinder communication between the
Black artist and other members of the Black lower class community.
In other words, at one time, the artistic traditions which influenced
LeRoi Jones provided him with a "hang-up" in terms of communicating with his people. While his tension or opposition between the
sensitive artistic protagonist of "A Chase" was symbolized in his
alienation from others, it is represented in the basic dissimilarities
between the leader and students and finally in the physical defeat
of the "leader."

Ray's sensitivity toward others causes him to object when a group
of students decides to intimidate a homosexual student, Hutchens,

and his lover. Upon revealing his own sympathy, Ray is accused of unnatural sexual liaison with the homosexual student. Ray is intimidated by the students even to the point that his speech is attacked:

> "Hee, that Ray sure can pronounce that word. I mean he don't say mutha' like most folks...he always pronounces the mother *and* the f----- so proper. And it sure makes it sound nasty..." "Hutchens teachin the cat how to talk...that's what's happening. Ha. In exchange for services rendered."   Tales., 20.

It is interesting that the students attack the leader's *propriety* in his use of words, the basic tools of the literary artist. It is almost as though they are attacking his artistic character. (Jones is structurally making another dialectical thrust against the bourgeois westernized Black artist.)

Later in "The Alternative" when a gang of students tries to force their way into the homosexuals' room screaming, "Whee! HEY LET US IN GIRLS!", Ray tries to intercede and is beaten to the floor by Rick, the mob's leader. For a brief time the students are silenced by Ray's defeat, but when Hutchens emerges from his room the crowd again erupts and Ray is left lying on the floor:

> The boys scream and turn their attention back to Love. Bald Lyle is in the closet. More noise. More lies. More prints in the sand...I am a poet. I am a rich famous butcher. I am the man who paints the gold balls on the tops of flag poles. I am no matter, more beautiful than anyone else...   Tales., 29.

By the thrust of the students' Black *machismo*, fiercely symbolized in the opposition leader, Rick, Ray is forced to retreat into the world of feeling and romantic notions "of painting the gold balls on top of flag poles," a world of art that is far removed from the mundane activity of the Black students. As a Black man the leader is alienated from his brothers because of his differences, his artistic and intellectual nature, and because of their immature unwillingness to accept those differences.

Words, as the basic tools of the artist, are also structurally important in the "Death of Horatio Alger." Here the protagonist's reality is shaped considerably by them. Initially the words he uses hinder communication with another member of his community, namely, J. D., his Black confederate. The portrait of the protagonist, Mickey, is one of a sensitive middle class oriented Black youth. Like

Ray in the "Alternative," Mickey is potential "establishment material" as opposed to "hard core ghetto material." The symbols
which shape his environment derive from a middle-class stereotype: "Light freckles, sandy hair…parquet floors." Mickey's pre-
dilection for these white middle-class symbols and values play a
large part in the failure of communication between him and J. D.
While initiating the cultural game of the "dozens" with J. D.,
Mickey's original words and intention are distorted by a group of
white friends:

> I had said something about J. D.'s father, as to who he was, or had he
> ever been. And J. D., usually a confederate and private strong arm
> broke bad because Augie, Norman, and white Johnny were there, and
> laughed, misunderstanding simple "dozens" with ugly insult, in that
> curious scholarship the white man affects when he suspects a stronger
> link than sociology, or the tired cultural lies of Harcourt, Brace
> sixth-grade histories.   Tales., 42.

Folklorist Roger Abrahams has identified two types of "dozens";
it is a version of the latter of those forms to which Mickey is referring:

> In the clean dozens some of the insults are directed at the other's
> mother, but most are directly personal. On the other hand, in the dirty
> dozens, the mother of the other person is almost always the subject
> of the slur, and she is commonly subject to aspersions of illicit sexual
> activity, usually with the speaker. Thus, the dirty dozens involve
> insults that also serve as boasts.[1]

J. D. has knocked Mickey down into the snow. Mickey's use of a
version of the "dirty dozens" contains an implicit cry of kinship
with J. D. It is possible, however, that the cultural kinship code is
violated when one plays the "dozens" around members of another
culture. The basis, however, for the conflict between Mickey and
J. D. is Mickey's improper use of the "game" in addition to a mis-
interpretation of his use of words by members of a different culture.
    After the initial incident Mickey is left lying in the snow (like Ray
on the floor of the dormitory) to ponder his attraction to the world
of white culture and "sandy hair." In Jones' philosophy the world of
white middle-class culture is identified with formal art, a world
which the narrator of this story calls a "stupid enterprise." Lying in
the snow Mickey begins to understand the illusory nature of his aspirations to become part of white culture: "I vaguely knew of a

[1]Roger Abrahams, *Positively Black* (New Jersey, 1970), p. 40.

glamorous world and was *mistaken* into thinking it could be gotten from books" (emphasis mine). (*Tales.,* 45.)

The story's anti-artistic strain results from the inner turmoil the protagonist experiences. He is an artist of sorts; former editor of his high school newspaper, he is extremely sensitive to the meaning of words, to the context in which they are used and to various interpretations people make of them. He fears that the worlds of art and words have forsaken him, a fear which is corroborated when his second attempt to communicate his true feelings to J. D. is thwarted. Mickey's plea to J. D. for help, through some freakish twist, metamorphoses into a vituperative attack against J. D. and his family:

> ...I pushed to my knees and could only see J. D. leaning there against the hydrant looking just over my head. I called to him, *for help really.* But the words rang full of dead venom. I screamed his mother a purple nigger with alligator titties. His father a bilious man with sores on his jowls. I was screaming for help in my hatred and loss, and only the hatred would show [emphasis mine].   Tales., 47.

There is a sense that the language Mickey uses is not his own but some foreign tongue, communicating the antithesis of what he really intends to say.

Mickey's second attempt at meaningful discourse with his ethnic brother, in a style and manner that reinforces kinship, is evident in his continued use of the dozens. Again, however, Mickey's original intention became distorted in the presence of the white children. (Because he continues to use the distorted method of communication, Mickey continues to fail in his effort to relate to his brother.) He is finally left with a kind of inescapable frustration, the result of a continued failure to communicate with J. D. Jones symbolized that frustration in Mickey's hands, which have been "frozen" by the *white* snow. The frozen hands also prevent him from returning J. D.'s blows. Thus he cannot fight his own ethnic brother:

> My mother stopped the fight finally, shuddering at the thing she'd made. His hands are frozen Michael. His hands are frozen.
>   Tales., 48.

Of course the "thing" Mickey's mother shudders at is a sensitive Black child, with misdirected aspirations, struggling to overcome his inability to communicate with members of his own culture and race.

In the tales discussed above, there is no mention of Jones' American Negro literary predecessors, but there are abundant references to William Butler Yeats, Walt Whitman, British Cavalier poets, Ford Maddox Ford, Paul Blackburn, Jean Genet, Jose Garcia Lorca, Albert Camus, Dante Alighieri, and others. The absence of references to Black literary artists in the early stories in *Tales* supports the underlying conflict between Black and white culture within the collection. The protagonist of each story mentioned above was directed toward or attracted to the alleged elegance, sophistication and intellectual prowess of white culture and art only to discover that this attraction alienated him from members of the Black community as well as from himself and his true artistic sources. With the appearance, midway in *Tales,* of climactic stories like "The Screamers" and "Words" we get an indication that the racial conflict and tension within the protagonist and the episodes are going to be resolved.

"The Screamers" invokes the spirit and tone of a Black musical whirlwind, a ritual of soul, in which a crowd of people are caught up. The allusions in this story are to young Black Newark street-corner men, to Charlie "Bird" Parker, Dizzy Gillespie and to a local Newark musician who did for his fans what James Brown does for contemporary Black youth.

As the police approach this crowd of Black people spilling from a dance hall into the streets, Jones invokes Bigger Thomas of Richard Wright's *Native Son:*

> Americas responsible immigrants were doing her light work again. The knives came out, the razors, all the Biggers who would not be bent, counterattacked or came up behind the civil servants smashing at them with coke bottles and aerials.   Tales., 79-80.

"The Screamers" in the context of the other tales represents a return to the world of the Black ghetto after a long departure from it. It, along with "Words," parallels Jones' actual return to Harlem after living in Greenwich Village.

"Words" is clearly a story about the artist's alienation from his kinsmen while it explores, for the first time in *Tales,* a way of eliminating that alienation. The nameless persona of the story has returned "home" to Harlem after a prolonged absence.

The sense of alienation is conveyed beautifully by the title of the story. It sits alone on the page surrounded by a mass of space, just as Ray McGhee and Mickey sat alone and defeated, surrounded by a vast, friendless void. The vagueness and emptiness of the title indicates that words themselves can be lifeless, emotionless objects. The words spoken by the artist-persona of the story have become vehicles of intellectual ideas void of actual feeling. The words themselves prevent the persona from conveying his true emotion in the same way that young Mickey's words were not his own but rather a foreign tongue communicating the antithesis of what he really intended to say. The character in "Words" feels like a foreigner in Harlem: "People look at me knowing the strangeness of my manner and the objective stance from which I attempt to 'love' them." (*Tales.*, 89.) Love is in quotes to underscore the irony of "loving" someone *objectively.*

The character's "words" and "manner" are strange to the Harlem Blacks because he represents an alien, not a native member of the culture. He discovers that his inability to feel himself in harmony with his people is also separating him from them. Thus the culture, the traditions he has followed and the use to which he has put his words all merge into a psychic prison from which he must escape to discover his own identity:

> In the closed circle I have fashioned. In the alien language of another tribe. I make these documents for some heart who will recognize me truthfully.
>
> The purpose of myself, has not yet been fulfilled. Perhaps it will never be. Just these stammerings and poses. Just this need to reach into myself, and feel something wince and love to be touched.   Tales., 90.

Thus the author and his quasi-fictional character merge and Jones reveals his aesthetic and his preoccupation with feeling as life forces in his art—something he believes Black people possess in abundance. By reaching this plateau in his quest for a more authentic voice, purpose and identity Jones penetrates the obfuscating wall which stood between himself and the Black community. His words no longer sidestep the minds and consciousness of those he loves and identifies with. A hint of the resolution of this conflict at the end of "Words" is portrayed stylistically by the shift from the individualistic first person narrative voice to the communal third person "we":

> We turn white when we are afraid.
> We are going to try to be happy.
> We do not need to be f---ed with.
> We can be quiet and think and love in silence.

> We need to look at trees more closely.
> We need to listen.   Tales., 91.

With the appearance of "Words" a new form begins to emerge from the collection and a kind of racial, spiritual and artistic rebirth seems to have been awakened in the writer. The incidental touches, the quick flashes of incidental experience and the poetic focus obtain, along with the telegraphic style of "A Chase." The extreme sensitiveness of the persona, and his visceral experience of his environment reiterate the notion that this version of the artist is a Blacker and uncompromised version.

After "Words" the style, tone and content of most of the remaining stories support Black culture and art. While earlier Jones quoted extensively from Yeats and other British poets to indicate that there was a significant European cultural influence on Afro-American culture and education, now he clearly gives priority to Black cultural figures whom he believes are more "expressive" than whites:

> The reflective vs. the expressive, Mahler vs. Martha and the Vandellas (a Black rock and roll singing group). It is not even an interesting battle.   Tales., 96.

Portions of the later stories are decided attacks on white cultural and artistic symbols. Herman Melville and Tony Bennett are viewed as weakling homosexuals in a tale entitled "Unfinished." This vindictive repudiation of Americanism and its cherished cultural symbols does not, however, characterize the final segments in *Tales*. It is, in fact, replaced by a growing *nationalist sentiment.*

The cultural manifestations of African creativity which Fanon describes in *The Wretched of the Earth*[2] chart a movement in the work of African intellectuals and writers which switches from *assimilation* to a disturbed *self-remembrance* and revitalization to a fighting *revolutionary national literature* which at once combines implicit elements of vindictiveness with a beautiful artistic lyricism surrounding items of national importance. Likewise, in *Tales* one finds an indication of this tendency.

Unlike the first, the final story in *Tales* is a vision of revolution, in part wild and comic, and in part stark and deadly serious. The vision, in which spacemen (emblems of spirituality) land on earth, in Newark, New Jersey, and immediately begin identifying with the

[2]Frantz Fanon, *The Wretched of the Earth* (New York: Grove Press, Inc., 1966), pp. 167-199.

quality and character of Afro-American culture, is saturated with references celebrating individuals and elements within Black culture. They include the mention of the West African deity Ogun, the Indian Buddha, musicians Art Blakey and the Jazz Messengers, Sun-ra, Albert Ayler, Smokey Bill Robinson, Charlie "Bird" Parker, artist Ben Caldwell, writer Claude McKay, and the nicknames of proverbial streetcorner brothers like Moosey, Pinball, Rodney, and Wingo. Within this story the author is stressing the transcendence and universality of Black spirituality and music. It is an affirmation and in many ways an extension of life styles in the average Black community. The poetic quality and feeling with which the author infuses this piece is captured in the prophetic poem or song rising up out of its mid-section:

> Walk through life/beautiful more than anything stand in the sunlight/walk through life/love all the things that make you strong, be lovers, be anything/for all the people of earth.
> You have brothers/you love each other, change up and look in the world/now, it's ours, take it slow we've long time, a long way/to go, we have/each other, and the/world, don't be sorry walk on through sunlight life, and know/we're on the go for love/to open/our lives/ to walk tasting the sunshine of life.   Tales., 129.

After reading the later *Tales* (and much of Jones' recent drama and poetry), one perceives that he has moved away from personally alienating European derived literary traditions and discovered for himself a meaningful form and unity of direction. The lyricism I spoke of earlier, fusing together images of Black experience, exemplifies, *not* a "whirlpool of hysteria," which is the "product of a monomaniacal obsession,"[3] but the voice of *artistic* genius. This voice and its utterances, while at once personal and private, singular and original, speaks of another kind of uniqueness, indeed of the originality and the sentiment of a whole people, born of an eclectic reach into the collective cultural and spiritual past of Black men and women everywhere—a reach destined to come up with the bits and pieces of flesh and blood, rhythm and energy that will help make his people whole again.

---

[3]Edward Margolies, *Native Sons* (Philadelphia and New York: J. B. Lippincott Company, 1968), p. 194.

Black Dada Nihilismus: Poetry

Imamu Amiri Baraka:
The Quest for Moral Order

by Lee A. Jacobus

LeRoi Jones' poetry describes a quest for a moral order which he feels ultimately impelled to create for himself and on his own terms. It begins as a moral order similar to T. S. Eliot's in *The Waste Land* and similar to the order insisted upon by the comic books and the radio serials of Jones' youth. The moral order Jones searched for is related to Eliot's hanged man, who appears frequently in Jones' work. But it is also related to the hero as something other than victim: to the existential hero who, like the Shadow, the Lone Ranger, and Green Lantern, can act individually to impose a strong moral order on a disordered world. Yet both of these visions are rejected. Of Eliot's Jewish God, he says, "jewchrist, that's hunkie bread, turned green";[1] the hanged man becomes not God, but a black, lynched granddaddy;[2] and "THE SHADOW IS DEAD."[3] All his heroes die; his values are inverted: "We are/ in love with the virtue of evil";[4] his only recourse is to become his own hero in the streets, to create his own black gods, and to preach a destruction of the old order as a means of preparing for the new. The pain and anguish he experienced in reaching this point—including the loss of faith in the old heroes and the old moral order—are the subject of the bulk of the poems in his three published volumes, *Preface to a Twenty*

"Imamu Amiri Baraka: The Quest for Moral Order" by Lee A. Jacobus. From *Modern Black Poets*, ed. by Donald B. Gibson (Englewood Cliffs, New Jersey: Prentice-Hall, Inc., 1973), 112-26. Reprinted by permission of the author.

[1]"Lowdown," *Black Magic* (Indianapolis and New York: Bobbs-Merrill, 1969), p. 74. Other volumes cited in the text are *Preface to a Twenty Volume Suicide Note* (New York: Totem Press and Corinth Books, 1961) and *The Dead Lecturer* (New York: Grove Press, Inc., 1964).
[2]"Biography," *Black Magic*, pp. 124-25.
[3]"THREE MOVEMENTS AND A CODA," *Black Magic*, p. 103.
[4]"Red Eye," *Black Magic*, p. 72.

Volume Suicide Note (1961), *The Dead Lecturer* (1964), and *Black Magic* (1969).

In view of the influences Jones recognizes in his own work, Baudelaire, Duncan, Olson, Ginsberg, to name a few, it may seem strange to isolate Eliot. But Eliot's influence is pervasive: it operates on many levels simultaneously. The fragmented structure of *The Waste Land* figures in many of Jones' more difficult poems, particularly in the poems of the fifties and early sixties. The vision of the world as wasted and infertile; the vision of a world having turned its back on God; the vision of rat's feet through the ruined city all seem as much a part of Jones' poetry as of Eliot's. Rhythms which are decidedly Eliotic crop up in crucial moments in the early—and sometimes the late—poems. And innumerable direct references and allusions to Eliot pepper all the poems, though they are most obvious and most frequent in the middle work. What all this seems to point to is an effort on Jones' part to understand the moral dilemma of his own situation as a black man in a white city, oppressed and displaced in his own land, in the mythic terms which satisfied Eliot and which concerned the ultimate problem of God, moral order, the disregard of man, and the hope of resolution through love and faith. In Eliot we find the thin edge of despair honed to razor sharpness only to be neutralized by faith in a God for whom justice is clear, unambiguous, and thorough—if not sudden and swift.

In a series of three poems called "From an Almanac," in *Preface to a Twenty Volume Suicide Note,* Jones talks about winter winds and words drowned in the wind, words at the mercy of the "clown gods." The connection with Eliot's God is unclear until the second of the Almanac poems, when the hanged man appears:

> Respect the season
> and dance to the rattle
> of its bones.
> The flesh
> hung
> from trees. Blown
> down. A cold
> music. A colder
> hand, will grip
> you. Your bare
> soul. (Where is the soul's place. What is
> its

nature?) Winter rattles
like the throat
of the hanged man.

It is almost impossible not to see in this an effort to describe a moral season, the cruelest season in Jones' terms, of nature battering man with cruel winds—with the hanged man himself "Swung/ against our windows"!

"From an Almanac (3)" is dedicated, "(For C. O.)," undoubtedly Charles Olson, since the poem is reminiscent of Olson's own work. But the influence is mingled with allusions, not only to Eliot, but to Milton as well. The question is the question of dancing, which interested Duncan and fascinated Olson enough that he wrote a syllabary on it. Jones propounds it, wondering how the children of winter could bring themselves, in this season, to dance at all.

This bizness, of dancing, how
can it suit us? Old men, naked
sterile women.
    (our time,
a cruel one. Our soul's warmth
left out. Little match children,
dance
against the weather.
)The soul's
warmth
is how
shall I say
it,
      Its own. A place
of warmth, for children
wd dance there,
      if they cd. If they
left their brittle selves behind (our time's
a cruel one.
      Children
of winter. (I cross myself
like religion
      Children
of a cruel time. (the wind
stirs the bones
& they drag clumsily
thru the cold.)

> These children
> are older
> than their worlds. and
> cannot dance.

If some of these images are reminiscent of *The Waste Land,* the themes are equally reminiscent of *Four Quartets.* The querulousness, the seasons, the children, and the dance are all important in the *Quartets.* But the differences in tone and the apparent loss of hope in Jones' poems are telling of a change. Where Jones talks about "Old men, naked/ sterile women" when he asks whether dancing is possible, Eliot sees a vision of a sacrament. Eliot sees dancing specifically as a metaphor for matrimony and "of the coupling of man and woman." He says, "The association of man and woman/ In daunsinge, signifying matrimonie —/ A dignified and commodious sacrament" ("East Coker," I). And later, in "Little Gidding," II, he says, "From wrong to wrong the exasperated spirit/ Proceeds, unless restored by that refining fire/ Where you must move in measure, like a dancer." For Jones the season is winter; his children are aged and infertile; and the only source of warmth is the soul, which is "Its own. A place," isolated and by no means a "refining fire." The children cannot dance. Their chances of taking part in "A dignified and commodious sacrament" are slight. They are match children whose refining fire is so slight it can neither refine nor support.

Jones' almanac is a moral almanac, like Eliot's record of the seasons; both their landscapes are moral landscapes, with the wind and the cold not only affecting, but reflecting the souls of men. The differences in their views lie perhaps in the feeling, on Eliot's part, that though the world has been wasted by man, God could somehow still inspirit it if he wished. Eliot's view is that there is a moral order in the nature of things which man has somehow lost the key to. Eliot's view in *The Waste Land* is certainly a despairing one, though the *Four Quartets* demonstrates that his ultimate faith is not shaken. The fact that man has defiled and destroyed is not sufficient grounds for ignoring the original moral order. But for Jones such is not at all so clearly the case. His almanac poems suggest a picture of despair. The winds are cutting, the people infertile, the children impossibly aged. The question of the soul and the question of religion figure strongly in the almanacs as they do in many of the rest of his poems. But Jones has no basic conviction that the basic moral order is there and needs only to be understood anew. Jones in no way renounces his faith in God, but he examines in painful detail his relation to Eliot's God. In these early poems the distinction between Jones' God and Eliot's God seems almost academic. The images Jones uses correspond closely enough to Eliot's to convince us that they are one and the same, the hanged man — Jesus Christ. But the fact seems to be that Jones is examining from the very first the nature of God, that he is trying to see himself in relation to Christ and Eliot's vision, and that he ultimately renounces Eliot's God on the grounds that the moral order is inverted because of the nature of the God himself. If he wishes to set things straight for himself, he must give up the Christian God and find his own.

The way in which the poems document the progression of his thought is remarkable. Jones is careful to tell us that he has put his poems together in as close to chronological order as possible, and consequently we can watch the progression in detail. Each of the following quotes and references will be accompanied by a page reference to the published volumes so that the nature of the progression can be fully appreciated at a glance.

In the first half of *Preface to a Twenty Volume Suicide Note* Jones does not worry himself directly about Eliot's God. He is more concerned with what he calls the "Mosaic of disorder I own but cannot recognize."[5] The word "disorder" appears frequently in the middle of *Preface:* in the misical poem for Bill Holiday called "Bridge"; in "Way Out West," in "the intricate disorder/ of the seasons"; and in "The Turncoat," in a mixing of memory and desire: "with dull memories & self hate, & the terrible disorder/ of a young man." Of course, self-hatred figures in other poems of this collection and it seems to be connected with disorder. The disorder of the season is reflected upon in the Almanac poems and becomes ultimately apocalyptic in "Roi's New Blues" (pp. 45-6) when he offers us an abrupt shift in address in the middle of the poem — recalling "Winter kept us warm" — in "Winter locked us in. (On/ the floor, at midnight/ we turned in blind/ embrace." He says, "Coldness will be/ stamped out, when those grey horsemen/ with sunny faces/ ride through our town. O, God/ we've waited for them. Stood/ for years with our eyes full/ of a violent wind." Though they have grey faces — "grey" becomes synonymous with "white" later, just as the sun is sometimes linked with white dominance — they are the horsemen of the apocalypse, and Jones somehow causes himself to feel that they will ride and revenge. They will set right the wrongs.

The Dead Lecturer is a more detailed search for God than *Preface.*

[5]"Vice," *Preface*, p. 28.

Jones is more explicit, as if he was taking more seriously the message
he himself sends us: "Let my poems be a graph/ of me" (p. 10). In "A
Poem for Willie Best," Section VII, Jones complains that he is treating
of "no God/ but what is given. Give me./ Something more/ than what
is here. I must tell you/ my body hurts" (p. 24). His need is clear, his
pain is somehow embedded in the pain of Willie Best, an actor like
Step'nfetchit whose degradation is shared by Jones. In his search for
something more, Jones dredges up several images from *The Waste
Land* in the ending of "A Poem for Democrats." The hanged man
merges with the Phoenician merchant to share a death by drowning, an
ironic mafia-style death with cement overshoes:

> (transporting your loved one
> across the line is death
> by drowning.
>   Drowned love
> hanged man, swung, cement on his feet.)
>   But
> the small filth of the small mind
> short structures of
> newark, baltimore, cincinnati, omaha. Distress,
> europe has passed we are alone. Europe
> frail woman, dead, we are alone.   (p. 39)

The echo of "Jerusalem Athens Alexandria/ Vienna London/ Unreal" is unmistakable, and the ironies in the poem are not confined
to the substitution of these middle-sized cities we now associate with
black unrest, if not despair. The chief irony is that the hanged man is
drowned in a manner which suggests the mafia—new Romans,
doing what old Romans did, but with the modern twist of premixed,
quick-drying overshoes.

Jones describes "a wreck of spirit,/ a heap of broken feeling," in
"Duncan spoke of a process" (p. 54), and talks of feeling that he must
cling to "what futile lies/ I have," though he begins to recognize them
as lies. Perhaps the beginning of the rejection of Eliot's God most
clearly comes in the two "Black Dada Nihilismus" poems. They are
remarkable in their clarity—once the trend of Jones' thinking and
feeling is seen. What Jones sees is history and the sins committed
in the name of Christ. He says, "God, if they bring him/ bleeding,
I would not/ forgive, or even call him/ black dada nihilismus" (p.
61). Jones speaks of "the umbrella'd jesus," as if he had mixed him
with the image of Gandhi, but he links Jesus with the alchemy of
conquest: converting flesh, not to bread, but to wealth:

            Trismegistus, have
    them, in their transmutation, from stone
    to bleeding pearl, from lead to burning
    looting, dead Moctezuma, find the West   (p. 62)

Then, in the second, and much more brutally forceful poem, Jones
speaks almost as if he were nostalgic for a Mau-Mau revolt: "Plas-
tique, we/ do not have, only thin heroic blades." Then, "Rape the
white girls. Rape/ their fathers. Cut the mothers' throats./ Black
dada nihilismus, choke my friends." And the poem ends with as
clear a call for revenge—or what some call justice—as Jones is capable of at this time:

    art, 'member
    what you said
    money, God, power,
    a moral code, so cruel
    it destroyed Byzantium, Tenochtitlan, Commanch,
        (got it, *Baby!*)
    For tambo, willie best, dubois, patrice, mantan, the
    bronze buckaroos.
        For Jack Johnson, asbestos, tonto, buckwheat,
        billie holiday.
            For tom russ, l'overture, vesey, beau jack,
    (may a lost god damballah, rest or save us
    against the murders we intend
    against his lost white children
    black dada nihilismus.   (p. 64)

The moral code is "so cruel" (a phrase he uses several times in his
early poetry to refer to something which is in him—is it this moral
code?) that it destroys not just men or races, but entire empires,
whole civilizations. It is no wonder that he renounces it. But he does
not renounce God, nor does he seem to slacken his quest:

        Who cannot but yearn
    for the One Mind, or Right, or call it some God, a thing beyond
    themselves, some thing toward which all life is fixed, some static,
    irreducible, constantly correcting, dogmatic economy
        of the soul.
                    "Green Lantern's Solo" (p. 70)

Critics who have seen nihilism and nothing more in these poems
and in Jones' work are simply wrong. He is looking for something
—for a God and a moral code—which will not destroy empires or

him. By no means is he fearful of violence or destruction so long as it produces the destruction of the code that destroyed Moctezuma. He sees no irony in the need for such violence: no more than one sees in the destruction of Sodom and Gomorrah, perhaps a reasonable analogy. In fact, by this time in his work, Jones has revealed himself—through his references to Sartre in the beginning of his second black dada nihilismus poem—as suffering an existential transmutation. He is passing, at the end of *The Dead Lecturer,* through a dark existential night of the soul, out of which an entire reordering must result. He reorders himself in relation to God, his soul, and his morality to begin to accept the existential role of action or of agent.

It is no accident and no irony that "Green Lantern's Solo" is one of the last poems of *The Dead Lecturer* and that it contains the kinds of existential sentiments that it does. Throughout the early work, Jones constantly links his comic book heroes with the search for moral order. Those heroes are not only men of action, but men of understanding: "'Heh, heh, heh,/ Who knows what evil lurks in the hearts of men? The Shadow knows.'/ O, yes he does/ O, yes he does./ An evil word it is,/ This Love."[6] Is it possible that even in this early poem Jones underlines his doubt by such insistent repetition, as he does with the capitalization and triple punctuation of "THERE *MUST* BE A LONE RANGER!!!"?[7] Love is easily reversed, naturally, and when it is it becomes evil—as Jones points out more than once. He seems aware, early on, in his frequently anthologized "The New Sheriff," that if there is no Lone Ranger, he may have to become himself a sheriff. As he says, what is in him is "so cruel, so/ silent," that "it hesitates/ to sit on the grass/ with the young white/ virgins."[8] The call to action is insistent, though "The New Sheriff" is more realistically considered a poem of hesitation, or perhaps preparation for action. But "Green Lantern's Solo" is more explicit. Green Lantern, one of the comic book heroes who is conspicuously less white than, say, Lamont Cranston or Superman, functions in the metropolis, working directly in the streets to cope with innumerable wrongs. Of all things, Green Lantern is an apotheosis of action.

What Jones seems to fear in "Green Lantern's Solo" is dying "without knowing life." He offers examples: "My friend, the lyric poet,/

---

[6]"In Memory of Radio," *Preface,* pp. 12-13.
[7]"Look for You Yesterday, Here You Come Today," *Preface,* p. 17.
[8]*Preface,* p. 42.

who has never had an orgasm. My friend,/ the social critic, who has never known society,/ or read the great italian liars, except his father." But for all his worry and all his concern, the poem ends not with a call to action, but with a series of questions and comments which challenge man's ability to act by himself. "What man unremoved from his meat's source, can continue/ to believe totally in himself?" Only the fully ignorant, like "our leaders," or the "completely devious/ who are our lovers./ No man except a charlatan/ could be called 'Teacher'." The truth and the lie are so similar as to be indistinguishable; and the poem ends with an ambiguous and unsettling comment about the fact that men demand knowledge of One greater than themselves ("Who cannot but yearn/ for the One Mind, or Right, or call it some God..."). Implying virtually that no man is an island, he says, "the islands of mankind have grown huge to include all life." Individual action is either anachronistic or impossible. Thus, Green Lantern in this poem is either solo or soloing. If he is solo, alone, it is only because he is fictional and removed "from his meat's source"; if he is soloing he is simply claiming the dependence he perceives in others.

The call to action is a call to violence in *Black Magic*. The machine gunners are called forward in "A Poem Some People Will Have to Understand" (p. 6), after the simple statement: "I am no longer a credit/ to my race." In "The People Burning," he talks about alternatives: about the fact that his friends (or someone) want him to be other than black: "Now they ask me to be a jew or italian, and turn from the moment/ disappearing into the shaking clock of treasonable safety, like reruns/ of films, with sacred coon stars. To retreat, and replay; throw my mind out,/ sit down and brood about the anachronistic God, they will tell you/ is real" (p. 11). As he says, "it is a choice, now, and/ the weight is specific and personal." He is prepared to make the choice, even if it is a choice which will wear him down: "The lone saver is knowing exactly/ how far to trust what is real. I am tired already/ of being so hopelessly right," he says in "Letter to Elijah Muhammad" (p. 12). In this first volume, *Sabotage*, of *Black Magic,* Jones' themes become steadily more involved in history and blackness. God is anachronistic if it is the Italian or Jewish God of his white friends. Even Eliot himself is repudiated openly in the final page of the volume: "Things/ shovel themselves, from where they always are. Spinning, a/ moment's indecision, past the vision of stealth and silence/ Byron thought the night could be. Death blow Eliot Silence, dwindling away, in the 20th century"

(p. 44). There are visions and revisions yet to come, while there is also the vision of stealth and silence, almost a Joycean cunning— along with an end to Eliot. A death blow.

Target Study begins, as it must, with an identification. Jones is concerned with the most central problem of all: who he is. He has revised his vision, chopped out Eliot and Eliot's God, and in a parody of the identity crisis (one of so many) in *A Portrait of The Artist as a Young Man* (when Stephen sees himself in terms of *"Europe/ The World/ The Universe"*) he says:

> I am real, and I can't say who
> I am. Ask me if I know, I'll say
> yes, I might say no. Still, aşk.
>
> I'm Everett LeRoi Jones, 30 yrs old.
> A black nigger in the universe. A long breath singer,
> wouldbe dancer, strong from years of fantasy
> and study.   "Numbers, Letters" (p. 47)

But there is a reality that Jones must deal with that is just as important as the reality of his own identity; it is the reality of the world and its ugliness. The early poems ("Confirmation," "Friday") mention its ugliness and describe it in almost the same surreal terms Eliot uses in his "bats with baby faces" passage. The world is ugly, the white God is a "dingaling god" ("I Don't Love You") and "A white man/ with/ a dueling scar" ("Dada Zodji"). Jones recommends revolution ("Ration," p. 68) and rejoices that things are so serious for "White Eyes" that even "mailmen grow murderous offspring" ("Lowdown," p. 74). Yet, he can take a moment, as in "Western Front" (p. 81), to consider Ginsberg, who went to India to "see God," even if God is "sole dope manufacturer of the universe" and a "baldhead faggot."

"Western Front" has a poignancy that leads one to think Jones sympathizes deeply with Ginsberg's faith—though he cannot by any means share it. There is no India for Jones to travel to: "God/ is not a nigger with a beard. Nor/ is he not" (p. 90), and no amount of search, at this point in his quest, seems likely to bring him to the kind of peace he imagines for "fools" like Ginsberg. But the poignancy of "Western Front" is only a shadow of the poignancy of "Cold Term," a poem that seems clearly wishful and idealistic. If action is essential, and if action is violence, then Jones in his enthusiasm for the machine gunners is not blinded to what might have been and to what ought to be:

Why cant we love each other and be beautiful?
Why do the beautiful corner each other and spit
poison? Why do the beautiful not hangout together
and learn to do away with evil? Why are the beautiful
not living together and feeling each other's trials?
Why are the beautiful not walking with their arms around
each other laughing softly at the soft laughter of black beauty?
Why are the beautiful dreading each other, and hiding from
each other? Why are the beautiful sick and divided
like myself?   (p. 91)

Such a lament is not novel and did not have to wait for LeRoi Jones
for it to be expressed, but it is nonetheless poignant and moving.
Jones has already admitted that men are islands operating independently ("Poem for Religious Fanatics," p. 89), and he sees that
black men living in a white city will become sick and divided. But
in "Cold Term," he admits that a beautiful thing has been lost, and
that if the black man is sick and divided, he is too. The call to
violence is by no means without its dues: and the black man has
historically paid his dues. The something in him that is so cruel
takes its toll, though not without his being aware of it.

The solution for reordering the future is not just to rid the land
of whiteness. In "I Am Speaking of Future Good-ness and Social
Philosophy," Jones declares, "Man is essential/ to my philosophy,/
man." And he says that the white man is a man, even though he is
also the beast of the age. Thus: "we must become Gods./ Gigantic
black ones./ And scare them back into the dirt" (p. 99). Eventually,
Jones sees black men as Gods in "The Test" (p. 188), but they are
Gods in the Miltonic (not the Dantesque) sense: Gods dispossessed
and in hell. "Like Gods we are in hell, fallen, pulling now/ against
the gravity of the evil one himself./ Black streak from sun power.
We are Gods, Gods, flying in black space." The entire poem is important; it establishes the end of the Jewish God—seen here with
four Italian "mobster cops" and with the "four dragons" of Revelation. White people are seen as driving black people against their
natures, and there is no alternative but "the upward gaze" "pulling
now/ against the gravity of the evil one himself." The black Gods
must displace the white God. In "The Black Man is Making New
Gods" (p. 205), Jones reviles the old hanged man as one who, by
mimicking the black man's suffering, may well have distracted him
from his purposes. He says, "The Fag's Death/ they give us on a
cross. To Worship. Our dead selves/ in disguise. They give us/ to

worship/ a dead jew/ and not ourselves." And then, "the empty
jew/ betrays us, as he does/ hanging stupidly/ from a cross, in an
oven, the pantomime/ of our torture."

What Jones is calling for is an inversion. The white God must go.
White morality—symbolized for Jones by the Italian mobster and
the Jewish merchant—must be turned around: "The magic words
are: Up against the wall mother/ fucker this is a stick up!" Such
an expression, in the final poem in the collection, effectively establishes, even in its "impolite" language, the purposes of inversion
which have been alluded to from the early poems onward. This last
poem, "Black People!" talks about robbery, taking what is needed,
dancing in the streets, turning things upside down: "We must make
our own/ World, man, our own world, and we can not do this unless
the white man/ is dead."

"Black People!" is a poem of finality; there are no alternatives,
no ambiguities. The call is to magic, the black magic of the title:
the dance is magic dance; the acts magic acts; the words magic words.
In all this there is no tinge of the white God, the white values: all
is expunged. The cross, we have been told, is "a double dirty cross,
to hang your civilization."[9] The naked man has long since been
dispensed of in "Biography" (p. 124), in an image of cruelty which
is impressive even in its economy: "hangs/ hangs/ granddaddy/
granddaddy, they tore/ his/ neck." The kyrie eleison is said for the
entire civilization, including all those blacks who wish to remain
aboard as servants, in "Madness" (pp. 162-65). So it should come
as no surprise that Jones' final poem is a call to arms, a call to turn
everything upside down. The disappointing part is that it is not so
much a vision of what has been promised as of what has been done:
"Black People!" is no vision of black men freeing themselves, of
finding the new black God; it is a vision of the rioting in Newark,
with all the streets and all the stores of Newark laid out for looting.
What is looted is not likely to be what is needed; this poem is, for
all its exhortatory power, short of the vision of the new blackness,
the new beauty. Yet Jones never denies this; his interest is in the
black man doing what he should not be doing: the black man cannot
be a credit to his race, since the very concept is a white concept, born
of worshipping the white God, the hero as victim. Evil has been
turned backwards, to live, though he hardly expects the white man
to understand this.

Yet, for all the inversions, God has not been lost sight of, and

---

[9]"Madness," *Black Magic*, p. 162.

Jones' identity is not abandoned. As he indicates in "Stirling Street September" (p. 177), "WE WORSHIP THE SUN,/ We are strange in a way because we know/ who we are. Black beings passing through/ a tortured passage of flesh." He even echoes Eliot again —despite his having formally given him the death blow earlier—in: "The will to be in tune/ the depth of god/ the will of wills thunder and rain/ silence throws light and decision/ to be in/ tune/ with/ God...to be alone with the God of creation the/ holy nuance/ is all beings./ Is the melody, and rhythm/ of/ the dancing/ shit/ itself" (pp. 182-83). In "Human to Spirit, Humanism to Animals," he says, "We are reaching/ as God for God/ as human/ knowing/ spirit" (p. 203). But Jones also knows that there is such a thing as backsliding, that "We are all spies for god,"[10] by which he seems to mean spies for the Jewish God, since he talks about betrayal, "coparmies," and the "jewish dog." "We expect some real shit. We expect to love all the things/ somebody runs down to us. We want things, and are locked here, to the earth,/ by pussy chains, or money chains, or personal indulgence chains" (p. 185). Such a moral view is almost puritanical, yet it is logical that Jones at this point would turn his back on material values. "Black People!" by comparison with this poem seems an earlier, less informed composition if only because the poem gives credence to the possibility that what black people take from white stores could be of use to them. But the "personal indulgence chains" seems a clear declaration of independence from a corrupt morality, or from a morality that is not dedicated to freeing black consciousness. Jones' contempt for what can be stolen from white stores figures plainly in one of the last poems in *Black Magic:* "Those Things. These refrigerators, stoves,/ automobiles, airships, let us return to the reality of the spirit,/ to how our black ancestors predicted life should be, from the/ mind and the heart, our souls like gigantic kites sweep across/ the heavens, let us follow them, with our trembling love for the world" (p. 223).

Thus the prose tracts Jones has written in recent years, since the publication of *Black Magic,* have consistently urged a firm moral position for the black man, one which unites him with his Black brothers and one that turns its back on white corruption. The logic of this position was begun in the earliest poetry and developed through the struggles with Eliot's conception of God, and through the ultimate creation of an alternative to Eliot's moral view.

It may be said that one of Jones' solutions to the dilemma of what

[10]"Are there blues singers in russia?" *Black Magic,* pp. 184-85.

to do about Eliot's God, and what to do about the existential heroes
of his comic book youth, is to supplant them both in his own person.
Eliot's God is seen as bankrupt and dangerous in *Black Magic*. If
he is not abandoned entirely, he is transformed and played against.
The comic book heroes change after "Green Lantern's Solo." One
of the last references is in "Madness" (p. 164), in which even the
Lone Ranger is untrustworthy. He says, "'i'm hurt, help me, no stay
with me nigger,/ die with me nigger...no one will remember/ Hi
Yo Silver...Away!!'" The last apparent reference to Superman is
ironic: "We have a nigger in a cape and cloak. Flying above the
shacks and whores" ("Election Day—2," p. 213), a reference apparently to the mayoral election in Newark. It may not be realistic to
see Jones imagining himself as a kind of God, though he has seen
black men as gods; but there is a curious passage near the end of
Black Magic that suggests the temptation may be present:

> I cd walk
> if I want to
> I used to run
> I can sing a little
> bit but that still
> don't say I can heal
> or bring back
> the dead.   "Bumi" (p. 196)

Facing this is a poem, "From the Egyptian," which issues forth a
doctrine of revenge which rings of Old Testament zeal, not to mention Old Testament language. It begins: "I will slaughter/ the
enemies/ of my father/ I will slay those/ who have blinded/ him."
And it ends: "car bashed into house fat legs/ upside down, and
smashed bloody JESUS/ whatill we do, lets geh-uh ohh ra-ze ra-ze/
I will slaughter the enemies of my father/ I will slay those who have
blinded him" (pp. 197-98).

Perhaps it is merely a vatic pose Jones adopts in these poems, and
he does not apotheosize himself at all. But there is a curiosity that
lingers in the imagination regarding the name he has assumed since
the publication of his poems, the Islamic name which appears in
the "Explanation" to *Black Magic*. One wonders if God and the
comic book heroes are dead forever, or if they have been absorbed
into Jones' poetic unconscious waiting to poke out again. His name,
Baraka, like Lorca's Duende, means many things. Its root is Hebrew:
Brk, and it means a number of things: lightning, the blessed of God,

virtue, inspiration, the muse. "Since lightning is a phenomenon everywhere attributed to the gods, *baraka* means the sudden divine rapture that overcomes either a prophet or a group of fervent devotees."[11] It makes one think of the lightning bolt on Captain Marvel's chest, the faith that transformed a Billy Batson at the altar of Shazam, and the consequent faith that out of the scourge of action will come a new order, a new wholeness.

[11]Robert Graves, "The Word 'Baraka'," in *Oxford Addresses On Poetry* (New York: Doubleday & Company, Inc., 1962), p. 110.

Baraka as Poet

by Clyde Taylor

The mark of LeRoi Jones' poetry is the mark of his personality on the printed page. He is the most personal so far of the Afro-American poets. For him poetry is the flow of being, the process of human electricity interacting with the weight of time, tapped and possibly trapped on paper. Feelings, impressions, moods, passions move unedited through a structure of shifting images. Quick poems, light on their feet, like a fancy middle-weight. Mostly, his poems carry no argument, no extractable, paraphraseable statement. They operate prior to the pros and cons of rational, persuasive, politic discourse. Even after several readings, one is likely to remember mainly a flavor, a distinct attitude of spirit, an insistent, very personal voice.

His poetry is written out of a heavy anti-rationalist, anti-didactic bias. Its obligation is to the intentions of its own feelings. Its posture is in defiance of criticism. The critic is for him the sycophant and would-be legislator of official (white) reality, an implacable enemy, the best symbol of the spiritually dead pseudo-intellectuality of the West. (Lula in *Dutchman* is a white *critic,* if you watch closely.) Against the strictures and constipations of this official reality, his poetry is an imposition upon the reader of the actuality, the majesty even (hence, LeRoi) of his subjectivity. The personalism of his earlier poetry, particularly, is a challenge to the ready-to-wear definitions of the sociologically defined "Negro writer" lying in wait for him.

The arrogance of *Preface to A Twenty Volume Suicide Note* and *The Dead Lecturer* is in this personalism and intimacy, not in any pretensions of impeccability of character. The poetry alternately invites the reader to jam his face into his own shit or to love or con-

"Baraka as Poet" by Clyde Taylor. From *Modern Black Poets,* ed. by Donald B. Gibson (Englewood Cliffs, New Jersey: Prentice-Hall, Inc., 1973), 127-34. Reprinted by permission of the author.

demn the poet. It is the work of a spiritual gambler who wants to think of himself as waging heavy stakes. A reflection of this spirituality is its absoluteness. All his poems give the notion of being end-of-the-line thoughts, where attempts to reach an understanding dance on the edge of ambiguity. They are the works of an apprentice guru, "stuntin' for disciples," he later decided.

A major source of this creative orientation came from the streets. The hipsterism that nourished his poetry has to be regarded respectfully since whatever its limitations hipsterism was the germ of several cultural and social revolutions still turning in the world today. Hipsterism was a counter-assertion to brand-name, white values and the conformism of middle America, a serio-comic celebration of energies and forms unaccounted for, a mysticism (with some odd resemblances to Zen and other spiritual disciplines) of rhythms and tempos inside of and beyond metronomic, bureaucratic time, reflective of the polyrhythmic time of black music (particularly bebop) and of the fluid, open time-space sensation of a pot high. Hipsterism was a new, Afro-American ontology, a style of knowing the world and acknowledging in the parody of one's own posture the craziness of a materialistic, hyper-rationalist, racist, self-contradictory square world on the one hand and the absurdity of a universe that mocked human values in its variousness and arbitrariness on the other.

An important aspect of hipsterism that LeRoi absorbed, less familiar than, say, the relationship to black music, was its deep fascination with the ghost-spirits and fantasy-figures of pop culture, the radio, movies, the comic book.[1] The connections between the aware black mind and these fantasy dramas are extremely complex, but a few linkages need to be suggested here. There was, first, the conviction that the world of sharp-edged pop invention, with all its ridiculous exaggeration, was a more accurate profile of the square world than it could afford to admit ("the white man, WHO AT BEST IS VERY VERY CORNY DUDE"—*BMP,* p. 163). There was also a contempt for the falsification of American manhood in its stoical cowboys and tough detectives and a preoccupation with drawing the the social-political-racial connotations of such characters as Gunga Din, King Kong, Rochester, Aunt Jemima and of such relationships as the Lone Ranger—Tonto hook-up.

[1]See the very thoughtful article by Lloyd Brown, "Comic-Strip Heroes, LeRoi Jones and the Myth of American Innocence," *Journal of Popular Culture,* III (Fall, 1969), 191-204.

My silver bullets all gone
My black mask trampled in the dust
& Tonto way off in the hills
moaning like Bessie Smith.

Preface...(p. 18.)

But there was also a kind of envy felt by the hipster toward the pop world in the feeling that its craziness was of an inferior aesthetic texture than his own and then in an unfulfillable identification with its outcast loner-heroes, many of whom (like Lamont Cranston and The Shadow, Bruce Wayne and Batman, etc.) lived secret, powerful identities apart from their bland but urbane public images and who had extraordinary energies and powers available to them, or who, like the detectives and cowboys, lived intense, dangerous, unsocial lives redeemed by the gloom and glamor of their inevitable defeats.

When LeRoi moved uptown from the East Village in 1965 — possibly the most momentous getaway in Afro-American or American letters — he left much behind, but took much of this aesthetic with him. Moving uptown, his poetry remained underground. To borrow a figure whose fascination Jones shares with Blake, his poetry passes through a vortex — a point at which physical forces converge — such as the center of a whirlpool. Graphically, this passage might be represented like this:

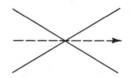

His development has been through one vortex into another (carrying a large segment of creative Afro-America with him). A reading of his works together shows that the crossing was not as sudden as its results were profound. More important, at the convergence-point of these two vortexes the themes, motifs, style, images are common to both, though sometimes inverted.

In brief, what we can see happening in *Black Magic Poetry, 1961-1967* is the despair without reference-point of the earlier volumes discovering its most sufficient cause in the enormity of the fall of man under whiteness. (See "Jitterbugs," *BMP*, 92.) Looking back, he admits, "I was under the spell of the whiteman," and *BMP* (and the plays, too) exhibits the violent and painstaking exorcism of the sick spirits that had possessed him. The fragments of a disjointed psyche crystallize themselves into new energies, heavier rhythms and shockingly concrete images:

> We want 'poems that kill.'
> Assassin poems, Poems that shoot
> guns. Poems that wrestle cops into alleys
> and take their weapons leaving them dead
> with tongues pulled out and sent to Ireland.

> *BMP*, 116.

The vagrant itches of his personal fantasies come home to a new cosmology, much indebted to Elijah Muhammad (see the dramatization of the Yacub myth in *Black Mass*). The natural order of the universe, in which "everything is everything" and man is in harmonious relation to nature and the gods, his imaginative and creative powers equal to his needs, has been interrupted disastrously by the intrusion of a counter-human homunculus (the white man) who maintains its parasitical existence feeding on the blood of living (nonwhite, essentially black) people and their cultures. A crucial image is the vampire: "...vampires, flying in our midst, at the/ corner, selling us our few horrible minutes of discomfort and frus/ tration." The homunculus and the spread of its civilization is the equivalent of the appearance of sickness, disease, maladjustment, and death into the universe, largely by virtue of its diabolical insinuation of abstraction (especially of time) and materialsm, but also through enslavement of living cultures under the notion that it is God. The sensitive reader of E. Franklin Frazier's cool, objective *Race and Culture Contacts in the Modern World* can find in *Black Magic Poetry* an appropriate moral and imaginative rendering of a certain, credible view of history.

But to characterize Jones' poetry rather than a particular segment of black nationalist ideology is to recognize the residue of the earlier, personal world-view transformed in the uptown work. For instance, the particular, non-conformist "craziness" of the be-bopper, one indigenous reference point for the adolescent Leroy, becomes the "black madness" of "Black Dada Nihilismus" and then the holier black madness of the intense, fiery, disorienting (to whites) commitment to blackness of the third section of *BMP*. Or, the Baudelairean, *fin du monde* despair of the downtown poetry becomes, after the crossing, a despair of the dying West and a determination to slick its way toward its self-destruction. One other hang-over Baudelairean feature is the posture of the innocent damned, the pure spirit confounded by stultifying orthodoxy into a rebellion that consists of an inversion of orthodox values.

What emerges is a diabolism, incipient from the earliest poems, whose main feature is the blaspheming of the hated religion, in this case the religion of whiteness. It is a commitment implied in the title, *Black Mass,* or in the poem "Black Art" (for some oblique but real parallels see Cavendish's book, *The Black Arts,* a primer of the unholy and occult sciences) or in the whole conception of *Black Magic Poetry.* The black magic motive (*black* meant ironically) is the drive to weave an imaginative spell powerful and compelling enough to counteract in the minds of black people the spell of the white man for "To turn their evil backwards/ is to/ live," or (see the last page of *Home*):

> We are unfair, and unfair.
> We are black magicians, black art
> s we make in black labs of the heart.
>
> The fair are
> fair, and death
> ly white.
> The day will not save them
> and we own
> the night.

It is as though his talent were lying around like an empty bag until filled by the spirit-breath of suddenly conscious black people and took stunning shapes from the idioms, rhythms, folklore, the needs and crises, the beauties of a self-defining Afro-America. Some of the *Black Magic* poems adapt the forms of blacktalk: the dozens in "T. T. Jackson sings" and "Word from the Right Wing"; wall-writings like "You cannot hurt/ Muhammud Ali, and stay/ alive"; hoodoo curses like "Babylon Revisited" and "Sacred Chant for the Return of Black Spirit and Power," raps such as "Poem for Half-White College Students," put-downs like "CIVIL RIGHTS POEM" and neo-African chants such as "Part of the Doctrine" (p. 200). But more of the poems are free-form reflective lyrics, alternately public and private, in which Jones shows remarkable growth as "a long breath singer" in contrast to the telegraphese of the earlier work. In these, where the inspiration is street talk and the long, cascading line of Coltrane and what might be called the Eastern-Astral school of black music, the utterance moves in one unimpedable breath, with its own swoops, cries, distributed vocal parts, sound effects and faultlessly chosen words to its cymbal-crash ending. Poems like "Poem for Black Hearts" and "Black People" are among the few works equal to the intensity and urgency of the black rediscovery years of the sixties.

The incandescent furies of *BMP* subside in subsequent poems, some of them collected in *In Our Terribleness* (1970). It is as though Jones sensed that simple, diabolical inversion of white values is another form of flattery and dependency and that the creative motif of de-spelling the white man had run its course. The later poems, more independently reflective of the spiritual needs of black people, are mellower, less satiric, showing a deeper turn into mysticism. This latest change in a poet who believes in change as a fundamental aspect of reality is signaled by the adoption of a new name, Imamu Amiri Baraka.

There are enough brilliant poems of such variety in *Black Magic* and *In Our Terribleness* to establish the unique identity and claim for respect of several poets. But it is beside the point that Baraka is probably the finest poet, black or white, writing in this country these days. The question still has to be asked whether he has fulfilled the vocation set for him by his own moves and examples. He has called himself a "seer" (one familiar with evil is the way he defined it) and holy man, but hesitates to claim (while vying for it) the fateful name of prophet.

The prophet differs from the poet and other word-men in his role of awaking and sustaining among his people a vision of their destiny set beside the criteria of their deepest values in the most fundamental though significant language. A poet's obligation, by contrast, is to the integrity of his verbal rendering of his individual sensibility. The problem is whether Baraka's creative impulse, which is essentially underground, hip, urban, and avant-garde, can be made to speak for a nation of black people rather than for a set of black nationalists. Can he transcend the inclination to ad-lib on the changes of black consciousness (the way be-boppers ad-libbed on "Indiana") toward redefining that consciousness in the light of enduring values and in major works of sustained thought and imagination?

"We need a heavy book, like the Bible or the Koran," he writes in *In Our Terribleness*. This is doubtless too much to ask of one man. There are qualities, further, in his creative armament that run

counter to that need. He seems to confuse fantasy, which is whimsical
and gratuitous (consider "Answers in Progress" in *Tales*, 1967, and
"All in the Streets" in *Terribleness*, both beautiful reveries) with
myth, which, however non-rational its basis, holds firmly to a certain
kind of cause-effect economy. His early avant-garde posture has
given way to a mysticism that depends upon other people's ortho-
doxies, a gnosticism, really, that carries with it the aura of initiates,
adepts and degrees of secret lore. The magic of his poetry owes almost as much to his enchantment with figures of pop culture like
Mandrake, Lamont Cranston, Plastic Man, and The Green Lantern
as it does to African cosmology and Arabic philosophers. Some of
his symbols look like paraphernalia left over from a Shriner's convention. In his later work, black nationalism moves toward becoming a subdivision of the occult sciences, whereas something more
broad-backed, comprehensive, open, accountable seems demanded
by the ethos of black people—the kind of poetry (groping for a reference) Malcolm might have written, had he turned his genius in
that direction.

The legacy of hipsterism, then, together with his still rather
Baudelairean spiritual elegance, places Baraka's work always underground or aloft in relation to the meat and potatoes' scene where
the straight world works out its dull, mediocre gimmicks. His peril
is that his work must pass close to that fearful terrain—not con-
ceding to whiteness all of the middle, ordinary world, where humans
play out their messy lives—if it is going to take on the amplitude
and range of black being.

The limitations I speak of, already dwindling in his latest pieces,
really go beyond a consideration of Baraka as poet. *There*, the same
qualities are adornments of his invented poetic cosmos, part of the
spellbinding conviction of the work, adding tones to one of the
distinctive, compelling, haunted modern voices, a voice like the
nerve-endings of our terrible times. They are part of the legend, a
legend supported by a list of accomplishments impressive in a writer
just reaching midcareer. And he *has* become a prophet in the literary sense, establishing modes in which some of the most stirring
impulses of black expressiveness have found form. Behind this record, still another title comes to mind for Baraka, one we used to
confer only upon ourselves; he is "The Kid" of Afro-American
writing.

The Changing Same:
Black Music in the Poetry of Amiri Baraka

by Nate Mackey

I

Consistency is one of the last words anyone would use in characterizing Baraka's thinking during the last two decades. Coming into his earliest prominence as a member of the Beat/Black Mountain avant-garde of the fifties and sixties, he wrote in 1959, still calling himself LeRoi Jones:

> For me, Lorca, Williams, Pound and Charles Olson have had the greatest influence. Eliot, earlier (rhetoric can be so lovely, for a time... but only remains so for the rhetorician). And there are so many young wizards around now doing great things that everybody calling himself poet can learn from...Whalen, Snyder, McClure, O'Hara, Loewinsohn, Wieners, Creeley, Ginsberg &c. &c. &c.[1]

Seven years later in an essay called "Poetry and Karma," having in the interim abandoned Greenwich Village for Harlen and the "New American Poetry" for the "Black Arts Movement," he writes of his earlier influences and associates:

> White poetry is like white music (for the most part, and even taking into account those "imitations" I said, which are all as valid as W. C. Williams writing about Bunk Johnson's band. Hear the axles turn, the rust churned and repositioned. The death more subtly or more openly longed for. Creeley's black box, Olson's revivification of the dead, Ginsberg's screams at his own shadowy races or the creepier elements completely covered up with silver rubied garbage artifacts and paintings and manners and ideas, my god, they got a buncha ideas, and really horrible crap between them and anything meaningful. They probably belch without feeling.[2]

"The Changing Same: Black Music in the Poetry of Amiri Baraka" by Nate Mackey. From *Boundary 2* 5 (1978). Reprinted by permission of the author.

[1]Donald M. Allen (ed), *The New American Poetry* (New York: Grove Press, 1960), p. 425.

[2]*Raise Race Rays Raze* (New York: Random House, 1971), p. 23.

Such openness not only to change but to about-faces of the most
explosive kind is typical of his career, an openness he himself acknowledges in "The Liar":

> Though I am a man
> who is loud
> on the birth
> of his ways. Publicly redefining
> each change in my soul, as if I had predicted
> them,
> > and profited, biblically, even tho
> > their chanting weight,
> > > erased familiarity
> > > from my face.[2]

Qualifications if not outright repudiations of earlier stances have
thus come to be expected. *Black Magic Poetry,* the collection of
poems written between 1961 and 1967, opens with "An Explanation
of the Work" written in 1968 in which he more or less dismisses
the work up to, say, 1965, calling it "a cloud of abstraction and dis-
jointedness, that was just whiteness."[4]

His latest collection of poetry, *Hard Facts,* comprised of poems
written between 1973 and 1975, announces yet another change of
direction. At the height of his Black nationalist phase, Baraka was
fond of countering any mention of Marxist theory by insisting that
socialism is contrary to the nature of whites and thus unattainable
by them in any form other than intellectual abstraction, whereas
Black people, being by their very nature communistic (generous,
non-exploitative, etc.), have no need of any such theories. Yet on the
back cover of *Hard Facts* we find a portrait of Marx, Engels, Lenin,
Stalin and Mao; and, in his introduction, Baraka explicitly disowns
his earlier nationalist position:

> Earlier our own poems came from an enraptured patriotism that
> screamed against whites as the eternal enemies of Black people, as the
> sole cause of our disorder + oppression. The same subjective mys-
> tification led to mysticism, metaphysics, spookism, &c., rather than
> dealing with reality, as well as an ultimately reactionary nationalism
> that served no interests but our newly emerging Black bureaucratic
> elite and petit bourgeois, so that they would have control over their
> Black market. This is not to say Black nationalism was not necessary,
> it was and is to the extent that we are still patriots, involved in the

[3] *The Dead Lecturer* (New York: Grove Press, 1964), p. 79.
[4] *Black Magic Poetry* (Indianapolis and New York: Bobbs-Merrill, 1969).

Black Liberation Movement, but we must also be revolutionaries who understand that our quest for our people's freedom can only be realized as the result of Socialist Revolution![5]

There are other changes. One notes another name change for example: the dropping of the Muslim title *Imamu* (meaning teacher), evidently bringing to an end his flirtation with Islamic religion. The poem "When We'll Worship Jesus" twice associates Allah with Christ, for several years now a villain in Baraka's work:

> jesus aint did nothin for us
> but kept us turned toward the
> sky (him and his boy allah
> too, need to be checkd
> out!)   (HF,7)

In addition, two poems attack Kenneth Gibson, whom he helped get elected mayor of Newark not long ago. One thing, however, hasn't changed. Black music continues to be invoked — respectfully invoked — serving in *Hard Facts,* as in earlier work, as a harbinger of change:

> hung out with any and all thats bad and mad and wont be had.
>   [In with
> all and all with in, out here stomping in the streets for
>   [the trumpeting
> dynamic of the people themselves — new and renew — Our Ex-
>   [perience
> Nows the time, charley parker sd, Now's the time. Say do it,
>   [do it, we gon
> do it.   (HF, 25)

In this essay I'll be talking about Black music in its dual role of impulse (life-style or ethos as well as technique) and theme in Baraka's work, exploring its usefulness as a sort of focal point or thread pulling together disparate strands of Baraka's thought. His early attraction to Projectivist and Beat poetics, for instance, bespeaks an attitude or stance which he and other spokesmen for those poetics repeatedly called upon "jazz" to exemplify. Kerouac, Ginsberg, Creeley, McClure and others glowingly referred to bop improvisation as a technique from which poets could learn. Olson remarked in a letter to Cid Corman in the early fifties: "how does — or is there — an anology to (as i'd gather any of us do) to jazz?"[6] Black music for

---

[5]*Hard Facts* (Newark, N.J.: Congress of Afrikan People, 1976).
[6]"Memorial Letter," *Origin,* 20 (Jan. 1971), p. 42.

Baraka, however, comes eventually to express the very spirit which leads to his repudiation of Olson, *et al.*—the Black nationalist ferment of the middle and late sixties. This ferment in his particular case, I'm suggesting, is itself impelled by certain attitudes and impulses which also motivated his Beat/Projectivist writings and with which this repudiation is thus not entirely inconsistent. What he rejects is an alleged failure of the Beat and Black Mountain writers to live up to the extra-literary (especially political) implications of their poetics—implications they themselves often insist upon in their pursuit of a relevance wider than the merely aesthetic.

Olson's insistence that "the projective involves a stance towards reality outside a poem as well as a new stance towards the reality of the poem itself,"[7] Duncan's sense of the poetic as a process of "ensouling" and Spicer's assurances that "the objective universe can be affected by the poet"[8] all attest to the importance of the notion of poetry as an agent of change and revelation to the poetic movement of which Baraka was—and remains—a part. The persistence of his celebration of Black music has to do with the persistence of a "will to change" (to use Olson's phrase)—a will common to his Projectivist, Black nationalist and Marxist periods—which the music invokes and exemplifies: "There is a daringly human quality to John Coltrane's music that makes itself felt, wherever he records. If you can hear, this music will make you think of a lot of weird and wonderful things. You might even become one of them."[9]

II

> ...Bankrupt utopia sez tell me
> no utopias. I will not listen. (Except the raw wind
> makes the hero's eyes close, and the tears that come
> out are real.)
>
> *Amiri Baraka,* "History As Process"

During the sixties assertions were often made to the effect that "jazz" groups provided glimpses into the future. What was meant by this was that Black music—especially that of the sixties, with its heavy emphasis on individual freedom within a collectively improvised context—proposed a model social order, an ideal, even utopic

[7]Allen and Tallman (eds), *The Poetics of the New American Poetry* (New York: Grove Press, 1973), p. 185.
[8]*Ibid.*, p. 230.
[9]*Black Music* (New York: Morrow, 1967), p. 67.

balance between personal impulse and group demands. The musicians' exhilaration at contributing to evolving musical orders rather than conforming to an already existing one seemed to anticipate the freedom of some future communalist ethic. Bill Mathieu, in a review of Roscoe Mitchell's *Sound,* stresses a communalist impulse he hears in the music: "There is emerging the sense of the holy tribal family as the primal artistic source."[10] In a review of Lester Bowie's *Numbers 1 & 2* he speaks of Bowie's music as an instance of a similar communalist experimentation, remarking at some length on a tuning-in process to which he applies the term *agreement:*

> In this music I hear the musicians making themselves fully known to each other. But the means are new. . . .
> In the old days, musicians used themes, rhythmic and harmonic inventions, expressive coloring, as the language of group play. These aspects are still present, but other work is done in other ways. The most important of these let us call *agreement.* The quality of agreement has always been a factor in making group music. Now, however, this aspect has become the illuminating aesthetic of contemporary music.[11]

Baraka's writings on Black music share with those of critics like Mathieu this tendency to discern inklings of an Edenic, open state or condition, though the terms of his particular sense of "agreement" are more insistently tribal or nationalistic—that is, Black. The music's communalist impulse is understood by him in terms of the synonymy of Blackness with collectivity. Accordingly, he interprets the interest in and experimentation with collective improvisation among the newer musicians as a return to the African ethic, a departure from which he takes the growth of the "jazz" solo to have been (see BM, 194-195). Something like the observation that this openness proceeds from an agreement which exists *above* the music also gets made in terms of Blackness (understood to be synonymous with spirituality as well). These notions of Black communality clearly carry the weight of a wished-for release from egocentricity, from the solipsism so rhapsodically lamented in poems like "The Death of Nick Charles," *"An Agony. As Now."* or "A Guerrilla Handbook":

> . . . Convinced
> of the man's image (since
> he will not look at substance
> other than his ego. . . .   (DL,66)

[10]*Downbeat,* June 15, 1967, p. 35.
[11]*Downbeat,* May 2, 1968, p. 26.

As this egocentrism is thought to be the issue of his white education, Blackness represents a liberating concern for as well as openness to others. The Black-musician-as-saboteur's target thus becomes the Western cult of individualism, the music an assault upon the ego. "New Black Music," Baraka writes in 1965, "is this: Find the self, then kill it" (BM, 176).

As if in preparation for the coming communalist ethic, Baraka's poems during the early sixties involve practices comparable to the surrealist *deréglèment de sens* as well as to the music's assault on the self. Like the surrealists—the analogy is enhanced by the fact that Baraka, as did Breton, Aragon and others, now espouses the Communist ideology—Baraka sought in these poems a derangement of the ratiocinative ego. Like Black surrealist Aimé Césaire, moreover, he saw this derangement as a plunge into previously repressed Black ancestral strata. The sense of "a plunge into the depths" is exactly what's evoked by Baraka's early poem "The Bridge," though the poem relies on musical terminology rather than surrealist imagery. The title refers to that portion of a "jazz" composition which leads the players back to the main melody line, referred to by musicians as the tune's "head." Baraka makes punning use of both terms, *bridge* and *head,* allowing his having "forgotten" the latter to suggest an experience of ego-loss, his having strayed beyond the former —"I can't see the bridge now, I've past/ it"—to suggest, again, a lostness which results in drowning, absorption into the oceanic All. The poem in full:

> I have forgotten the head
> of where I am. Here at the bridge. 2
> bars, down the street, seeming
> to wrap themselves around my fingers, the day,
> screams in me; pitiful like a little girl
> you sense will be dead before the winter
> is over.
> I can't see the bridge now, I've past
> it, its shadow, we drove through, headed out
> along the cold insensitive roads to what
> we wanted to call "ourselves."
> "How does the bridge go?" Even tho
> you find yourself in its length
> strung out along its breadth, waiting
> for the cold sun to tear out your eyes. Enamoured
> of its blues, spread out in the silk clubs of

this autumn tune. The changes are difficult, when
you hear them, & know they are all in you, the chords
of your disorder meddle with your would be disguises.
Sifting in, down, upon your head, with the sun & the insects.

(Late feeling) Way down till it barely, after that rush of
wind & odor reflected from hills you have forgotten the
        [color
when you touch the water, & it closes, slowly, around your
        [head.

The bridge will be behind you, that music you know, that
        [place,
you feel when you look up to say, it is me, & I have for-
        [gotten,
all the things, you told me to love, to try to understand,
        [the
bridge will stand, high up in the clouds & the light, & you,

(when you have let the song run out) will be sliding through
unmentionable black.[12]

On a strictly musical level "The Bridge" evokes the tendency towards deconstruction or defamiliarization among players of what
was then—the poem was written sometime between 1957 and 1961—
beginning to be called "the new thing." This tendency involved a
departure from—even outright abandonment of—bebop's reliance
on the recurring chords referred to as "the changes" of a particular
piece. Rather than basing their improvisations on the chord structure of the tune's head, the "new thingers" began to venture into
areas not so patly related to the harmonics of the piece being played.
To listeners accustomed to recurrent reminders of a tune's head in
the form of the soloist's confinement to the changes, the new music
seemed structureless and incoherent. These "nonchordal" excursions
were often put down as unmelodic ("Save the Popular Song") or as
evidence of the musicians' confusion. The players were frequently
said to sound *lost.* What Baraka does in "The Bridge" is make a
poem of this charge—"I have forgotten the head/ of where I am"—
making this "confusion" suggest a descent into the Black sub-
conscious, into "unmentionable black." "The Bridge" is still, however, a poem which *refers to* rather than *enacts* the sort of derangement I've been talking about. We find in it very little of the "dif-

----

[12]*Preface to a Twenty Volume Suicide Note* (New York: Totem Press/Corinth
Books, 1961), pp. 25-26.

ficulty in focusing on its controlling insights" M. L. Rosenthal sees
as the characteristic defect in Baraka's first two books of poems.[13]
The poem's "controlling" musical conceit remains very much in
view throughout.

Rosenthal, as have others, remarks on "the structural similarity
of some of its [*Preface to A Twenty Volume Suicide Note's*] pieces
to jazz improvisation" and observes, "The spiraling, dreaming movement of associations, spurts of energetic pursuit of melody and
motifs, and driftings away of Jones's poems seem very much an expression of a new way of looking at things, and of a highly contemporary aesthetic, of a very promising sort."[14] He fails, however, to
appreciate the connection between this "jazz" aesthetic and the "difficulty in focusing" he finds so disappointing. My own sense is that
this difficulty is not so much a defect as a principled outgrowth of
the African aesthetic underlying Black music and Baraka's poetry.
In *Blues People* Baraka quotes a passage from Ernest Borneman's
"The Roots of Jazz" which is worth quoting again, a passage in which
a description is offered of the African aesthetic in language and
music:

> In language, the African tradition aims at circumlocution rather than
> at exact definition. The direct statement is considered crude and un-
> imaginative; the veiling of all contents in ever-changing paraphrases
> is considered the criterion of intelligence and personality. In music,
> the same tendency towards obliquity and ellipsis is noticeable.[15]

Baraka echoes Borneman when, in the course of his liner notes to
Archie Shepp's *Four for Trane,* he applauds a certain "tendency
towards obliquity" in the playing of altoist John Tchicai (whose solos
he elsewhere describes as "metal poems"): "John Tchicai's solo on
'Rufus' comes back to me again. It slides away from the proposed"
(BM, 160).

Baraka's poems, especially those in *The Dead Lecturer,* likewise
tend to slide away from the proposed, to refuse to commit themselves
to any single meaning. The beginning of "The Measure of Memory
(The Navigator," for example, leads one to expect some sore of
theodicy, but by the second line conceptualization has given way to
a stream of images the relationship or relevance of which to the
poem's opening assertion is nowhere made explicit:

[13]*The New Poets* (New York: Oxford University Press, 1967), p. 191.
[14]*Ibid.,* p. 190.
[15]*Blues People* (New York: Morrow, 1963), p. 31.

> The presence of good
> is its answer (at the curb
> the dead white verb, horse
> breathing white steam
> in the air)
>   Leaving, into the clocks
> sad lovely lady fixed by words
> her man
> her rest
> her fingers
> her wooden house
> set against the rocks
> of our nation's
> enterprise.

The second stanza follows from—in the sense of being logically or thematically related to—the first only in that its image of disappearance echoes that of "leaving" in the poem's sixth line:

> That we disappear
> to dance, and dance
> when we do,
> badly.

The third stanza follows from the second in that it continues to describe what "we" do, but the discontinuity between it and the fourth stanza is not only tolerated by Baraka but accentuated by the double line he inserts between them:

> And wield sentiment
> like flesh
> like the dumb man's voice
> like the cold environment
> of need. Or despair, a trumpet
> with poison mouthpiece, blind player,
> at the garden of least discernment; I
> stagger, and remember/ my own terrible
> blankness and lies.
>
> ————————————————
>
> The boat's prow angled at the sun
> Stiff foam and an invisible cargo
> of captains. I buy injury, and decide
> the nature of silence. Lines of speed
> decay in my voice.   (DL,40-41)

The image of the boat in this final stanza recalls the word *navigator* in the poem's title, but what does it or any of the poem's other images and assertions have to do with the proposition that "the presence of good/ is its answer"? The connective is neither logic nor discourse, but the poet's voice. Adhering to and putting into practice Olson's *dictum* that "in any given poem always, always one perception must must must MOVE, INSTANTER, ON ANOTHER,"[16] the poem has a mercurial, evanescent quality, as though it sought to assassinate any expectations of traceable argument or logical flow. This is exactly the quality Baraka praises in Shepp's "Rufus," going on in the liner notes to *Four for Trane* to speak of the music in terms more commonly applied to poems:

> "Rufus" makes its "changes" faster. *Changes* here meaning, as younger musicians use that word to mean "modulations," what I mean when I say *image*. They change very quickly. The mind, moving.
>
> (BM, 160, Baraka's italics)

The mind, moving. Poems like "The Measure of Memory (The Navigator)" seek to circumvent stasis, to be true to the essential mobility of the psyche. Their "tendency towards obliquity" is a gesture in the direction of totalization, towards an enlargement of the realm of that we take or will accept as being meaningful. "Poetry aims at difficult meanings," Baraka writes. "Meanings not already catered to. Poetry aims at reviving, say, a sense of meaning, or meaning's possibility and ubiquitousness" (BMP, 41).

This gesture towards totalization has to do with an anti-Western, anti-rationalist feeling, the West and its cult of rationality epitomizing a pursuit of order at the expense of the All. The West's exclusionary practices against non-white peoples are seen as one with its attempted suppression of the non-rational. The dreamish, arational quality of his poems is thus of a piece with Baraka's contempt for the confusion of rationality with rationalization ("Bankrupt utopia sez tell me/ no utopias"). Hence his espousal of "insanity," the ultimate irrationality, in the form of a Black dadaistic uprising in the poem "Black Dada Nihilismus" and in the essay "Philistinism and the Negro Writer."

At its worst Baraka's praise for the emotively expressive veers towards the anti-intellectualism — which, as usual, sounds a bit lame coming from an intellectual — of pieces like "New-Sense," in which

[16]"Projective Verse," *Human Universe and Other Essays* (New York: Grove Press, 1967). p. 53.

he sets up an opposition between the expressive and the reflective.[17] In its best aspects this anti-intellectualism is not so much a repudiation of thought as an effort to *re*think, to as it were *un*think the many perversions of thought — rationalization, "institutionalized dishonesty" and so forth — endemic to an unjust social order. The anti-reflective position, that is, having been arrived at by way of reflection, represents an instance of dialectical thinking, as in "Hegel":

> Either I am wrong
> or "he" is wrong. All right
> I am wrong, but give me someone
> to talk to. (BMP, 24)

An ongoing oscillation between these two impulses — or more exactly these alternate modes of a single impulse (towards totalization) — is what makes for the characteristic unrest of Baraka's thought. The unrest itself bespeaks a desire to transcend conditionality, the very desire with whose futility the poem "Jitterbugs" has to do:

> The imperfection of the world
> is a burden, if you know it, think
> about it, at all. Look up in the sky
> wishing you were free, placed so terribly
> in time, mind out among new stars, working
> propositions, and not this planet where you
> cant go anywhere without an awareness of the hurt
> the white man has put on the people. Any people. You
> cant escape, there's no where to go. They have made
> this star unsafe, and this age, primitive, though yr mind
> is somewhere else, your ass aint. (BMP, 92)

This repudiation, it perhaps bears repeating, comes of Baraka's own desire for some such transcendence, of the idealist, Hegelian, sub-tilizationist (call it what you will) impulse from which his poetry's obliquities derive.

The defamiliarization encountered in the poems, that is, betrays a sense of the world as not only determined or conditioned but *over*-determined. This overdetermination is what their obliquities do battle with, seeking to expose, by circumventing, the partiality of common sense, of any consensually-constituted reality's necessary eclipse of unassimilable truths. The totalization at which they aim being outside their reach, they put in its place a vigilant sense of the

---

[17]See *Tales* (New York: Grove Press, 1967), p. 96.

patencies towards which consciousness tends as inescapably con-
ditional, thus neverendingly susceptible to qualification. Baraka
hears this spirit of interrogation and discontent in the most moving
of Black music, especially that of John Coltrane ("the heaviest spirit").
Of the version of Billy Eckstine's "I Want to Talk About You" on the
Coltrane Live at Birdland album he writes:

> ...instead of the simplistic though touching note-for-note replay of
> the ballad's line, on this performance *each note is tested,* given a slight
> tremolo or emotional vibrato (note to chord to scale reference), which
> makes it seem as if *each one of the notes is given the possibility of*
> *"infinite" qualification.*   (BM,66, my italics)

A similar "testing" can be heard in most of Baraka's poems, giving
them that hesitant, stuttering quality suggestive of a discomfort with
any pretense of definitive statement. What this "testing" projects is
a world of uncertainties or of expanded possibilities, a world of shifting, unsettled boundaries in which any gesture towards definition is
unavoidably tentative, self-conscious and subject to revision. This
"uncertainty principle" often takes the rather obvious form of a pre-
ponderance of questions, as in "The Clearing," where repetitions of
and variations upon the questions "Where are the beasts?", "What
bird makes that noise?", "Were you singing?" and "What song is
that?" occur throughout:

> Your voice down the hall. Are
> you singing? A shadow song
> we lock our movement
> in. Were you singing?
> down the hall. White plaster
> on the walls, our fingers
> leave their marks, on
> the dust, or tearing
> the wall away. Were you
> singing? What song
> was that?   (TVSN, 30)

Another characteristic use of repetition has much the same effect.
While not one of outright questions as in "The Clearing," the repetition of such phrases as *or pain, the yes* and *flesh or soul* in *"An*
Agony. As Now." suggests a state of astonishment if not one of confusion. Each repetition being followed by a staccato burst of imaged
evocation, the sense of a wrestling with definition is given, of an ob-

sessive anxiety towards the impossibility of any settled sense of what
these phrases mean:

> It can be pain. (As now, as all his
> flesh hurts me.) It can be that. Or
> pain. As when she ran from me into
> that forest.
>   Or pain, the mind
> silver spiraled whirled against the
> sun, higher than even old men thought
> God would be. Or pain. And the other. The
> *yes.* (Inside his books, his fingers. They
> are withered yellow flowers and were never
> beautiful.) The yes. You will, lost soul, say
> 'beauty.' Beauty, practiced, as the tree. The
> slow river. A white sun in its wet sentences.
> Or, the cold men in their gale. Ecstasy. Flesh
> or soul. The yes. (Their robes blown. Their bowls
> empty. They chant at my heels, not at yours.) Flesh
> or soul, as corrupt. Where the answer moves too quickly.
> Where the God is a self, after all.)   (DL, 15-16)

Something of a treadmill or a stuttering effect results, the sense of
someone caught in a rut being heightened by the dead-ending op-
tions—the word *or* occurs twelve times in the poem—created by
posing the same word as an alternative to itself ("Or pain. ... Or
pain. ... Or pain"). This effect, as I've already tried to suggest, is a
very salient feature of the playing of those Black musicians Baraka
most admires. (Listen, for example, to Sonny Rollins' "Green
Dolphin Street," Coltrane's "Amen" or John Tchicai's "Everything
Happens to Me."[18]) In some poems, in fact, the use of repetition is
almost purely musical, in that sound seems to take precedence over
sense:

> say day lay day may fay come some bum'll
> take break jake make fake lay day some bum'll
> say day came break snow mo whores red said they'd
> lay day in my in fay bed to make bread for jake
> limpin in the hall with quiverin stick.   (BMP,169)

Another statement Baraka has made about Coltrane can very fitting-
ly be applied to such gestures as these:

[18]On the albums *Sonny Rollins on Impulse!* (Impulse! A-91), *Sun Ship* (Impulse!
AS 9211) and the New York Art Quartet's *Mohawk* (Fontana 881 009 ZY), respectively.

One night he played the head of "Confirmation" over and over again, about twenty times, and that was his solo. It was as if he wanted to take that melody apart and play out each of its chords as a separate improvisational challenge. And while it was a marvelous thing to hear and see, it was also more than a little frightening; *like watching a grown man learning to speak*...and I think that's just what was happening.

(BM,59, my italics)

III

Baraka's poetry (to borrow his own description of the new music) "began by calling itself 'free'" (BM, 193). "MY POETRY," he wrote in 1959, "is whatever I think I am. ... I CAN BE ANYTHING I CAN. ... I *must* be completely free to do just what I want, in the poem."[19] This declaration of poetic freedom is likewise "social," a "direct commentary on the scene it appears in." So assertive an espousal of or aspiration towards poetic freedom implies the absence of any such freedom outside of poems. It may have been this absence Baraka had in mind in 1960 when he remarked, "I'm always aware, in anything I say, of the 'sociological configuration'—what it *means* sociologically. But it doesn't have anything to do with what I'm writing at the time."[20] Though he seems to have at this point believed in poetry as an actual, albeit fleeting transcendence of material constraints, only a few years later he insists in "Green Lantern's Solo":

> ...Can you understand
> that nothing is free! Even the floating strangeness of
>   [the poet's
>   head
> the crafted visions of the intellect, *named, controlled,*
>   [beat and erected
> to work, and struggle under the heavy fingers of art.

(DL, 68, Baraka's italics)

So, just as he's able to discern the "sociological configuration" from which the freedom-thrusts of Black music derive, he's also aware of the contingencies his poems' obliquities seek to deflect. In fact, the poems become increasingly concerned with explicit statements regarding these contingencies, thus making for a certain tension between such directness and any attempts to "slide away from the proposed." Such attempts all but disappear, in fact, from the poems of

[19]*The New American Poetry*, p. 424.
[20]David Ossman, *The Sullen Art* (New York: Corinth Books, 1963), p. 81.

the early seventies, poems such as those in *It's Nation Time* or, a bit more recently, a poem like "Afrikan Revolution":

> We are for world progress. Be conscious of your
> life! We need food. We need homes; good
> housing—not shacks. Let only people who want to
> live in roach gyms live in roach gyms
> We do not want to live with roaches. Let
> Nixon live with roaches if he wants to. He
> is closer to a roach. What is the difference
> between Nixon and a roach?
> Death to bad housing
> Death to no work
> We need work. We need education. ...[21]

This contentment with the explicit (the sloganistic in fact), while inconsistent with "the denying or withholding of all signposts" so essential to the "jazz" aesthetic, is nonetheless consistent with and in fact articulates the "message" implied by—the "enraged sociologies" (*Tales*, 77) Baraka hears in—Black music.

The poems in *Hard Facts* appear to signal an arrest of this trend towards utter directness, a return to the blend of the explicit with the oblique characteristic of *Black Magic Poetry*, a work in which one finds statements as outright as "President Johnson/ is a mass murderer" (p. 93) or "The white man/ at best/ is corny" (p. 162), and images as indecipherable as "a black toe sewn in their throats" (p. 154). The poems in *Hard Facts*, while generously laced with an unambiguously Marxist line— "fight for the dictatorship until it is reality. The dictatorship of the proletariat, the/ absolute control of the state by the working class" (p. 31)—nevertheless allow for the warp introduced by such lines as "In rag time, slanting/ stick legs, with a pocket full of/ toasted seaweed" (p. 12). Baraka appears to be attempting an accord between the conflicting claims of the accessible and the esoteric—for which also read the contingent and the indeterminate, the social and the spiritual, the Marxist and the Hegelian, *ad nauseum*—("the spiritual and free and soulful must mingle with the practical"). This is the synthesis, significantly, whose weight he envisions a future Black music carrying, a music wherein all the dichotomies he's troubled by will have been rescued from conflict:

---

[21]*Black World,* May 1973, p. 45.

But here is a theory stated just before. That what will come will be a
Unity Music. The Black Music which is jazz and blues, religious and
secular. Which is New Thing and Rhythm and Blues. The consciousness of social re-evaluation and rise, a social spiritualism. A mystical
walk up to the street to a new neighborhood where all the risen live.

(BM, 210, Baraka's italics)

*(Except the raw wind makes the hero's eyes close, and the tears that
come out are real.)*

The Search for Identity
in Baraka's *Dutchman*

by Sherley Anne Williams

I

Dutchman is a two-scene, two-character play of powerful dimensions and chilling implications. Ostensibly, it is the story of a young, Ivy League Black man, Clay, who allows himself to be picked up by a white woman, Lula, on a New York subway. When Clay refuses to conform to Lula's vision of the Black man as a "hip field-nigga," she taunts him into revealing his antagonism toward all whites as well as revealing the self which he hides under his Ivy League front, his facade, and then she kills him. And the audience's smug agreement with Lula's charge that Clay is nothing more than a third-rate imitation white man changes to shock and surprise as Clay reveals the awareness which looks out from behind his front.

The plot line in itself has several implications, the most important being that the survival of the Black man in America, or the Western world, for that matter, is predicated upon his ability to keep his thoughts and his true identity hidden. As Baraka himself has stated in "A Poem for Willie Best," the Black man thus becomes "A renegade/ behind the mask. And even/ the mask, a renegade/ disguise." And when one views the implicit assumption that Black people hide behind stereotyped images through the prism of the three myths embodied in the play, further dimensions are added to this theme.

The myth or legend implicit in the title "Dutchman" is that of the ghost ship, the *Flying Dutchman,* which roamed the seas and added unwary ships to its phantom entourage. As though to underline the spectral implications of the title, Baraka sets the scene for the open-

"The Search for Identity in Baraka's *Dutchman*" by Sherley Anne Williams. From *Give Birth to Brightness* (New York: The Dial Press, 1972). Copyright © 1972 by Sherley Anne Williams. Reprinted by permission of the Dial Press and the author.

ing of the play: "In the flying underbelly of the city. Steaming hot, summer on top, outside. Underground. The subway heaped in modern myth."[1] One does not want to push this opening statement too much, but Lula's action at the end of the play, after she has killed Clay and, with the help of the other occupants of the subway coach, thrown his body overboard, tends to confirm the supposition that Clay's death is no instance of mere feminine caprice or a random act.

> Lula busies herself straightening her things. Getting everything in order. She takes out a notebook and makes a quick scribbling note. Drops it in her bag. The train apparently stops and all the others get off, leaving her alone in the coach.
>
> Very soon a young Negro of about twenty comes into the coach with a couple of books under his arm. He sits a few seats in back of Lula. When he is seated, she turns and gives him a long slow look. He looks up from his book and drops the book on his lap.

The implication seems plain that the young Black man will be pushed into playing Clay and Lula will perform her ritual murder again. Lula is thus subtly aligned with the supernatural, the ghostly, the powers of death and destruction. She is likened to a ghost ship, cruising the city's underbelly, asking Black men the question, Which side are you on? and murdering those who, like Clay, respond, My own. One realizes that had Clay continued to hide, had he traded his Ivy League front for that of the hip field-nigga as Lula wanted, she would have allowed him to live. For it is she, as a representative of the white power structure and a symbol of the sexuality which white men have used, both as justification of Black castration and oppression and as an inducement to Black men to accept that castration, who has the power of life and death over him.

The historical dimension to the title is equally significant, for it was a Dutchman, a Dutch man-of-war, which brought the first Black slaves to North America. America symbolically comes full circle through Lula's — the *Dutchman's* — murderous actions. The economic foundations of the nation were contained in the Dutchman's Black cargo and that cargo, as slave, freedman and would-be citizen has been the source of controversy and conflict. America's economy is no longer based on chattel slavery yet the issue of how Black people are to live and prosper continues to be a problem, a festering irritant under the nation's skin. The problems raised at Jamestown are re-

[1]LeRoi Jones, *Dutchman and The Slave* (New York: Morrow & Co., 1964), p. 3.

solved on the subway: What the Dutchman has given, the *Dutchman* also takes away. The other occupants of the coach, sitting quietly as she leads up to her murderous finale, helping eagerly to "bury" Clay, these are Lula's crew. It is not without significance that this crew is both Black and white, that it apparently changes with each of Lula's victims. The Blacks, the Negroes, are what Lula has accused Clay of being, imitation white men with no traitorous awareness peeking from behind their various facades. The whites are the power structure of which Lula is so vocal an exponent. The crew changes, making every segment of American society a participant, if silent, in the murder of Black men.

The apples which Lula enters the subway eating so daintily at the beginning of the play seem to bear some resemblance to the biblical fruit of the tree of knowledge in Christian mythology. For, as Lula tells Clay after he has accepted an apple from her, "Eating apples is always the first step." Clay's acceptance of the apple is, presumably, the first step in his "quest" for carnal knowledge of her or at least submission to the idea of knowing her. One is tempted to ask, just where was Eden that a Black man could be tempted from it by a white woman? But it is not Eden from which Lula seeks to tempt Clay. Rather, she seeks to tempt him from behind the safe, assimilationist facade under which Baraka seems to feel Black people have sought refuge. The shared apples seem to establish the needed intimacy for Lula to metaphorically catapult Clay onto the exposed, untenable promontory from which she pushes him to his death.

But for one splendid moment he reveals not only himself but also Lula and through her the ignorance and hypocrisy of the structure which she represents; reveals that the pretense in which she wants him to join—"And we'll pretend the people cannot see you. That is, the citizens. And that you are free of your own history. And I am free of my history. We'll pretend that we are both anonymous beauties smashing along through the city's entrails"—is not lightly self-mocking or even hip. It is bogus and sinister and Clay's distant observation of it is his only possibility of salvation. And his observation of Lula and her world is distant, despite Lula's charge that Clay "crawled through the wire and made tracks to her side." But Lula assumes that Clay's front is an accurate reflection of his pumping Black heart. Hence, her plea, "Clay, you got to break out," is rather hollow and is perhaps more a plea for her own salvation than for his.

Lula is in many ways the prototype of the white hipster who presumes to know Black people and their culture better than Black people know it themselves. It is her insistence that Clay conform to her view of him which brings about the outburst which leads to his death. As she says early in the play, lying helps her to control the world. This particular lie is what Lorraine Hansberry has called the image of the "eternal exotic,"[2] another of the images which Blacks have hidden behind in order to survive and which whites have promoted, have in fact gloried in, in order not to see the humanity of Black people. To see that humanity is to confront their own guilt, Clay strips aside his "renegade mask" and the violent Black heart is illuminated:

> You telling me what I ought to do. *(Sudden scream frightening the whole coach)* Well, don't! Don't tell me anything. If I'm a middle class fake white man...let me be. And let me be in the way I want. *(Through his teeth)*...Let me be who I feel like being. Uncle Tom. Thomas. Whoever. It's none of your business. You don't know anything except what's there for you to see. An act. Lies. Device. Not the pure heart, the pumping black heart.

The world in which Clay moves is revealed as a shadowy world filled with images and illusions, where one's true self, one's true identity is hidden, revealed to members only, where manhood is a secret between a man and his horn or a man and his Ivy League suit, and image and illusion, horn and suit form a barrier against the sanity which can only bring death.

The central concern of the play is not identity as one knows it from contemporary literature. For Clay's whole life is predicated upon the conscious effort of hiding what he knows is his own Black self from his eyes and the eyes of others. Rather, the concern is with a denial, not only of identity, but of heroism. As Clay says, "[I'd] rather be a fool. ... Safe with my words and no deaths and clean, hard thoughts urging me to new conquests." Black heroism for Clay would be a clear rational solution for white pollution, for the "hurt the white man has put on the people..."[3] He prophesies the time when whites will be caught in their own trick, be victimized by their own game:

[2]Lorraine Hansberry, "Me Tink Me Hear Sounds in de Night," *Theatre Arts,* XLIV (Oct. 1960), p. 9.

[3]LeRoi Jones, "Jitterbugs," *Black Magic: Poetry 1961-1967* (Indianapolis: Bobbs-Merrill, 1969), p. 92.

Tell him [Lula's father] not to preach so much rationalism and cold logic to these niggers. Let them alone. ... Don't make the mistake, through some irresponsible surge of Christian charity, of talking too much about the advantages of Western rationalism, or the great intellectual legacy of the white man, or maybe they'll begin to listen.... And on that day, as sure as shit, when you really believe you can "accept" them into your fold, as half-white trustees late of subject peoples...all of those ex-coons will be stand-up Western men, with eyes for clean hard useful lives, sober, pious and sane, and they'll murder you. They'll murder you, and have very rational explanations. Very much like your own. They'll cut your throats, and drag you out to the edge of your cities so the flesh can fall away from your bones, in sanitary isolation.

But he backs away from this vision, tries to climb back into his buttoned-up suit, collect his books and get off the train in which he has journeyed in time as well as space. His retreat from participation in this solution is again a denial of his identity. But once having shown himself to the white world, he learns that there is no retreat and he becomes just another dead nigger.

II

As just another dead nigger, Clay takes his place in a long line of fallen Black males who believed that the solution to their Negro problem was for Black people to be less Negro. He is heir to the tradition which Robert Bone calls assimilationism.[4] As heir apparent, Clay differs from his forebears in the fact that he is brought to the realization that no matter how many nigger characteristics he drops, no matter how assimilated he becomes, he is still Black, he is still one of the subject people. He learns, also, that despite all the accouterments of status, the clothing, the education, he can still be commanded to drop back into that old role. But even this knowledge which he is goaded into acquiring is flawed, for he does not learn—or learns too late—that it is impossible to exhibit his newly found learning before the oppressor and live.

[4]*The Negro Novel in America,* Rev. ed. (New Haven: Yale University Press, 1965). Bone's definitions do not lend themselves to paraphrasing or interpretation—at least with any reasonable assurance that one has captured what he is trying to convey (as Darwin T. Turner points out in *"The Negro Novel in America:* In Rebuttal," *CLA Journal,* X (Dec. 1966), 122-134). The reader is therefore advised to consult Bone, pp. 25-28.

It is open to question whether Clay's analysis of Soul is a knowledge which he has consciously lived with for some time and merely verbalizes as a result of Lula's prodding or whether Lula's verbal slashing and jabbing unlock a door which has kept this knowledge hidden away from even his own private eye. One does not, of course, see a light bulb go on in Clay's mind or hear him exclaim, "Aha, color is the issue." One does, however, watch him try valiantly to play Lula's game, to be that which she desires him to be. His explosion, as her thrusts become more painful and her conduct more outrageous, is uncontrollable, at least by him, and once his rage is vented, he turns away from his exposition of the Black heart to give Lula some world-weary advice, as though acknowledging the futility of words as a medium for understanding Blackness or, perhaps, having blown his own game, trying to save Lula from the consequences of hers.

The makings of a hero are there in Clay, the convention breaking, the front, but they never come to fruition. As an Ivy League negro he is by definition an affront to convention, not only because he has stepped out of his assigned place in the social order, but also because he has turned his back upon Black people, or at least the masses of them. An Ivy League or bourgeois negro embraces those social structures or traditions which have oppressed Black people and has, himself, become another kind of stereotype. The narrow shouldered suit, the beard, the aping of Baudelaire are all efforts to forge a new self which has little or nothing to do with Blackness in America. Ironically, all the facades in the world can never hide Clay's skin color which in itself is looked upon as the biggest departure from, and affront to, convention.

Thus Clay's front does not give him that element which is essential to the success of any game, the element of control. He is a victim of his own game; rather than using his front to manipulate others, Clay uses it as a protection not only from white power, that is, the white power structure, but from Black power as well. And, from the moment she enters the coach, Lula does control the situation. *She* picks Clay up. *She* encourages him. And it is she who goads him into revealing things which must have been carefully hidden deep in the most secret places of his heart. Clay denies himself even the simple and logical action of walking away from Lula. He attempts to transmute this rejection of action, this denial of heroism, of identity, into a metaphor ("[*suddenly weary*] Ahhh. Shit. But who needs it? I'd rather be a fool"). Perhaps he would have written a poem—had he survived.

Dutchman and The Slave:
Companions in Revolution

by John Lindberg

LeRoi Jones' two plays, *Dutchman* and *The Slave,* published together as one book, offer many striking parallels, each the reverse of the other, in character and theme. These reverse parallels are so strong that the plays, though published as distinct works, make sense as a single piece. The two important themes are the theme of search and the theme of sanity. They develop through the time-lapse between plays, because each play gives a stage in Jones' view of black revolution as one phase of a continuing race-war.

I

Many obvious reversed parallels bring us to an enriched under-standing of the themes of search and sanity. Both plays present a race-war, and in *Dutchman* the white wins, and in *The Slave* the black wins. The winners are opposite sexes representing opposed cultural goals. The black loser in the first play is a would-be revolutionist who prefers the comfortable role of an artist-intellectual following white models. The black winner in the second play is a one-time artist-intellectual who has rejected white models to achieve violent black-nationalist goals.

The white victor-woman in *Dutchman* imposes her values on her black male victim. The black victor-male in *The Slave* forces his triumphant philosophy on his white ex-wife. Lula, Western culture's bitch-goddess, first entices and then denies the sexual urge of Clay, whose death is only the final version of his emasculated life. Walker Vessels taunts his ex-wife's white husband with impotence, and the artillery barrage of Walker's vigorous black soliders kills the white

"*Dutchman* and *The Slave:* Companions in Revolution" by John Lindberg. From *Modern Black Literature,* ed. by Dr. S. Okechukwu Mezu (Buffalo, New York: Black Academy Press, 1971), 101-7. Reprinted with permission of the publisher.

woman he loved and then rejected when she could not continue to love him as he worked for a black victory. Walker with his penis-gun replaces Lula with her gelding knife. His last name, Vessels, has male erotic meaning to contrast with the pun in the name of his white male victim, Easley. And his first name, Walker, has the purposefulness missing in the malleable character suggested by the name Clay of his black opposite in the first play.

How do these reversed parallels help us understand the themes of search and sanity? Only when we view·the plays as complementary do we know the full meaning of several actions and lines. Lula enters eating an apple, in the role of temptress, searching for knowledge and corrupting her men by insisting they help her search in her own way. She invites Clay with words echoing the Fall from Innocence, when Adam and Eve discover their nakedness: "I...saw you staring...down in the vicinity of my ass and legs"; "Eating apples together is always the first step"; "What've you got that jacket and tie on in all this heat for?" Clay is only the next in a series of relationships she has discarded as phony: "Walked down the aisle... searching you out"; "Dull, dull, dull. I bet you think I'm exciting"; "I told you I didn't know all about *you*...you're a well-known type"; "My hair is turning gray. A gray hair for each year and type I've come through"; "Everything you say is wrong. That's what makes you so attractive."

> [Searching aimlessly through her bag. She begins to talk breathlessly, with a light and silly tone.] All stories are whole stories. All of 'em. Our whole story...nothing but change. How could things go on like that forever? Huh?
> [Slaps him on the shoulder, begins finding things in her bag, taking them out and throwing them over her shoulder into the aisle.] Except I do go on as I do. Apples and long walks with deathless intelligent lovers.

Searching through her bag and discarding things—we imagine symbols of dominance like wallet, car keys, lipstick, compact, comb, sexy-cover paperbacks filling the air—she has exhausted her repertoire of cultural plays, and confronts Clay on what she considers to be ultimate ground, the question of his sincerity. This confrontation is the climax of the play. When Clay turns to stone defiance, her only recourse to protect herself from her own ignorance is to kill him. She has always looked for a master, but Clay has loved her white world so well he is unwary and falls to her surprise knife.

The best lines are Lula's. She is the protagonist, the hysterical bitch of white values. But Clay's own search has fed her the lines, because he has admired success that she can scorn. He wallows in lubricious pleasure at the picture of himself at a party with a white beauty, on a long delicately delaying evening ending in bed with her. She makes him sneer at his name, his parents, their dreams, and their past: "Take your pick. Jackson, Johnson, or Williams"; "My grandfather was a night watchman"; "My mother was a Republican"; "Plantations were big open whitewashed places like heaven, and everybody on 'em was grooved to be there. Just strummin' and hummin' all day"; "And that's how the blues was born." Everything he says justifies her contempt:

LULA. ...About your manhood, what do you think? What do you think we've been talking about all this time?

CLAY. Well, I didn't know it was that. That's for sure. Every other thing in the world but that.

Thus Lula can rage at his hypocrisy and taunt him by claiming to know more about blacks than he does, with her insulting invitation to the dance: "You middle-class black bastard. Forget your social-working mother for a few seconds and let's knock stomachs."

The climax of the play, the confrontation which now occurs, relates the search theme to the sanity theme. Both Clay and Lula have searched for themselves by playing roles, and now they test their final roles. Lula has become a destroyer in her search for integrity. She is past sanity though sanity is her search: "Red trains cough Jewish underwear for keeps! Expanding smells of silence. Gravy snot whistling like sea birds. Clay. Clay, you got to break out. Don't sit there dying the way they want you to die." In these lines Lula actually begs Clay to save her from her own kind. But when he is only embarrassed, she makes the mistake of taunting him with his acceptance of white values and makes him speak the truth they have both avoided: "If I'm a middle-class fake white man...let me be. And let me be in the way I want. ... You fuck some black man, and right away you're an expert on black people. What a lotta shit that is." For the moment Clay refuses to accept the lies Lula uses to "control the world...I lie all the time. Draw your own conclusions."

But she wants to believe in her version of funky black vitality so she can deny Clay's view of the blacks' arts as an escapist sublimation of hate for dominant whites, a response as ineffective as his own imitation of whites:

Some kind of bastard literature…all it needs is a simple knife thrust.
… A whole people of neurotics, struggling to keep from being sane.
And the only thing that would cure the neurosis would be your
murder.… But who needs it? I'd rather be a fool. Insane. Safe with my
words, and no deaths, and clean, hard thoughts urging me to new
conquests.

In choosing insanity he accepts Lula's false view of blacks, knowing it is false, confirms her in error, and accepts the knife thrust he
knows could be his to give when Lula kills him rather than admit
she has wasted her life fighting unreal enemies. For she has not won.
Clay knows with a foresight of his reincarnation in Walker that the
blacks are truly sane: "My people. They don't need me to claim
them. They got legs and arms of their own.… They don't need all
those words. They don't need any defense.… They'll murder you,
and have very rational explanations."

II

Clay's choice of insanity places the motivation of the characters in
both plays outside of individual values, "[p]ersonal insanities."
Lula seems to accept this relative view of personal responsibility
when she says playfully: "We'll pretend that we are both anonymous
beauties smashing along through the city's entrails." The opening
stage directions read: *"In the flying underbelly of the city.… Underground. The subway heaped in modern myth"*; men are caught in
the development of their institutions.

History seen as a black revolutionary process is the value-ref-
erence in both plays, a reference that shows clearly to help us grasp
the significance of the action in either play only when we consider
both plays together. Clay has foreseen the eventual victory of his
own people, whom Walker, in the next play, leads to the brink of
that victory. Walker has rejected Grace, his white ex-wife, because
she cannot reconcile his personal love for her with his political action to kill white people. Brad Easley, Grace's new white husband,
cannot tolerate Walker's black revolution because it makes impossible "life as a purely anarchic relationship between man and God…
or man and his work." Walker has grown beyond his role as Brad's
pupil. Personal relationships, individual reputation must emerge
with the socializing imperative of the black revolution.

The themes of search and sanity appear again in *The Slave* after their first appearance in *Dutchman,* this time in an obvious physical way because the race war is now open. Lula can no longer knife Clay by surprise. The roles are now actual, not symbolic. Prologuizing, Walker begins: "Whatever the core of our lives. Whatever the deceit. We live where we are, and seek nothing but ourselves. We are liars, and we are murderers." The universal pronoun in these lines states the implicit theme in *Dutchman* that history no longer allows private compromise but throws individuals into public roles. Ideas—personal justifications—no longer have meaning even when honest: "The very rightness stinks a lotta times." "I am an old man," Walker complains, and in the prologue he is older than in the play, because the prologue shows us Walker after he has lived through the play. In the play, he is a liar and murderer to the whites who deny his public role.

For the playing-time of the play Walker has deserted his public role to return to his private past, partly in genuine regret, mainly to break his last ties with his earlier self when he was still a non-historic personality. He checks his watch to keep track of the pace of history so he will not be caught by his men on the scene of his shame, his outdated white loyalties. The action of the play speeds up as the bombardment approaches, and Walker finally frees himself from his white past as the house collapses under black shells. He has now shed false roles and lived into his destiny—search and sanity coincide as he makes his way back to his men. But for the space of the play he has returned to an insane part of his life, and the action consists of his trying to explain to Grace and Brad why he is not the liar and murderer they call him.

While working up to a climactic scene, Walker plays mock-roles as a stupid darkie, a stage Irishman, a Japanese torturer, because Brad and Grace refuse to take him seriously as a militant leader:

GRACE. ... It must be a sick task keeping so many lying separate ug-
linesses together ... and pretending they're something you're made
and understand.

WALKER. What I can use ...

EASLEY. ... What is this, the pragmatics of war? ... I thought you
meant yourself to be a fantastic idealist? ...

WALKER. ... Now you can call me the hypocritical idealist nigger
murderer.

The argument over the girls arises because the whites refuse to believe a killer can love his children. They do not understand when he claims the girls for the black revolutionary future. He agrees with the whites that this future is created by violence and betrayal, and insists that the end justifies the means. Nearly every speech by Grace and Brad in this part of the play uses words like *lying* and *insane*. Walker's sanity is their insanity: "You thought I betrayed you... And don't, now...start thinking he's disillusioned...cynical, or any of these...liberal definitions of the impossibility or romanticism of idealism."

At this point the dialogue again places values in the historical destiny of black triumph and rejects conventional morals: "What does it matter if there's more love or beauty [in black victory]? Who the fuck cares?... The point is that you had your chance, darling, now these other folks have theirs." And when Brad stresses the ugliness of this idea, Walker again admits that in the past he valued personal ideas but had to give them up as luxuries in the need for revolt: "No social protest...right is in the act! And the act itself has some place in the world...it makes some place for itself." These words reverse Walker's mockery of non-historical private values when he says in the prologue: "But figure, still, ideas are still in the world. They need judging." And ideas are judged by the act.

No understanding is possible any more between Walker and his whites. His new true role inevitably leads to Brad's death, when Grace repeats four times in a crescendo of horror: "You're an insane man." Grace calls him insane because she is unable to see him as a superman now that he had fulfilled his destiny. His old values must die to make room for his new life: "There is no reason he [Brad] should go out with any kind of dignity. I couldn't allow that." To which Grace repeats three times: "You're out of your mind." And Walker retorts: "...being out of your mind is the only thing that qualifies you to stay alive. ... Easley was in his right mind. ... That's the reason he's dead." These lines echo the cross-accusations between Lula and Clay with the difference that Walker has consciously passed into the historic personality that Clay foretold for his people.

When we learn that Walker has killed his children, this knowledge completes his reversal of Clay. He has jived Grace and Brad with his assumed role of concerned black parent who risks death to rescue the girls from a life as whites. Lula had taunted Clay for playing a white role. Walker makes his point by playing a role when it suits his purpose in the argument, but the whites are the deluded ones. And while Clay falls easily to Lula's knife because he admires her whiteness, Walker kills his children to free himself from all white taint. He has become the man without a past, the stone revolutionist, clay no more.

This totally new man, committed to a historical imperative, has passed beyond conventional human roles. The play opens and closes with stage directions calling for children crying. Walker quotes a Yeats poem ironically, a poem about wounded innocence. But his irony arises from the fact that he no longer copies Yeats by writing poems; he has become the intolerable music Yeats foretells—he has just murdered his children. In the prologue he is unsure of his age, after the success of his revolt. In the play, he admits to Brad that the black revolution may build no better world than the whites have done. He fulfills Brad's dying mockery, for the character of Walker complements that of Clay, and the two plays compose a ritual drama symbolizing LeRoi Jones' conviction that history develops through cycles of race-war.

The Corrupted Warrior Heroes:
Amiri Baraka's *The Toilet*

by Robert L. Tener

Among the few who have written critically and favorably about Amiri Baraka's (LeRoi Jones') *The Toilet,*[1] Paul Witherington in "Exorcism and Baptism in LeRoi Jones' *The Toilet*" has demonstrated that the play is "the acting out of a ritual"[2] dramatizing the passage from boyhood to manhood of a group of black teenage boys. The final events signify their leader's "mature victory over the hyper-masculinity of the gang and over his own divided self."[3] Embedded in this essay, however, is another idea that Witherington has not developed as fully, namely "that private level of response is the only feasible one for expressing genuine mature feeling in a world dominated by stereotyped responses."[4] That this is one of the major concerns of the play can be shown by examining the ritual which Baraka develops, the movement from boyhood to manhood.

But the concept means more than what Witherington suggests. It is not just the exit from the maternal world in the house into the arena of the gang. Instead it is the ideological drift from the sense of what is a boy to the sense of what is a man. Indeed the remove is marked by the gradual development of an inner picture or concept (often a stereotype) of what is a man. Its form can be simplified through a syllogism: a man is so and so, or does this and that, or thinks in such a way; when a boy becomes so and so, or does this and that, or thinks in such a way, then he is a man.

"The Corrupted Warrior Heroes: Amiri Baraka's *The Toilet*" by Robert L. Tener. From *Modern Drama* 17, no. 2 (June 1974), 207-15. Reprinted by permission of *Modern Drama.*

[1]Amiri Baraka (LeRoi Jones), *The Baptism and The Toilet,* New York, 1966. All references hereafter to *The Toilet* are to this edition.

[2]Paul Witherington, "Exorcism and Baptism in LeRoi Jones' *The Toilet,*" *Modern Drama* 15, Sept. 1972, p. 159.

[3]*Ibid.,* p. 162.

[4]*Ibid.,* p. 163.

What is the concept of maleness that the gang members have accepted and from whence is it derived? How does it affect their relationships and ability to cope with their emotions? These are some of the important questions to ask about the play. Their answers bear on the physical actions and language strategically assigned to each character by Amiri Baraka. But the inner sense of masculinity on which the play is anchored cannot be separated from Amiri Baraka's image of what is a man, or more specifically from his vision of the black male intellectual and his relationship to his black brothers in a white society.

The problem in *The Toilet* is part of the larger issue of who are the mythic black heroes and models from whom young black boys derive their images of what is a man. The source of their heroes like their idols determines not only their psychological awareness of self but also helps shape their daily behavior. As the promising young intellectual, the writer of a book of poetry, *Preface to a Twenty Volume Suicide Note* (1961), and the recipient of a Whitney fellowship (1961-1962), Amiri Baraka was most clearly aware that what he had studied in college was primarily the literature and the heroes of white societies. His writings are filled with allusions to Dante, Shakespeare, Baudelaire, and others. But he was also aware that the heroes of a white society, especially middle class, are frequently drawn from other than literary sources.

When he was going through his period of intense introspection, transmuting his own image from the man who had become a literary hero in the white world to the man who conceived of himself as a leader of his people, he was obviously aware of mythic heroes and their impact on the development of the individual psyche. In his poem from that first book of verse, "Look for You Yesterday, Here You Come Today," wherein he refers to the great Spanish poet Federico Garcia Lorca and to his own play *The Toilet,* he explores the idea that his life is like the white man's myths. Humming lines from Lorca's biting poetry on New York and reflecting a mood reminiscent of Strindberg's marital difficulties, he exclaims "It's so diffuse/ being alive. Suddenly one is aware/ that nobody really gives a damn."[5] As his introspective mood shifts to include his specific problems in writing *The Toilet,* he adds "An avalanche of words/ could cheer me up, Words from Great Sages." Clearly con-

---

[5]Amiri Baraka (LeRoi Jones), "Look For You Yesterday, Here You Come Today," *Black Voices,* ed. Abraham Chapman, New York, 1968, p. 485.

cerned at this time with the nature of self and personal meaning and engaged at the same time in the creation of *The Toilet,* he leaps mentally to his new heroes and asks "was James Karolis a great sage" and why did he "let Ora Matthews beat him up." Baraka's thought now drives him to the feeling that all his "piddling joys retreated/ to their own dopey mythic worlds."[6]

His responses to the indecisiveness of life and the lack of identity remind him of the Baudelairean flowers of evil, "cold & lifeless." At the moment Amiri Baraka's identity seems to be a composite of the white man's heroes whom he had digested as a young boy. They are Tom Mix, Dickie Dare; the heroes associated with box tops created by the ad men, Captain Midnight, Superman; and, as he capitalizes in heavy print, even the "LONE RANGER."[7] These are the heroes of brute force, of guns and violence; they are mechanical characters largely unaffected by sex and emotions, superficially aware of puppet-like females called women whom they only rescue but never become involved with. In the world of radio, T.V., and comic books, the mythic hero cannot be damaged; his powers are superhuman. He is fast, agile, keen, alert, strong, and unbeatable. Indeed if he is taken as a boy's hero, he is ultimately without human limitations and emotions. His problems are always external, never internal; his solutions work through the sudden application of force, never through compassion. As the heroes for a boy's inner vision, they are mechanically perfect creatures disguised as human beings who operate in terms of absolutes in a black and white world of evil and good and are void of emotional problems. Thus for Baraka the earth and his life thereon turns out to be an "alien planet."[8] As he points out, if one looks to the mythic past, it is seen today in the lost people around one. They have been dehumanized by a process which causes Baraka to say "'Look for you yesterday/ Here you come today/ Your mouth wide open/ But what you got to say?'"[9] In the end Baraka sees the society around him as though it were a cowboy and Indian movie with the reel running out.

For Amiri Baraka the days of the silver bullets are gone and his black mask is "trampled in the dust." He had discarded the childhood or white man's heroes; he would no longer appear in blackface, but would be a black man. But what could he replace those

[6]*Ibid.,* p. 486.
[7]*Ibid.,* p. 487.
[8]*Ibid.,* p. 486.
[9]*Ibid.,* p. 487.

heroes with? As he says, Tonto is "way off in the hills/ moaning like Bessie Smith."[10]

Does *The Toilet* offer the viewer the new black identity or does it reveal the black psyche dehumanized by its imitation of white models? It would seem in *The Toilet* that Baraka is trying to show how the black youths, except for Foots, act according to their inner vision of what is a man, an image affected by the white mythic heroes, and have, consequently, lost some of their dignity and worth as black boys. They have been corrupted by the white society. In addition it also seems possible that Baraka is intending to reflect the black experience under the eroding influence of the white middle-class society which not only debases the black identity but also destroys the vitality of the white group. The only two positive characters in the play are Ray (the name Karolis uses for Foots, the gang leader) and Karolis. Both have some dignity as human beings and are involved emotionally with each other. Ray resists fighting Karolis; he returns after the gang members have left to share himself with Karolis. On the other hand Karolis is willing to fight Foots but loves Ray, as though he senses the split identity of the young gang leader. Of importance also is Baraka's strategic conception of Karolis, the only white in the play, as a homosexual. The characterization suggests perhaps the demoralization and confusion of standards for behavior within the white system.

The operating world of the gang is the urine stinking toilet in a high school with white and black students. It is a male world. Here, the image of a man, derived partly from heroes in the outer world, stigmatized by the stench of man's excremental functions and his sexual confusions, is incompletely expressed by the boys. That image is an epic one minus its heroism. It captures the heroic warrior from a classic past with its emphasis on physicality, but it is transmuted by the alchemy of the white dream into the picture of a fighter or athlete. It is reflected in the gang's emphasis on physical contact, in their tough talk, their games, their actions, their assumptions, and especially in their limitations.

The male relationships in their world are given in terms of physical contact. It is boy strength versus boy strength as muscle tests muscle. Love holds the door against Ora who thumps the door but does not get angry (p. 38); Holmes and Love spar a few minutes with each other (p. 38), then Hines joins in the action (p. 39). In another

[10]*Ibid.,* p. 488.

instance Holmes and Ora square off, after Ora has already punched Holmes, *"both laughing and faking professional demeanor"* (p. 41). Love and Hines play an imaginary game of basketball. In all of these examples the physical involvement shifts its emotional strength, always threatening to move from fun to violence. Ora nudges Karolis with his foot (p. 50), or he pushes Karolis into Foots. In turn Foots pushes Karolis away (p. 58). Except in the relationship with Karolis, the rules of the physical contact game do not allow the contact to turn into serious fighting. Their function apparently is to allow the gang members to express in an acceptable but restricted manner their contradictory impulses to be both dominant and dominated, to be both independent as well as bound by some cohesive force. Ora clearly threatens the group physically, but he cannot subdue George and he accepts Foots as the leader.

The emphasis on physical contact, like that expressed in the training of some warrior or athlete, is reinforced in their male world by their excessively tough language. But it is a young male world activated by the image of man as a fighter-hero who battles the forces of evil mechanically (not all know why Karolis must be forced to fight) and who ignores the effects of his sexual changes. But such a warrior-athlete, if he is successful, is rewarded with sexual adulation, his female counterpart being reduced to serving him. The inhabitants of this male arena talk about the two characteristics of a man related to that image: fighting (what all their physical contact is directed towards as though they were going through a training process) and sex (what their changing glandular systems are preparing them for).

Their talk about fighting is always done in the context of their still being boys. The proposed fights are imagined, not real. Those in between are affairs of honor, involving an imagined or felt ideal, and following a definite ritual, borrowed possibly from white western movies or Batman comics. When Foots asks Knowles to stop drumming on the walls, Knowles threatens to drum on Foots' head (p. 53). Ora threatens to "stomp mudholes" (p. 48) in Farrell's head if he doesn't shut up.

The central incident, however, is a matter of honor. The gang has dragged Karolis to the toilet room where he is supposed to fight their leader Foots. According to Hines the gang does not intend to beat him up (p. 49). But by the time that they get him to his destiny, he has been considerably mauled. Foots pays homage to Ora who has hit Karolis by saying "You a rough ass cat, Shot. He sure don't look like he's in any way to fight anybody" (p. 52). But Foots is supposed to fight Karolis because the white boy had written him a letter calling him beautiful and saying "that he wanted to blow him" (p. 56). The talk among them is of killing as though the fighting were to be for real on some battlefield. But it is not. When Karolis pulls himself up unsteadily and says that he wants to fight Foots, Knowles exclaims "You mean that sonofabitch wasn' dead?" (p. 57). Or when Foots comes in and first sees Karolis on the floor, he asks "Damn! What'd you guys do, kill the cat?" (p. 52). Even Karolis says "I want to kill you" (p. 58) to Foots. All such comments refer not to the actual destruction of a human being but more than likely to an emphasis on fighting, hitting, or beating up, to some process not likely to end in death but which releases their internal tensions. Their language thus continually suggests that they are in a probationary period when all their actions are training sessions for the real thing. In the world of the play, however, they can never have the real thing.

But it is their language about sex and their sexual terms that most readily reveals their participation in a male world where their concept of maleness is affected by the masculine images provided by a white society. In the first place the emphasis is on their talking about sex; nowhere in the play do they actually engage in sexual activities. While they are not necessarily virgins or neophytes, they are certainly in that transition period where they lose their sexual innocence. But their uncertain sense of masculinity and of heroism has not taught them how to cope with their ambivalent sexual feelings and responses or how to express them. Under their internal pressures they play the game of the dozens in which they insult each others' mothers. As Ora says, he would "rub up against" Love's mother, and Love replies "Ora, you mad cause you don't have a momma of your own to rub up against" (p. 51).[11] But it is a game. They do not rub up against real women, not yet. They are not free enough of their maternal-female image to develop a separate sexual-female concept. In their rhetorical playing, the force is on talk and male dominance, as in the love of tall talk on the American frontier. Their language does not reflect the subtleties of the sexual feelings between men and women and the ways in which those feelings permeate all other relationships. Their vocabulary reveals their almost new yet crude concern for their penises, a self-interest which bothers them somewhat, perhaps even embarrasses them. They

[11]See: Roger D. Abrahams, "Playing the Dozens," *Journal of American Folklore* 75, 1962, pp. 209-10.

relish the names for their sexual masculinity which has suddenly become important to them. Perhaps that is why they want Foots to fight a duel with Karolis. As Perry says, Karolis wanted to "blow him" (p. 56) and Ora calls the white boy a "dick licker" (p. 57).

Their sexual reactions have yet to be directly transferred to women. They do not discuss going with girls, or bedding with them, or marrying them. They are still boys and apparently embarrassed or confused by their bodies and sexual stirrings. They conceive of sex in the terms of comic books, of sexual relationships in the metaphors of the white mythic heroes. They relate sex to their male egos and their need to dominate. Almost in retaliation for their changing selves, they stress their obvious maleness to each other in ritualized language which is often euphemized. They refer to a penis as a "joint" (p. 37). In the toilet or commode, like little boys they want to play with their urine. Even Ora, the most obviously physical boy, tends to giggle and grin as he pees over the seat of a commode; he flushes all the urinals in a row when he leaves (p. 37). Hines tells Holmes that Love is in the toilet "pulling his whatchamacallit" (p. 38). And when Holmes asks him why he doesn't get Gloria to do that, Love says "She-et. [*Grinning.*] Huh. I sure don't need your ol' lady to be pullin' on my joint. [*Laughs....*] " (p. 38). They even call each other "cocksucker" (p. 41), a term which when it applies to them is less pejorative, perhaps even complimentary, than the term "dick licker" which they apply to Karolis.

When Love says that Karolis never bothered him, Ora turns his reply into the dozens by saying that Karolis always tells everybody that "he bangs the hell out of Caroline, every chance he gets" (p. 43). Holmes answers by asking if that's the name of Love's mother. Even Ora calls his own penis a "nice fat sausage" for Karolis (p. 50). Such excessive use of euphemisms suggests their sense of embarrassed delight and highly limited response to their sexual organs. For them it is insulting to be compared with a girl. Knowles says to Ora, after Karolis had struggled to his feet, "Shit, Big Shot, you must hit like a girl" (p. 57).

Their range of emotional responses to each other is apparently limited by their inner sense of manhood. They tend to eschew girls; they emphasize physical touch; they pretend to play basketball. In general they tend to transfer their sexual impulses into such games as the dozens, bluff, or the affair of honor. Their reaction to their emotions and to the problems of personal involvement with each other suggests the same mechanical quality that strikes one in the

behavior of the Lone Ranger, Superman, or any of the other mythical heroes of white society.

The actions of the gang members, furthermore, strengthen their
unconscious imitation of such models. The boys stress agility,
strength, a super-masculinity. They feel insulted by the thought of
a white boy calling one of them beautiful and wanting the pleasure
of intimacy. Perhaps their unconscious image of a super, but false,
masculinity can best be seen in their relationship with their leader
Foots.

It is Foots whom Karolis says that he wants to kill, not Ray. The
implication is that Karolis sees Foots as two different persons: Ray,
a human being, beautiful, whom he wishes to be involved with; and
Foots, a stereotyped leader of a gang of corrupt heroes. Like Foots,
Karolis has some dimension to his development in the play. But the
other persons are nearly caricatures in Baraka's strategy. They are
hardly the models for black dignity. Their stereotyping is most
obvious. Foots, the leader, is short and intelligent. On the other
hand Ora is short and ugly. Most of the others are tall, like Hines
who is "big" and "husky" (p. 35). Foots does not rule the gang through
physical strength. He cannot even break Karolis' choke hold. Instead he rules by cleverness, by wit, or by some charisma he holds
for the other boys. The authorities in the high school, whom he
mocks, find him smart, a credit to his race. In explaining why he is
late for the duel, Foots says that he was detained by Van Ness, symbol of the high school authorities, who wanted him to help keep all
the unsavory boys in line. Foots directly implies in his statement
that his gang are some of the "unsavory…elements" (p. 51). Neither
the gang members nor the high school authorities, apparently, accept Foots as a person. Rather both groups see him as an agent whom
they can exploit for some particular quality he has, perhaps his
cleverness or sure intelligence. Whatever it is, their relationship
with him is mechanical and stereotyped.

What does Foots receive from them? From the high school authorities, he probably gets a good laugh; what he receives from his gang
cannot be so easily answered. In terms of his reaction to Karolis,
what Foots desires is some acceptance of himself as a young man, a
recognition of his feelings. Karolis has appealed to him in a way
that his gang friends cannot. The white boy sees beauty and love in
him. Instead of trying to use Ray, Karolis is willing to risk his person for the black boy's love. As a human being needing and responding to love, Foots has to return, therefore, to the beaten boy. In the

solitude of the room, the loneliness and stench intensifying his compassion, as Ray he holds Karolis' head in his arms. At that moment with another human being, Ray expresses a mature tenderness and love which his mythic destiny had denied him with his gang. The relationship between the two has to be private to be meaningful, to take place in a toilet in order for it to rise above the stereotyped and artificial responses of the other boys.

In its dramatic strategies *The Toilet* implies Amiri Baraka's awareness of how a white society has affected the lives of black boys. At a critical time in their passage from boyhood to manhood, their conceptions of manly behavior, conditioned as they are by the mythic heroes of a white culture, have made them incapable of responding fully as complete human beings. They have no expression for beauty, for compassion, for selfless love. No black music penetrates their world; no blues affects their body rhythms. To all appearances the gang members are alienated from the world at large. Their center of operations is a crude and foully smelling toilet room where they stand revealed as rough caricatures of mythical heroes, like puppets created in some lesser image of an imperfect dream.

They leave the room carrying their wounded, Foots, after what has been a mock battle of honor. The stage is left for those who have some acceptance of their new sexual feelings; the future belongs to Foots. He leaves the gang for love and tenderness. He is needed for himself, not for his leadership qualities or his ability to be a credit to his race. He has become a man, or at least he alone has the possibility of becoming a man. In his past are the unhuman mythical heroes of his gang. Perhaps his future is to be a human being, black, a different kind of model for his gang.

Great Goodness of Life: Baraka's Black Bourgeoisie Blues

by Owen E. Brady

Imamu Amiri Baraka's play, *Great Goodness of Life: A Coon Show,* translates the revolutionary potential of E. Franklin Frazier's *Black Bourgeoisie*[1] into art through techniques drawn from the blues[2] and through an invocation of the ritual aspects of minstrelsy. Baraka's acute awareness of the Black cultural tradition, especially of the blues and minstrelsy, helps him humanize the bleak chronicle of Black middle class life described by Frazier in *Black Bourgeoisie.* In depicting the inner life of Court Royal, a representative protagonist, the play becomes, as Ellison in *Shadow and Act* says of the blues, "an autobiographical chronicle of personal catastrophe expressed lyrically"[3] that can be used as a critique of life. The achievement of the play is that it goes beyond a dogmatic critique of middle class life. In drawing Court Royal, twisted and comic as he is, Baraka shows us the human spirit in motion, surviving as it does anywhere, through self-accommodation. He achieves this depth of character through pathos and bitter, comic irony which squeeze from the protagonist's experience what Ellison calls "a near-tragic, near-comic lyricism" (90) characteristic of the blues.

The play's subtitle, *A Coon Show,* recalls the minstrel tradition and the classic blues which Baraka contends arose from minstrelsy. The play is, as Baraka says of minstrelsy, a parody "of certain as-

[1] E. Franklin Frazier, *Black Bourgeoisie: The Rise of a New Middle Class in the United States* (New York, 1962). All references are drawn from this edition; page numbers are cited parenthetically in the text.

[2] Baraka's criticism of the Black middle class in the blues idiom has an antecedent in Leadbelly's "Bourgeois Blues" recorded in 1939. See Paul Oliver, *The Meaning of the Blues* (New York, 1960), pp. 209-210; 358.

[3] Ralph Ellison, *Shadow and Act* (New York, 1966), p. 90. All references are drawn from this edition; page numbers are cited parenthetically in the text.

pects of Negro life in America."⁴ The main title, *Great Goodness of Life*, points out the aspect satirized: Black middle class life which is, according to Frazier, a search for status and acceptance by the white mainstream through adherence to the values of the white middle class without regard for the harsh psychological and social consequences of such adherence (28). In the play, Court loses his identity in a house of distorting mirrors because he sees himself from the perspective of an off-stage Voice representing the white mainstream, which traditionally projects debased stereotypes of Black life. Court makes his life's goal, as Frazier says the Black bourgeoisie has made its, the unconditional acceptance of "the values of the white bourgeoisie world: its morals and its canons of respectability, its standards of beauty and consumption" (28). The play's ironic core is the tension between Court's longing to taste the great goodness of white middle class life and his fate to remain a comically inept imitation of a white man in the eyes of the group to which he seeks admission.

As the play opens, the audience sees a log cabin, a reminder of the Black man's rural, Southern past, and an allusion to Uncle Tom's cabin, the home of the docile slave. The protagonist's name, the play's first word, recalls the first freedmen—specifically those of Port Royal, South Carolina⁵—a group whose disillusioning experience of citizenship Frazier views as the prototypical Black middle class experience (21-22).

The action opens as an eery electronic Voice calls Court to account for his life and begins the conditioning program which will eventually dictate the terms of Court's existence. Goading Court to center stage, the Voice accuses him of "shielding a wanted criminal. A murderer."⁶ There is irony and comedy in the accusation and Court's response. The Voice recognizes the Black man's right to murderous hostility because of historical experience, while Court denies these feelings, comically asserting his innocence and re-

---

⁴LeRoi Jones, *Blues People: The Negro Experience in White America and the Music that Developed from It* (New York, 1963), p. 85. *Blues People*, published three years before *Great Goodness of Life* was written, cites *Black Bourgeoisie* and borrows heavily from it.

⁵See Willie Lee Rose, *Rehearsal for Reconstruction: The Port Royal Experiment* (Indianapolis, 1964). Rose chronicles the changing, but always ambiguous, status of Black Americans in their movement from slavery to freedmen to citizenship.

⁶LeRoi Jones, *Great Goodness of Life* in *Four Black Revolutionary Plays* (Indianapolis, 1969), p. 46. All references are drawn from this edition; page numbers are cited parenthetically in the text.

spectability by referring repeatedly to his quintessentially Black middle class civil service job: "I work in the Post Office. . . . I work in the Post Office and have done nothing wrong" (46). Court's autonomy is stripped away as he enters a not quilty plea, an action which allows the Voice domination over his identity. Court's proud but ludicrously pathetic assertion of status implicit in his rejection of a court-supplied attorney also diminishes his stature: "I don't need a legal aid man. I have money. I have an attorney. I work in the Post Office" (48).

The entrance of John Breck, Court's lawyer, begins an expressionistic scene exposing justice as an illusion and revealing the relationship between the Black professional class and the dominant mainstream. Baraka's depiction of this relationship borrows from Frazier's delineation of it as an historical pattern derived from the house-slave/white-master relationship (17.18). Breck's character is depicted in visual terms worthy of the concrete, hyperbolic imagery of the blues: Breck is "a smiling house slave in a wrinkled dirty tuxedo. . . a wire attached to his back leading offstage. A huge key in the side of his head. . .motors 'animating' his body groaning like tremendous weights. He grins and slobbers" (48).

Breck ostensibly comes to help Court resolve his problem, but, as in the blues, the solution to a problem is phrased in ironic terms. Breck, a sycophant obviously wired to a mainstream power source, advises Court "to plead guilty" despite his innocence so that he can avoid severe punishment (49). Breck's solution echoes a traditional survival technique for the slave and the Black bourgeoisie: play a demeaning role; you'll survive and perhaps even be rewarded. Court, too, might be allowed the threadbare status of the Black bourgeoisie represented by Breck's wrinkled dirty tuxedo. Implicit in this tactic, however, is a rejection of the positive aspects of one's Black identity and an acceptance of Blackness as a social liability. Rejecting Blackness on those terms will fix Court through legal ritual in a state of self-alienation. He will begin to conform to the psychological displacement pattern noted by Frazier: his hostility at the injustice will turn inward against himself and outward against other Black people, especially the lower class, with whom he is always associated because of his Negro characteristics (186).

As Court considers Breck's temptation to suffer guilt and alienation in exchange for middle class status, a second off-stage voice, "strong, young, begins to shout in the darkness at Court" (50). It militates against Breck's advice and poses another ironically structured solution. Like Breck, the second voice, perhaps the repressed murderous self, encourages Court to plead guilty: its motive, however, is quite different from Breck's. This voice demands that Court accept the guilt of Blackness (50), which would bind him to all Black people and enable him to recognize himself as one historically fated to be a victim. If Court accepts this voice's viewpoint, then fate can be changed through revolutionary action based on group solidarity. But Court's attraction to middle class status keeps him color blind to Blackness as a force for change. Stage gesture illuminates Court's abortive attempt to fathom the second voice's revolutionary logic; he "Peers into the darkness" trying to see "who's that talking to me" (51).

Breck's pathetic, crawling exit intensifies Court's anxiety. Court is alone, isolated in a pool of harsh white light. Not having accepted guilt, Court feels the threat of force become as palpable as weather on stage. Sirens wailing, lights pulsating, machine guns chattering and cell doors clanging ensnare Court in a maelstrom of theatrical effects representing the history of violence that has conditioned Black people. Court is reduced to a network of raw nerves: "His eyes grow until he is almost going to faint" (52).

Stage gesture reveals Court's inner torment and his response to the cultural conditioning. As the violence subsides, we see Court "frozen, half-bent arms held away from his body, balancing...in his terror" (51-52) and imploring the Voice not to kill him because "I'm not trying to escape" (52). Frozen in place, Court becomes a visual metaphor for the Black middle class in America; he maintains a place or status by means of a precarious, self-distorting balance between life and death, pathos and comedy, manhood and some imposed imitation of manhood. The legal subterfuge in the scenes with Breck and the threats of violence just experienced leave Court feeling guilty and unable to stand upright in the dignified posture of manhood.

Court's balancing act, his tragi-comic stance in the world, reflects his fear and anxiety; but to the Voice representing the mainstream, the act seems absurdly comic, confirming Court as a subhuman species. Almost choking with capillary-popping shriek-laughter, the Voice articulates traditional mainstream views of the Black man as beast of burden, insensible thing and unassimilated waste product of the American body politic: "You donkey. ... You piece of wood. You shiny shuffling piece of black vomit" (52).

Court's pathetic "corny tinny stupid" pleas to find out "Where I am" (52) emphasize his dependence on the mainstream for a place in America and precipitate an excursion into racial memory. His generalized fears become specifically associated with slave experience. Expressionistic stage effects externalize Court's rattled state of mind, reminding him that his place is a kind of slavery:

> A chain, slightly, more, now heavier, dragged bent, wiggled slowly, light now heavily in the darkness, from another direction. Chains. They're dragged, like things are pulling them across the earth. The chains. And now low chanting voices, moaning, with incredible pain and despair, the voices press just softly behind the chains, for a few seconds, so very very briefly then gone. And silence (53).

The vision evoked by the rhythmic sounds of slave agony and the profound, protracted silence which follows cause Court to swoon and moan. But the silence also prepares the audience for the tragicomic laughter of the blues which the next snippet of dialogue provokes.

Court breaks the silence imploring, "Just tell me where I am." The Voice replies in the "cool and businesslike" tone of the supreme ironist: "HEAVEN" (53). In his desire to resolve his guilt and be redeemed into the middle class, Court seems to believe the Voice. He claps his hands together in a gesture of stereotypical gratitude and joy, releasing himself from the tensions of his balancing act. But the blues roll in to inform the moment: A white man's heaven is a black man's hell. Blues wisdom and slave memories, which bind all Black people, must be repressed if Court is to escape into the middle class. He rejects the communal experience, this blues consciousness, as Frazier notes the Black bourgeoisie does (98), for an illusory middle class status. But the act of repression befuddles Court; he mumbles, "these things are so confusing" (53).

As the lights dim, Court assumes the "redeeming" minstrel mask. Breaking into a clownish song and dance for the Voice's amusement, Court seems to accept a debased, comic blackface role. But minstrel tradition and its ritual functions inform the action.[7] On the one hand, Court's use of the minstrel mask, developed by white actors, seems to signal an abandonment of a dignified Black identity and

[7]Clinton F. Oliver and Stephen Sills, "Introduction," *Contemporary Black Drama from A Raisin in the Sun to No Place to Be Somebody* (New York, 1971), p. 5. See also, *Blues People*, pp. 83-86.

an acceptance of a distorted, white-derived image—the "jiggedy bobbity fool" (53). To the white audience, uninitiated in the ambiguities of the blues and minstrelsy, Court's scat singing seems to be the jibberish of either a true subhuman or of a man who chooses to be a fool, a performance motivated by what Ellison, discussing minstrelsy's ritual function, terms "the profit motive" (65). In the latter case, any white guilt for the Black man's debasement is relieved ritually because Court is exercising the American values of free choice and the right to make a profit: exploitation of a willing victim is not exploitation. On the other hand, to a Black audience, the self-maiming of a Black man blackening his face to perform a white-derived role can signify, a hidden revolution. In the face-blackening ritual, the Black actor makes clear that he is consciously putting on a mask and dissociating himself in the audience's mind from, as Ellison puts it, "a symbol of everything [Black people] rejected in the white man's thinking about race, in themselves and in their own group" (65). Court's use of the mask can be deceitful, a way of signifying to those baptized in the blues that his acceptance of the stereotype in grotesquely comic terms is a mode of guerilla warfare—what Ellison calls "a jiujitsu of the spirit, a denial and rejection through agreement" (70). Ears attuned to the covert rebellion in Court's song listen and begin to know what the "devil-meant" in offering Black people middle class status: self-distortion. The audience can be, if it hears Court truly, "*Dig*gedy dobbidy cool" (my italics) and begin thinking about self-reference and the real meaning of "what was heaven, heaven, heaven" (53-54).

Using the ambiguity of the minstrel mask and ritual to inform his characterization of Court, Baraka humanizes and deepens the stereotype created by Frazier in *Black Bourgeoisie*. He pays grudging homage to the Black middle class in its quiet rebellions and understands the desire to be respected and to live in peaceful prosperity. Moreover, he understands the historical necessities—institutionalized injustice and violence—that forced people to assume the minstrel mask.

In the next sequence of three incidents, however, Baraka rejects any accommodation made by the Black middle class as an ultimate substitution of the minstrel mask for reality, an action hostile to Black communal interests.

First, "a greasy-head nigger lady" (54) is pushed in front of Court by two hooded figures. Court's response typifies the Black bourgeoisie's reaction to the Black lower class. Court is "frightened...

sickened...embarrassed" and rejects this image of Blackness that "drinks and stinks and brings down our whole race" (54). This rejection allows the Voice to perpetuate the woman's shameful condition: "Grind her into poison jelly. Smear it on her daughter's head" (54). The second incident typifies the Black bourgeoisie's fear of being associated with Black militant movements. This time, the hooded figures bear in the body of an assassinated Black "Prince" (55) representing Malcolm X. Sensing the Voice's fear of militant ideas, Court rejects them and tries to gain the Voice's acceptance by mustering the symbols of middle class life to his defense: "I have nothing to do with any of this. ... I have a car. A home. A club. ... I work in the Post Office,...and then home, and television, dinner, then bowling" (56). Again, the possibility of social change is aborted.

In the climactic third incident, Court is brought to a recognition of his own Blackness and of his part in creating Black victims. The Voice asks, "Do you know this man?" (56) as sounds "like secret screaming" (57) underscore slide projections of "Malcolm. Patrice [Lumumba]. Rev. King. Garvey. Dead nigger kids killed by police. Medgar Evers" (56) which flash behind and wash over Court. Asserting his individuality and, thus, rejecting a communal identity, Court claims that the images represent many people and that he does not understand the meaning of the phantasmagoria. As the pictures flood over Court, and the sounds build to "point thrusts" (57), the Voice, seeing all Blacks as one, badgers him into identifying with "the murderer" in the images. As Court wheels around to face the images of victims with whom he sympathizes but rejects because the Voice calls them murderers, the agony of his accommodation to a white viewpoint erupts:

> No, I've tried...please I never wanted anything but peace...please, I tried to be a man. I did. I lost my...heart...please it was so deep, I wanted to do the right thing. I wanted...everything to be...all right. Oh, please...please (58).

Any revolutionary consciousness based on a communal identity is short-circuited for Court by his self-protective instincts and materialism. Though frightened by his guilt, Court soon bows his head and resigns himself to the mainstream's summary judgment in hopes of preserving his middle class status. In a stroke of mercy made possible by its own cruelty, the Voice spares Court's life because he has accepted the guilt of his Blackness and, thus, the beauty of his sharply delimited place in America:

> We have decided to spare you. We admire your spirit. It is a compliment to know you can see the clearness of your fate, and the rightness of it. That you love the beauty of the way of life you've chosen here in the anonymous world. ... You are absolved of your crime, at this moment, because of your infinite understanding of the compassionate God Of The Cross. Whose head was cut off for you, to absolve you of your weakness. The murderer is dead. The murderer is dead (59).

Court's adherence to middle class values in the face of his own outrage has shriven him. His act of repression has, indeed, killed the murderer that lurks in the heart of the oppressed. Court's acceptance of a decapitated savior alludes to his practice of a headless or unreasonable Christianity which preaches patience rather than rational rebellion. Court trades a search for life's mysteries for the Black middle class view, which Frazier says, sees religion as an instrument for the advancement of social status (111-112). Court's purchase of the unrealistic philosophy of assimilation draws "Applause from the darkness" (59); the mainstream cheers the absolution of its own guilt.

The play's ritualistic conclusion proves the minstrel mask no longer viable: assuming the mask relieves only the mainstream's guilt. Ironically, the Voice promises Court release from all guilt if he will sacrifice the "last fleeting astral projection" (61) of the murderer. Sacrificing the murderer will deprive Blackness eternally of its potential for revolutionary change. Having a Black middle class man perform the ceremony confirms the Voice's value, laissez-faire individualism, and frees the mainstream of guilt and fear.

Two hooded figures lead in the ritual victim, a young Black man wearing an ankh who symbolizes Black life and a potentially positive self-identity. The ritual instrument, a gun made of diamonds and gold and loaded with a silver bullet (60), represents middle class status symbols which Frazier notes "are of a material nature implying wealth and conspicuous consumption" (181). Using the status and power derived from material consumption to kill a symbol of Black life is the ultimate act of self-hate—a symbolic suicide and genocide that will wash Court "white as snow" (62).

When Court balks at shooting the young man, the Voice, now itself under the compulsion of the American guilt-relieving ritual, repeatedly assures him that the victim is only a "shadow" (61). Under the pressure to maintain the *status quo* and his own limited status, Court kneels, praying as the Voice instructs him, to become "as the centuries pass" a member of "the covenant of guiltless silence" (62). Finally, Court shoots the young man. The rite performed, the Voice is absolved. The victim's dying word, "Papa," however, reveals his relationship with Court and deprives Court of an unambiguous salvation.

Even in the didactic ending, which scrupulously adheres to a structure provided by Frazier, Baraka turns to the idiom of the blues for artistic effect. A final comic twist follows the pathos of the sacrifice scene and, ironically, intensifies it. Suddenly, the twilight world of Court's inner life dissipates as the stage lights come up full. Reality replaces ritual. Court, happily reiterating the ironic words of his salvation, "My soul is as white as snow," discards the gold and diamond gun (63). Thus he accepts status without substance. His joy at being accepted by the Voice causes him to forget about the social and economic power attributed to status.

As Court wanders around the stage muttering about being free and white as snow, a brighter mood strikes him; his life assumes new focus and meaning. He calls out, full of purpose: "Hey, Louise, have you seen my bowling bag? I'm going down to the alley for a minute" (63). The play ends with Court frozen, hand raised, beckoning for his bowling bag. His baptism into the Black middle class over, Court stands motionless in his bleak, peculiar and very separate place.

The lighthearted bowler, the last image of the play, operates like the last line of a blues stanza; it resolves the questions raised in the story, which precedes it, and it provides a philosophic comment on the situation.[8] It squeezes a lingering near-tragic, near-comic lyricism from the chronicle of the Black bourgeoisie. It is comic because bowling can, momentarily, relieve Court's tremendous guilt. But it is bitterly comic, almost tragic, because Court trades personal and communal freedom from oppression for ephemeral joys. He cultivates what Frazier calls "an attitude of play" (169) as a philosophic consolation for acceptance of his marginal existence. In so doing, his life, in Frazier's words about the Black bourgeoisie, loses "both content and significance" (195). In the words of the old

[8]Eileen Southern, *The Music of Black Americans: A History* (New York, 1971), p. 334.

blues, however, Baraka has brought us to a recognition that in Court's case, "When you think I'm laughin', I'm just laughin' to keep from cryin'."

The play's revolutionary function is to chastise the Black middle class, in Frazier's words, for struggling "to gain acceptance by whites" rather than being "a responsible elite in the Negro community" (193). But by using the blues and minstrelsy to inform the dramatic action, Baraka harmonizes art and politics through artistic form. Like the blues man or the Western moral artist, Baraka goes beyond propaganda to teach his lesson and to reveal the humanity of the man behind the minstrel mask.

Myth, Magic, and Manhood in LeRoi Jones' *Madheart*

by Charles D. Peavy

"For the black man in this country, it is not so much a matter of acquiring manhood as it is a struggle to feel it his own. Whereas the white man regards his manhood as an ordained right, the black man is engaged in a never-ending battle for its possession. For the black man, attaining any portion of manhood is an active process. He must penetrate barriers and overcome opposition in order to assume a masculine posture. For the inner psychological obstacles to manhood are never so formidable as the impediments woven into American Society."[1] This statement, made by the black psychiatrists, Grier and Cobbs, explains the motivation for certain recurrent themes in current black revolutionary drama, and certainly the emphasis on *maleism* in many of the plays of LeRoi Jones. Some of the indications of the black man's psychological predicament are reflected in the hostility he feels toward black women as inhibiting instruments of an oppressive social system and the attraction he feels toward the white female as a desirable (but forbidden) sex object. For the more militant black man, the attitude toward the white woman often becomes an ambivalent blend of attraction-repulsion. This dilemma forms the opening chapter of Eldridge Cleaver's *Soul on Ice*, "On Becoming."[2] It is also reflected in LeRoi Jones' play *The Slave,*[3] and has apparently been a problem in his own personal life. Indeed, even such an ardent Black Nationalist as Askia Muhammad (Roland Snellings) has criticized some of Jones'

"Myth, Magic, and Manhood in LeRoi Jones' *Madheart*" by Charles D. Peavy. From *Studies in Black Literature* 1, no. 2 (Summer 1970), 12-20. Copyright © 1970 by Raman K. Singh. Reprinted by permission.

[1]William H. Grier and Price M. Cobbs, *Black Rage* (New York: Basic Books, 1968), p. 59.

[2]New York: McGraw-Hill, 1968, pp. 3-18. See particularly the poem, "To A White Girl," pp. 13-14.

[3]New York: William Morrow, 1964.

[4]See *Black Dialogue, III* (Winter, 1967-68), pp. 3-5, 16.

dramas as projections of his own "hang-ups concerning whites"[4] and his love-hate affairs with them.

There is a constant assertion of black masculine identity in many of the plays of Jones—usually at the expense of the white male. Jones often portrays the white man, and the pro-white black man, as effeminate or homosexual. (See, for example, the white and Negro police in *Police*,[5] the white father in *Home on the Range,* the white professor in *The Slave,* Karolis and Foots in *The Toilet.*) In Jones' dramas, however, the chief impediment to the black male's realization of his identity is the white woman.

Jones' first dramatic portrayal of the confrontation between white woman and black man occurs in *Dutchman.* The action of *Dutchman* should be viewed as symbolic and ritualistic, rather than only realistic. Indeed, the name of the female temptress (it is Lula rather than the more traditional Lulu) is an allusion both to lullaby and, even more significantly, to Lilith.[6] A lullaby is a soothing song, often used to induce sleep. When Lula sits next to Clay she pushes her legs out "as if she is very weary," and she converses with him in a sharp city coarseness "which is still a kind of gentle, sidewalk throb" (see stage directions, p. 9). The seductive, soothing, and somnolent quality of her voice persists through the apple-eating— temptation scene, where she continues "speaking in a loose sing-song" (p. 11), or "humming snatches of rhythm and blues songs" (p. 12). The various meanings of the word *lull* are also suggested by Lula's name: to soothe with sounds or caresses; to induce to sleep or to pleasing quiescence, to quiet (suspicion) by deception, to delude into a sense of security. Lula also embodies certain characteristics of Lilith, the demon woman of the Talmudic tradition (cf. Babylonian or Assyrian demons, Lilit, Lulu). Lilith is usually described as a vampire and a seductress (note all the talk about Clay's manhood during Lula's seductive conversation, pp. 25-26). If Lula is not specifically the traditional blood-sucking vampire, she is a *vampire* or *vamp* in the early 20th century sense, i.e., a *femme fatale,* or beautiful but heartless woman that lures men to their destruction.

---

[5]In *Police* the white police are portrayed as simpering homosexuals who react orgasmically as a black policeman commits suicide with a "penis-pistol." *Police* is included in the collection of black drama printed in a special issue of *The Drama Review, XII* (Summer, 1968), pp. 112-15.

[6]Indeed, there is some evidence that both words are connected. A commentator on Skinner's *Etymologicon Linguae Anglicanae,* quoted in the *Encyclopedia Metropolitania,* says that the English word lullaby is derived from *Lilla, abi!* (Begone, Lilith!).

In a later play by Jones, *Madheart*,[7] the character of Lula is transposed entirely into the realm of mythology. In Arabic mythology Lilith married the Devil and became the mother of evil spirits. In *Madheart*, the apple-eating temptress of *Dutchman* is reincarnated as Devil Lady, while the slain Clay is resurrected as the personification of the black man in a continuance of the ritual confrontation of the black man and the white witch. The Devil Lady, the latest avatar of the Lilith type, appears in an elaborately carved white Devil mask. BLACK MAN is more hip than the uptight Clay of the earlier play; he recognizes immediately that the white goodess is not divine at all, but a devil ("God is not the devil"). "Why aren't you dead?" he asks her, and DEVIL LADY admits "I am dead and can never die,"[8] thus setting up the necessity for the particular ritual of her killing by BLACK MAN, who realizes that she will have him in her power until he destroys her ("You will die only when I kill you"). The DEVIL LADY, in the guise of Great White Goddess, would lead BLACK MAN to his destruction by placing him under the same spell that has his MOTHER and SISTER in thrall. Again, as in *Dutchman,* the spell is woven upon the man through seduction; the DEVIL LADY rolls on her back and lifts her skirt provocatively to reveal a cardboard image of Christ pasted over her genitals. BLACK MAN attempts to counter her evil *white* magic with his own *black* magic.[9] The lights come up to reveal the DEVIL LADY

[7]*Madheart* is printed in LeRoi Jones, *Four Revolutionary Plays* (New York: Bobbs-Merrill, 1969), and in LeRoi Jones, *Black Rage* (New York: Morrow, 1968). All page references to *Madheart* in this study are from the Bobbs-Merrill text.

[8]*Madheart*, p. 70. DEVIL LADY is referring to her vampire nature. Vampires are the "living dead" who can only be killed by a stake driven through the heart.

[9]Jones has often made ironic use of the traditional concept of white magic versus black magic. For instance, in a poem included in his essay, "State/meant" (*Home: Social Essays,* New York, 1966, p. 252) he writes:

> We are unfair, and unfair
> We are black magicians, black art
> s we make in black labs of the heart.
>
> The fair are
> fair, and death
> Ly white.
>
> The day will not save them
> and we own
> The night.

See also his poems "Black Art" and "Black Dada Nihilismus." Jones' Spirit House, located in Newark, New Jersey, may be considered the center of the Black Arts movement in America (see BLACK MAN's remark about the Black Arts, *Madheart,* p. 77).

sprawled mid-stage with many arrows impaling her abdomen and vagina. She forms a life size (and living) voodoo doll, and BLACK MAN is seen gesturing over her with his hands and "conjuring" (see stage directions, p. 71). "You will always and forever be dead, and be dead, and always you will be the spirit of deadness. ..." he chants. But the DEVIL LADY has already admitted she is dead and yet undying, in short, she is a vampire, a parasite that sustains itself by sucking the life blood of its victims (an allegory of the white culture's relationship to the blacks). His voodoo conjurations failing, BLACK MAN drives a wooden stake through the heart of DEVIL LADY (the traditional method of killing vampires).

His desire for the temptress is not completely banished, however. The ritual killing of seductive DEVIL LADY may also have Freudian implications—the arrows impaling her abdomen and vagina are obviously phallic in their symbolism, as is the wooden stake he drives through her heart. In a frenzy BLACK MAN withdraws the stake and prepares to penetrate her body again, muttering "Beautiful, Beautiful!" He is so preoccupied with the ritual "murder" of the desirable devil that he fails to notice the entrance of the three BLACK WOMEN. These three figures, identified only as MOTHER, SISTER and BLACK WOMAN, represent three aspects of black womanhood. MOTHER and SISTER attempt to stop BLACK MAN from killing DEVIL LADY, but BLACK WOMAN suggests "Perhaps we are intruding." The MOTHER is drunk, and wears a red wig, the SISTER is clad in mod clothes and wears a blonde wig, and the BLACK WOMAN wears her hair in a soft "natural" style. To the first two women the white DEVIL LADY represents all that is beautiful, pure and good. The "fairness" of her hair and skin, the sanctity of her sex, are part of the iconography of the white devil worship to which these women have fallen prey. MOTHER and SISTER so worship DEVIL LADY that they try to emulate her even though her hair, skin, and whiteness are the antitheses of their own blackness. BLACK MAN is appalled at the idolatry of his wig-wearing MOTHER and SISTER. "This is the nightmare in all of our hearts. Our mothers and sisters groveling to white women, wanting to be white women, dead and hardly breathing. ..." He rips the blonde wig from his sister's head and hurls it at DEVIL LADY. "Take off filth. Take your animal fur, heathen. Heathen. Heathen." The SISTER figure offers an interesting example of psychological transference. When BLACK MAN impales the DEVIL LADY a second time with his stake, SISTER screams "Oh God, you've killed me, Nigger," grabs her heart, and falls as if dead. So intense is the psychological transference of the sister that she actually believes she is killed when the DEVIL LADY dies; her self-image is so deficient that she has transferred her identity to the idealized person. Such transference results in complete ego destruction, a psychological death.

The "death" of SISTER can be viewed from a cultural as well as a psychological perspective, however; she has become so "white" (clothes, wig, attitudes) that the stabbing of the white devil has the same effect upon her as pins in a voodoo doll. At one point, SISTER refers to the dead DEVIL LADY as "my dead sister reflection," and after she revives and finds that BLACK MAN has thrown the corpse of DEVIL LADY into a pit she screams "Where's she...ooh...Where's my body...my beautiful self?...Where'd you hide me? Where's my body?" SISTER works herself into a frenzy and runs about the stage screaming. MOTHER finally soothes SISTER by feeding her some collard greens from a small pot. This action presents a parodied pieta; the grief-stricken mother attempts to restore her child through the ingestion of soul food. Significantly, the soul food comes from the bosom of the mother; a stage direction (p. 85) indicates that she extracts it "from her brassiere."

The three BLACK WOMEN in *Madheart* are used to show how different black women have survived in a predominantly white society. The older woman, MOTHER, has survived through obsequious conformance and will have nothing to do with the new social revolution. "What is wrong with the niggers, this time," she says. "I'm old and I hump along under my wig. I'm dying of oldness. I'm dying of the weight" (p. 74). When the burden of conformity becomes unbearable she, like so many of her generation, retreats into alcoholic escapism: "I slap around drunk up Lenox. Stumble down 125th into the poet who frowns at me, lost in my ways."

SISTER, on the other hand, aspires to the American dream through assimilation. Warped by her worship of the meretricious beauty of the bitch goddess, she dons blonde wigs, discotheque boots, Carnaby Street clothes, and imagines herself white. When she first sees her fallen goddess, slain by her brother, she weeps, "It's just...that I wanted to be something like her, that's all."

BLACK WOMAN, on the other hand, is, as her name implies, the new generation of Afro-American woman. Proud and defiant ("I am black black and am the most beautiful thing on the planet"), she is instrumental in BLACK MAN's gaining his own masculine identity after he has escaped the DEVIL LADY. She scorns the red and blonde wigs affected by MOTHER and SISTER, and "her natural hair cushions her face in a soft remark." She overcomes the lingering influence of the DEVIL LADY by her own natural allure. "What can I give you?" she asks BLACK MAN in a calm, loving voice. "Is there a heart bigger than mine? Is there flesh sweeter, any lips fatter and redder, any thighs more full of orgasms?" (p. 75). When BLACK MAN begins to notice the beauty of BLACK WOMAN, she tells him, "Be alive, BLACK MAN. Be alive, for me."[10] She encourages him to assert himself, to discover his manhood. "I am the black woman," she says. "The one you need...Now you must discover a way to get me back, BLACK MAN... Or you'll never... be a man. My man. Never know your own life needs" (p. 81). But when BLACK WOMAN persists and says, "You better get me back, if you know what's good for you" BLACK MAN slaps her repeatedly in the face, and forces her to kneel in submission. "Go down, submit, submit...to love...and to man, now, forever," he commands (p. 81). This scene might appear somewhat brutal, but the entire action is a symbolic ritual and the final phase in the achievement of BLACK MAN's identity. In the past, BLACK WOMAN has seen BLACK MAN humbled, has seen him crawl. He could do nothing then, but that is now over, and he must assert himself before MOTHER, SISTER, and BLACK WOMAN.

This final phase in BLACK MAN's self-realization is necessary. BLACK MAN discovers BLACK WOMAN, and finds that he loves her. But she, in her own way, tries to dominate him just as the mother and sister and the white woman had done, for she tries to prescribe his behavior. He must symbolically (and physically) dominate her so that he can become her man, and the strongest of God. Through he assistance of BLACK WOMAN, BLACK MAN has gained his identity, and he is now able to reject anything "white," even, if necessary, MOTHER and SISTER.

BLACK MAN's progress toward the achievement of his *soul*, from the initial emergence from the hold of the DEVIL LADY to the destruction of the false god's body, not only bears close resem-

---

[10]P. 76. This urgent appeal of BLACK WOMAN is contrasted with the sexual preferences of MOTHER and SISTER. "If I have to have a nigger-man," says SISTER, "give me a faggot anyday." "I know the kind you mean," replies the mother, "But...a white boy's better, daughter. Don't you forget it" (pp. 76-7).

blance to the conventions of the morality play[11] but also includes a good deal of mythology, both Christian and non-Christian. There are also present the traditional Christian concepts of the anti-Christ, post-lapsarian Adam and Eve, the sacrifice, the Eucharist (the collard greens or "soul" food), the Baptism (with the fire-hose phallus) and the messianic hope at the end of the play.

[11] Jones subtitles *Madheart* "a morality play."

Vision and Form in *Slave Ship*

by Kimberly W. Benston

When Amiri Baraka called for an "anti-Western" theatre in his post-1965 manifestoes, he spoke as both Black Power Nationalist and black visionary artist. The dramatic event he envisaged was therefore one in which black people could experience the growth toward communal identity and solidarity during the theatrical happening itself. The dramas discussed in this volume's preceding essays share the theatrical problem of communicating to an audience whose members are to be integrated into a new wholeness, of unleashing an emotional response in a community which has been treated and has seen itself as an object in a brutally impersonal system for such a long time as to have been deadened to such an appeal. These plays had only limited success in achieving this goal. But in Baraka's latest major drama, *Slave Ship,* the objectives of the "revolutionary theatre" are fully realized.

Slave Ship has no definite plot. There is very little use of discursive speech and almost no dialogue. Every theatrical device is directed toward creating an "atmosphere of feeling,"[1] one appropriate to a slave ship, the attendant horrors of the Middle Passage, and the grim consequences that comprise the history of the Afro-American experience. Baraka transforms the entire theatre into the slave ship whose black passengers' historical journey is from first enslavement to contemporary revolution, and whose mythical journey is from African civilization through enslavement to spiritual reascendancy. With the abandonment of traditional plot, Baraka

"Vision and Form in *Slave Ship*" by Kimberly W. Benston. From *Baraka: The Renegade and the Mask* (New Haven: Yale University Press, 1976). Copyright © 1976 by Yale University. Reprinted by permission of the publisher.

[1]My discussion of *Slave Ship* is based upon the text published in *Negro Digest,* April 1967, pp. 63-74 (from which all following quotations are drawn) and a performance of the play by Detroit's Concept East Theatre on November 18, 1973. Having seen Concept East's brilliant realization of the script, I can confidently assert that the possibilities and objectives evident from the text have been fully achieved where they count: in the theatre.

moves us along these historical and mythical paths by a series of tableaux and symbolic actions. It should be clear from this brief description of *Slave Ship* that any discussion of the play is immediately an interpretation. Accordingly, I shall proceed to analyze its essential motives in the hope that the simple level of action will gradually unfold.

History and Community: The Vision

Baraka calls *Slave Ship* "a historical pageant." From this alone it is clear that the play is a radical departure from the norm of Afro-American theatre which, as Harold Cruse has lamented, tends to be ahistorical[2] Baraka's abilities as a playwright, so frequently used to mount attacks upon his "grey" brethren *(Dutchman, The Slave)* and to expose the torments of heroes trapped by history (Clay, Walker), are directed in *Slave Ship* toward the formation of a nationalist historical consciousness. The Afro-American historical experience appealed to in *Slave Ship* is the product of event, memory, and communal emotion. Baraka perceives the importance of this history not so much in its "facts" as in their moral significance. For Baraka, *slavery* is the key to interpretation of Afro-American history: it is both the central, finite epoch and the general, persistent condition of Afro-American life. Appropriately, slavery is also, dramatically speaking, the condition of the audience caught with the actors inside the hold of the slave ship. The audience's consequent alienation is a perfect analogy to that of the black slave, the latter's struggle for communal identity becoming ultimately the entire theatre's concern. This struggle, which takes place in the Afro-American psyche as it does in history, accompanies the succession of "images"[3] that identify the origin, evolution, and eventual transcendence of the slave condition.

The glory of the primeval African community is the first image. The African sensibility is depicted as quintessentially religious. We witness a complex fertility rite involving the dances of warriors,

[2]"Harold Cruse: An Interview," conducted by C. W. E. Bigsby. *The Black American Writer: Vol. II* (Baltimore: Penguin Books, 1971), p. 229.

[3]I borrow this term to describe *Slave Ship's* episodic scenes from Stefan Brecht's "LeRoi Jones' *Slave Ship,*" *The Drama Review* 14, no. 2 (1970): 212-19. Though I identify a few more such "images" than does Brecht, his tripartite division of the play ("deprivation of identity, alienation, retrieval of identity") is a provocative and informative approach to which I am much indebted.

farmers, and priests; chants and praises to harvest and protective gods; the whirling dance of the masked fertility goddess; and the culminating expression of social order through a hierarchical procession leading from youngest child to head priest. The ritual is nearly complete when the white slave-trader enters, destroys the tribal harmony, and rounds up his black cargo for the Americas. The black prisoners, proud and once powerful, are dragged from their homeland calling vainly upon their gods and fighting to maintain contact with mates, children, kindred.

In the second image, the slaves are brought aboard one by one. Chains rattle, sea-smell mixes with that of excrement, women moan. Soon suffering begins to overwhelm African strength. A man curses the highest of gods, the creator *orisha* Obatala: "Where you be? Where you now, Black God?" The tribal leader, once holiest of holy high priests, attacks a black girl. Unity dissolves as old people call on God, the young for war; others are merely confused, hurt, and fearful. Worst of all, "families [are] separated for the first time." The community is fractured into an anarchy of individual wills; their isolated cries, rapes, songs, and moans define a moving, tortured existence. Whereas Baraka's earlier plays were characterized by long, illuminating orations, in *Slave Ship* he emphasizes in every way *concrete* aspects of pain, the heavy reality of chains, the screams and smells of degradation. There is horror but there is also life, and we feel it all. The agonized cry—signaling both suffering and survival—echoes in the hold while the white man howls laughter at the condition of the black people.

The third image opens to us the complexity of black life in America. The survivors of Middle Passage are herded onto land. The auction block severs man from wife, mother from child. As in the slave narrative tradition (from which Baraka draws many specific physical details in *Slave Ship*), the break-up of the family is accompanied by the emergence of cultural conflict and debasement. The latter state is portrayed by the archetypical "house-nigger," the grinning assimilationist who predicates his life upon white recognition. The epitome of Baraka's "slave" figures, he dances about the auction block for his master's pleasure and approval:

> Yassa, boss, yassa massa Tim, yassa, boss I'se happy as a brand new monkey, yassa boss, yassa, massa Tim, Yass, massa Booboo, i'se so happy, i'se so happy i jus don't know what to do. Yass, massa, boss, you'se so han'some and good and youse hip, too [...] *(Lights flash on*

slave doing [a] dance for the boss; when he finishes he bows (p. 68) and scratches).

Despite disruption of the community, the African sensibility remains in most others: the tribal rhythms, the pride, the unfetterable urge for freedom. Reverend Turner prepares plantation slaves for rebellion. Some are afraid, but the leader is resolute:

> *Slave 1.* Reverend Turner, sir, what gon' do when the massa come?
> *Slave 2.* Cut his Godless throat.
>
> (p. 69)

Yet the master's Tom betrays the conspiracy for a pork chop and, as the white man laughs in triumph, the others are crushed. The white man seems all-powerful.

The next images deepen the complexity of the African endurance in America. The Tom becomes a modern version of the housenigger, the comically "proper" Reverend who preaches a self-negating gibberish devoid of Africanisms, absent of meaning. African chants—"Moshake! Moshake! Moshake!...beeba...beeba" —are intoned against the preacher's tomming—"We Kneegrows are ready to integrate." African names—Olabumi, Dademi, Aikyele— mingle with slave names—John, Luke, Sarah. The prayer to Obatala, the African God, dies into cries for "Jesus Lord." African rhythms are beaten while spirituals rise up. Historical degradation is overshadowed by spiritual transference; African sensibility fuses itself into Afro-American culture. The call for war, for revolt, comes from the old African warrior with remembered religious invocations: "Beasts. Beasts. Ogun. Give me spear and iron. Let me kill."

The African power, always present and merely molded in the alien land for survival purposes, builds up until the liberating revolt can take place. This is the final image. The chant swells as in tribal ritual:

> Rise, Rise, Rise
> Cut these ties, Black Man Rise
> We gon' be the thing we are...
> (Now all sing "When We Gonna Rise")
> When we gonna rise/up
> When we gonna rise/up
> When we gonna rise/up
> When we gonna rise...
>
> (p. 72)

The preacher and the white man (now Uncle Sam) first ignore the rising black anger, then begin to lose confidence. The group converges upon the preacher and kills him. The white Voice's laugh, so powerful throughout the play, as in *Great Goodness of Life,* "gets stuck in his throat." His dying protest—"You want to look like me. You love me. You want me. Please. I'm good"—indicates that the reemerging Africans are killing off the insidious myths by which the oppressor controlled the oppressed.

The revolt has really been immanent throughout, from the first crossing of the gangplank to Reverend Turner's rebellion to final victory. The true victims, symbolized by the heads of the preacher-Tom and Uncle Sam, were always just waiting to be killed. At every stage of his evocation of Afro-American history, Baraka insists upon the survival of aboriginal African communalism in the black slave population. Following the black nationalist thesis of *Blues People,* he shows this survival to be a function of collective separation from the white mainstream. Thus Baraka's energetic revaluation of history does more than prophesy liberation; it teaches the audience that no complete dissolution of the black will has resulted from the inherited burdens of slavery.

Afro-American identity, then, is a function of collective impulses. From African nation practicing holy ritual to the liberating group descending en masse on the two lonely enemies, the entelechy of the black spirit is communality. Mutual concern and reverence for familial forces are the lifeblood of the black nation. A major emblem of the play might be the mother and child, murdered in the village, dying in the slave ship, separated on the auction block, but united (with the male leader) at the end. This communal power of the Afro-American sensibility is sharply contrasted with the oppressive power's individuated sense of self; the latter condition is symbolized by the single actor playing each successive white man from slave-trader to Uncle Sam.

The condition of slavery, which Baraka has chosen as the metaphor for the Afro-American historical process, is metamorphosed at the end into a celebration of liberation with the audience participating. The actors get the audience to come to the ship's center and dance to the jazz that has continued from the final death-acts. Once everyone is involved in the general festivity, the heads of the preacher and the white man are thrown amidst them. What had appeared to be didactic (if existentialized) historical drama is swiftly transmuted into an integral ritual of triumph involving the entire theatre collective. In the flow of images that comprise *Slave Ship's* "historical pageant," Baraka has left out one crucial event: Emancipation. By omitting this favorite story of textbook historians, the play tells the Afro-American spectators they are still slaves. As Stefan Brecht put it in his astute review of *Slave Ship,* "by having the slave ship be the stage, it tells [them they are] still on that boat."[4] The scene de-Americanizes the black spectators and returns them to their African roots.

Thus it might be quite helpful to think of the final communal dance in terms of African ritual. When the African dancer puts on his mask, he is divesting himself of his own identity and assuming instead the identity of the spirit for which the mask was created. The demon lives in the mask and, through it, lays a spell on all assembled, sweeps them along, fascinates them even to the point of hypnosis. Such is the nature of *Slave Ship's* final rite, for the entire assembled black community dons the mask of its ancient spirit and comes to full life as a potent, physical manifestation of the forgotten, but historically nourished, national power. In *Slave Ship,* the black nation promptly transforms itself into history, for the imitation of suffering has conferred on it a collective past and assigned it a triumphant future.

Music and Dance: The Form

In the mid-1960s, strong criticism of the Afro-American playwright's failure to make any progress toward realizing the demands of the new, music-oriented aesthetic began to emerge from various black theorists. It was pointed out that the native Afro-American theatrical form is really not a typically European dramatic form but a musical one that has its roots in such expressions as the minstrel show. Thus Harold Cruse asserted that black originality in nonmusical modes would come when "the blacks in America attempt to reclaim their musical tradition in terms of pantomime, music, movement, dance, in a theatrical form, which is more natural to them because for many years the Negro's chief form in the theatre was a musical form."[5] *Slave Ship* is the most successful dramatic work to emerge from the Black Arts Movement precisely because it "re-

[4]Brecht, p. 218.
[5]"Harold Cruse: An Interview," p. 236.

claims" and utilizes the musical base of the Afro-American genius. Baraka galvanizes a communal response to his vision by calling upon collective creation and participation in the play's musical life. However, before we can fully appreciate the ways in which music services thought (dramatic and conceptual) in *Slave Ship*, we must first briefly consider music's role in Baraka's earlier poetry and drama.

As a poet, Baraka has seen music as an integral part of the black tradition. His verse evolves from the songless deprivation of *Preface to a Twenty Volume Suicide Note* to the transcendent lyricism (both subject and style) of *In Our Terribleness*. Baraka uses musical metaphors in his poetry in several complementary ways. Music is the energy of the black spirit and the bedrock of black strength. In the mythic return to holiness, this musical energy manifests liberty, services prophecy, and signals immanent ascendance:

> Our strength is in the drums,
> the sinuous horns, blow forever beautiful princes, touch
> the spellflash of everything, all life, and the swift go on
> go off and speed. Blow forever, like the animals plants and
> sun. Forever in our universe there is beauty and light, we come
> back to it now.   "Distant Hearts"

Music aids the transformation of reality but it is at the same time the affirmation of this process. Thus Baraka speaks of "the possibilities of music" ("Leadbelly Gives an Autograph") but also, as his concerns move from personal dilemmas to communal issues, of music's confirmation of being itself (see, for example, "Planetary Exchange"). The pulse of black rhythms (not just musical, but those expressing The Life's total style) cements the multiple aspects of the black soul, communicates a lyric lightness with heavy Dionysian intuitions; rhythm—tom-tom, jazz, field hollers, street shouts, the horns of Armstrong, Trane, and the mythical Probe—represents the temporality of black existence while carrying messages from beyond. When Baraka as black poet prophesies to his brothers a better future, he portrays deliverance as

> the melody, and the rhythm
> of
> the dancing
> shit
> itself.

"For All Matter"

Energy, prophecy, judgment, affirmation, the naked thing itself—black music is for Baraka all of these at once. It is the spark of being and of needing-to-be; it makes the "total jazzman" and he makes it. In his drama Baraka has constantly used music. In *Jello,* Rochester dances soul-steps while robbing Bennie. In *A Recent Killing,* dances and songs help fill empty dramatic spaces and serve as entertainment. In *Home on the Range,* music becomes a metaphor for judgment and apocalypse in the wild "nigger" party. The most interesting use of music before *Slave Ship* is in *Dutchman,* where Lula's dance, Clay's discussion of the blues and Charlie Parker, and the Negro conductor's final soft-shoe are crucial theatrical and thematic elements of the play.

It is with *Slave Ship,* however, that Baraka elevates music to the dual position of central metaphor and primary theatrical vehicle. While this total unification of drama with music was prepared for in the visions of Baraka's poetry and in the experiments of his plays, the conceptual root of *Slave Ship's* African/American synthesis can be traced back to the basic music aesthetic explored in several of the essays collected in this volume. The drama of *Slave Ship* is fundamentally the same as that of *Blues People:* African Spirit endures Western (specifically, American) oppression and rises to perfection in musical form. The genius of Baraka's play lies in the manner in which the complex black music aesthetic is given precise theatrical embodiment.

These, then, are the primary forces that inform the nature and use of music in *Slave Ship.* As one might expect from this diverse background, music operates on many levels and in many ways to give form to Baraka's thought in the play. Every effect of feeling and every physical condition is portrayed through sound. The props call for ship "noises," ship "bells," sea "splashing," whip and chain "sounds." The slave-characters evoke the state of misery with constant moans, cries, curses—all bare intonations which, rather than describing a condition, become its essence. Baraka's observation in the poem "Ka'Ba," that "our world is full of sound," is concretized in *Slave Ship:* here, sound fully becomes the world.

The experience of the play, then, is less one of watching than of listening. If sound is the world's substance, then the particular organization of sound into music is the world in process. Music in *Slave Ship* is the form of idealized historicity as projected by the successive "pageant" images. Thus religious, civilized Africa *is* the music and dance-oriented rite of the opening image. Africa survives on the slave ship and in America in the incessant drumbeats, ritual chants, and tribal dances that remain a basic means of expression among the slaves. On the slave ship, the life of the black people is assured almost thoroughly through the rising "chant-moan of the women [...] like mad old nigger ladies humming forever in deathly patience," and in the percussional beating upon planks and walls. The white man's being *is* his hideous laughter; the entire Middle Passage is composed by Baraka as a sound-war between this laughter and the music of the black collective will (which is also internally threatened by "the long stream of different wills, articulated as screams, grunts, cries, songs, etc."). At times, the "laughter is drowned in the drums," but these moments are always followed by silence (a stand-off) or the rise of white laughter (repression). The tribal humming endures; the African civilization is brought to America with the slaves.

The musical expression of the Afro-American does not simp¹⁻ parallel history; again, it is the complexity of the slaves' alienatᴜu existence. The gospels, presaged by the patient moans of women in the hold, take over as the constant undertone of black resistance. The traitorous Tom's shuffling, jeffing "dance" represents the degradation of the masked dancer of the opening fertility rite. Yet subversively, in darkness, the pure and ancient culture remains, juxtaposed to the Tom image:

> *(Lights off...drums of ancient African warriors come up...hero-warriors. Lights blink back on, show shuffling black man, hat in his hand, scratching his head. Lights off. Drums again. Black dancing in the dark,...scratching his head. Lights off. Drums again. Black dancing in the dark, with bells, as if free, dancing wild old dances. Bam Boom Bam Bomma Bimbam Bomama boom beem bam. Dancing in the darkness... Yoruba Dance/ lights flash on briefly, spot on, off the dance. Then off.)*   (p. 68)

With the suppression of the plantation revolt, African war drums subside into "the sound of a spiritual," a song of American experience and African spirituality: "Oh, Lord Deliver Me...oh Lord." White laughter howls in triumph; for a moment, it drowns out what has now become the complex African/ American musical fusion.

Now, modern rhythms: the gibberish of the preacher-Tom takes up the gospel's "Jesus, Jesus, Jesus..."; against him; the African/ American voices sing new notes—jazz and blues scatting—and "new-sound" horns scream the old war chants. The drums persist as the unvarying keeper of the old rhythms. As the community coalesces once again, the original humming gathers and reaches toward climax. White laughter rises sporadically above the swelling sounds of chant, scream, hum, scat, horns, drums; all is "mixed with sounds of [the] slave ship." History gathers all its imagined moments in an anarchy of sonority and becomes imminently apocalyptic. The chant of "when we gonna rise/up" grows with the music; "the white man's laughter is heard trying to drown out the music, but the music is rising."

Eventually, the chant becomes song; African drums, slave-ship noises, and contemporary visionary jazz (Sun Ra, Archie Shepp) become one poem of black experience, one tangible weapon of black revolt. The preacher's voice "breaks" before he dies; the white man gasps on his laughter as the horde descends. Finally, the triumph — spiritual and physical — is expressed as dance. Again, this is an African/American synthesis, "Miracles'/Temptations' dancing line" merging with African movement in a "new-old dance": what Baraka amusingly but pointedly calls "Boogalooyoruba." The improvisational essence of this Afro-American musical sensibility becomes the ultimate statement of transcendence, and this is the audience's achievement. The quickly created "party" is an ecstasy of "fingerpop, skate, monkey, dog" in which each participant's thing is everyone's thing and individual improvisation becomes communal form: in the words of the street-wise saying, "everything is everything."

Music is thus strength, memory, power, triumph, affirmation — the entire historical and mythical process of Afro-American being. The mythical curve of return to primordial power is enacted in the dance, for the final dance of the audience in the womblike hold returns us to the site of the whirling fertility goddess. By integrating the spectator with the opening dance, Baraka has moved *Slave Ship* out of drama and into ritual; that is, he has reversed the process by which the Western (particularly Greek) theatre evolved from rite to drama. In Greek theatre, the spectators became a new and different element added to original ritual. The dance was not only danced but also watched from a distance; it became a "spectacle." Whereas in ritual nearly all were worshippers acting, the spectators added the elements of watching, thinking, feeling, not-doing. The *dromenon* or rite, something actually done by oneself, became *drama,* a thing also done but abstracted from one's doing. The members of Baraka's audience, on the contrary, are transformed from spectators of drama as "a thing done" but apart from themselves, to partakers of ritual, "a thing done" with no division between actor and spectator. Just as the opening African ritual is refashioned at the end into a higher act, one of communal triumph as well as celebration, so the audience is brought to a higher role. No longer merely observers of an oft-forgotten tradition, they themselves now perform a ritual, affirming by their deed the complete communality of the theatrical event. The collectivity of ritual has supplanted the individuation of drama.

The final rite, with its mimed cannibalistic aspect, is apocalyptic in both a mythical and a religious sense. In its mythical dimension, the ending completes the absorption of the natural, historical cycle into mythology. Its mythical movement is one of comic resurrection and integration, completed by the marriage of the spectator into community and the birth of the "old-new" black nation. This fertility ritual clearly has a religious dimension that has been prepared for by the continuous prayers to Obatala and Jesus, curses of the "Godless, white devil," and litanies such as "Rise, Rise, Rise, etc." Indeed, by creating basic images of resurrection with accompanying sensations of magic, charm, and incantation, Baraka returns the black audience to the most fundamental religious ground of tribal ceremony from which sprung the two greatest epochs of Western theatre (Greek and Christian), and which gave life to the archetypical African spirit. The spectators are as integral a part of the work as the congregation of a black Baptist church is of its service, and they function in much the same way. The nationalist myth of African-inspired renewal and Afro-American triumph is taken up by the audience because Baraka has called upon the community's shared aesthetic—the genius for musical improvisation.

This re-creation of the mythical and religious through music points Baraka's art toward the Nietzschean Dionysian state. Here the end of individuation becomes possible, for the Dionysian essence for Nietzsche was a musical one: "In song and dance man expresses himself as a member of a higher community; he has forgotten how to walk and speak and is on the way toward flying into the air, dancing."[6] By claiming African roots in their totality, the

---

[6]*The Birth of Tragedy,* trans. Walter Kaufmann (New York: Vintage Books, 1967), p. 37.

black community controls its destiny as Clay, the middle-class greyboy, could not. Now, Baraka's black heroes, not the witch-devil Lula, dance in triumph. The tragedy-burdened slave ship of *Dutchman* has become the dance-filled celebration of *Slave Ship;* musical transcendence has risen from the spirit of tragedy.

Chronology of Important Dates

1934	Everett LeRoi Jones born in Newark, New Jersey, October 7, son of Coyt LeRoy Jones and Anna Lois Jones.
1950	Graduates from Barringer High School in Newark.
1954	Graduates from Howard University in Washington, D.C.
1954-57	Service in the U.S. Air Force.
1957	Moves to Greenwich Village.
1958	Marries Hettie Cohen.
1958-63	Edits *Yugen* with Hettie Cohen.
1959	Robert F. Williams advocates armed self-defense for Afro-Americans in Monroe, North Carolina.
1960	Travels to Cuba with a group of black intellectuals.
1960-61	Whitney Fellow.
1961	*Preface to a Twenty Volume Suicide Note.*
1961-62	Edits *Floating Bear* with Diane di Prima.
1962	"The Myth of a 'Negro Literature,'" an address before the American Society for African Culture, later published in *The Saturday Review.*
1963	Murders of John F. Kennedy and Medgar Evers occur, and four young black girls are killed in a Birmingham, Alabama, church bombing. March on Washington, led by Martin Luther King, Jr., occurs. Edits *The Moderns: An Anthology of New Writing in America.* *Blues People.*
1964	Murders of civil rights activists James Chaney, Andrew Goodman, and Michael Schwerner occur in Mississippi. Obie Award winning *Dutchman* opens at the Cherry Lane Theatre, New York, in March.

The Baptism first produced at the Writers' Stage Theatre, New York, in March.

The Slave first produced at St. Mark's Playhouse, New York, in December.

The Toilet first produced at St. Mark's Playhouse, New York, in December.

The Dead Lecturer.

1965   Murder of Malcolm X occurs.

Leaves Hettie Cohen and the Village for Harlem.

Directs the Black Arts Repertory/ School.

"The Revolutionary Theatre" published in *Liberator.*

The System of Dante's Hell.

1965-66   Guggenheim Fellow.

1966   Returns to Newark and founds Spirit House.

Marries Sylvia Robinson (Amini Baraka).

A Black Mass first produced at Proctor's Theatre, Newark, in May.

Home.

1967   LeRoi Jones becomes Imamu Ameer (later Amiri) Baraka, a minister of Kawaida.

Arrest during summer disorder in Newark leading to trial, conviction, and eventual dismissal on appeal on charge of unlawful possession of firearms.

Great Goodness of Life first produced at Spirit House, Newark.

Madheart first produced at San Francisco State College.

Slave Ship first produced at Spirit House, Newark.

Tales.

Black Music.

1968   Founds the Black Community Development and Defense Organization (BCD).

Murder of Dr. Martin Luther King, Jr., occurs.

Edits *Black Fire: An Anthology of Afro-American Writing* with Larry Neal.

1969   "A Black Value System" published in *The Black Scholar.*

Black Magic Poetry.

1970   Aids Kenneth Gibson's campaign for the mayoralty in Newark.

First meeting of the Congress of African Peoples in Atlanta, Georgia.

In Our Terribleness.

It's Nation Time.

1971   *Raise Race Rays Raze.*

1972   National Black Political Convention in Gary, Indiana.
         Kawaida Studies: The New Nationalism.
         Spirit Reach.

1974   "Toward Ideological Clarity" published in *Black World*, pro-
         pounding the ideology of international socialism ("Marxism-
         Leninism-Mao Tse Tung Thought").

1976   *Hard Facts.*

1977   *The Motion of History.*

Notes on the Editor and Contributors

KIMBERLY W. BENSTON is the author of *Baraka: The Renegade and the Mask.* Presently he is at work on a study of Christopher Marlowe.

OWEN E. BRADY is Assistant Professor of Humanities at Clarkson College. He has taught at the University of Notre Dame and the University of Sierra Leone (West Africa).

CECIL M. BROWN, author of the novel *The Life and Loves of Mr. Jiveass Nigger,* now lives in Berkeley, California.

LLOYD W. BROWN, Professor of Comparative Literature at the University of Southern California, is the author of *Bits of Ivory: Narrative Techniques in Jane Austen* and *West Indian Poetry,* and is editor of *The Black Writer in Africa and the Americas.* Presently he is completing a manuscript entitled "The African Woman as Writer."

LARRY G. COLEMAN is Assistant Professor in the School of Communication and the African and Afro-American Studies and Research Center at the University of Texas at Austin. He has published in the fields of communication theory, message analysis, and performance in black culture.

RALPH ELLISON, the celebrated author of *Shadow and Act* and *Invisible Man,* is Albert Schweitzer Professor of the Humanities at New York University.

WILLIAM C. FISCHER teaches American literature in the Department of English at the State University of New York at Buffalo. He has written on Jean Toomer, Amiri Baraka, and other Afro-American literary figures.

THEODORE R. HUDSON is Professor of English at Howard University. A contributor to *Contemporary Poets in the English Language,* he is the author of *From LeRoi Jones to Amiri Baraka* and of numerous articles in a variety of journals.

LANGSTON HUGHES (1902-1967), the masterful poet, playwright, historian, essayist, critic, humorist, and anthologist, was at the heart of Afro-American culture for nearly half a century.

189

ESTHER M. JACKSON, Professor of Theatre and Drama at the University of Wisconsin, Madison, is author of *The Broken World of Tennessee Williams* and of many essays on American and Afro-American literature.

LEE A. JACOBUS is Professor of English at the University of Connecticut. His publications are primarily in seventeenth-century English literature, with recent books on John Cleveland and John Milton's *Paradise Lost.*

JOHN LINDBERG, Professor of English at Shippensburg (PA) State College, has written many essays on Victorian literature and black American literature. He is a contributing editor of *North American Review* and an associate editor of *Anima, An Experiential Journal.*

NATE MACKEY is Assistant Professor in the English and Ethnic Studies departments at the University of Southern California. His poems have appeared in such journals as *Isthmus, Gumbo, Credences, Hambone,* and the *Yardbird Reader.*

LAWRENCE P. NEAL, poet, playwright, and essayist, is the author of *Black Boogaloo* and *Hoodoo Hollerin' Bebop Ghosts,* and was coeditor with Baraka of *Black Fire: An Anthology of Afro-American Writing.* He is currently director of the Washington, D.C., Commission on the Arts and Humanities.

CHARLES D. PEAVY is Professor of English at the University of Houston. He has written several books, monographs, and articles in the fields of American and Afro-American literature and popular culture.

CLYDE TAYLOR is Head of the Ethnic Studies Department at Mills College. A Blake scholar, he has also published widely on Afro-American literature.

ROBERT L. TENER, Associate Professor of English at Kent State University, has published numerous articles on English and American drama and on dramatic theory. He is presently completing a book on concepts of space in modern drama.

SHERLEY ANNE WILLIAMS is Chairwoman of the Literature Department at the University of California, San Diego. She is the author of *Give Birth to Brightness: A Thematic Study in Neo-Black Literature* and *The Peacock Poems.* A second volume of poetry is forthcoming.

Selected Bibliography

Works by Baraka

Arm Yrself or Harm Yrself. Newark, N.J.: Jihad Productions, 1967.

The Baptism and The Toilet. New York: Grove Press, 1966.

Black Magic Poetry. New York: Bobbs-Merrill Company, 1969.

Black Music. New York: William Morrow and Company, 1967.

A Black Value System. Newark, N.J.: Jihad Productions, 1970.

Blues People: Negro Music in White America. New York: William Morrow and Company, 1963.

The Dead Lecturer. New York: Grove Press, 1964.

"The Death of Malcolm X," in *New Plays from the Black Theatre,* ed. Ed Bullins. New York: Bantam Books, 1969.

Dutchman and The Slave. New York: William Morrow and Company, 1964.

Four Black Revolutionary Plays. New York: Bobbs-Merrill Company, 1969. Includes *Experimental Death Unit #1; A Black Mass; Great Goodness of Life;* and *Madheart.*

Hard Facts. Newark, N.J.: Congress of African People, 1976.

Home: Social Essays. New York: William Morrow and Company, 1966.

In Our Terribleness. New York: Bobbs-Merrill Company, 1970.

It's Nation Time. Chicago: Third World Press, 1970.

Jello. Chicago: Third World Press, 1970.

Kawaida Studies: The New Nationalism. Chicago: Third World Press, 1972.

Preface to a Twenty Volume Suicide Note. New York: Totem Press, 1961.

Raise Race Rays Raze: Essays Since 1965. New York: Random House, 1971.

"Slave Ship: A Historical Pageant." *Negro Digest* (April, 1967), 62-74.

Spirit Reach. Newark, N.J.: Jihad Productions, 1972.

The System of Dante's Hell. New York: Grove Press, 1965.

Tales. New York: Grove Press, 1967.

Works about Baraka

I. GENERAL ASSESSMENT

Baker, Houston A., Jr. "'These Are Songs if You Have The/Music': An Essay on Imamu Baraka." *Minority Voices* 1 (1977), 1-18.

Costello, Donald P. "LeRoi Jones: Black Man as Victim." *Commonweal,* June 28, 1968, pp. 436-40.

Dennison, George. "The Demagogy of LeRoi Jones." *Commentary* (February, 1965), pp. 67-70.

Jackson, Kathryn. "LeRoi Jones and the New Black Writers of the Sixties." *Freedomways* 9 (1969), 232-46.

Margolies, Edward. "Prospects: LeRoi Jones," in *Native Sons: A Critical Study of Twentieth-Century Negro American Authors.* Philadelphia: J.B. Lippincott Company, 1968, pp. 190-99.

Munro, C. Lynn. "LeRoi Jones: A Man in Transition." *CLA Journal* 17 (1973), 57-78.

Schneck, Stephen. "LeRoi Jones, or Poetics and Policemen, or Trying Heart, Bleedin Heart." *Ramparts,* July 13, 1968, pp. 14-19.

Sollors, Werner. "LeRoi Jones (Imamu Amiri Baraka)." Stuttgart: A Kroner, 1973, pp. 506-22.

II. BIOGRAPHY

Benston, Kimberly W. "Baraka: An Interview." *Boundary 2* 6, no. 2 (Winter 1978), 303-18.

Cruse, Harold. *The Crisis of the Negro Intellectual.* New York: William Morrow and Company, 1967, pp. 355-68.

Faruk and Marvin X. "Islam and Black Art: An Interview with LeRoi Jones." *Negro Digest* (January, 1969), pp. 4-10, 77-80.

"Jones, (Everett) LeRoi." *Current Biography* (May, 1970), pp. 16-19.

Llorens, David. "Ameer (LeRoi Jones) Baraka." *Ebony* (August, 1969), pp. 75-78, 80-83.

Ossman, David. "LeRoi Jones." *The Sullen Art: Interviews by David Ossman With Modern American Poets.* New York: Corinth Books, 1963, pp. 77-81.

Reilly, Charles E. "The Former LeRoi Jones." *The Drummer,* August 17, 1976, pp. 7,21.

Watkins, Mel. "Talk with LeRoi Jones." New York *Times Book Review,* June 27, 1971, pp. 4, 24, 26-27.

III. MUSIC CRITICISM

Goldberg, Joe. "Music, Metaphor, and Men." *Saturday Review,* January 11, 1964, p. 69.

Hentoff, Nat. "The Square Route to Blues is White." *Book Week,* October 20, 1963, p. 5.

Howard, Richard. "Some Poets in Their Prose." *Poetry* (March, 1965), pp. 397-404.

Keil, Charles. *Urban Blues.* Chicago: University of Chicago Press, 1966, pp. 39-44, 56.

IV. PROSE

Brown, Lloyd W. "LeRoi Jones as Novelist: Theme and Structure in *The System of Dante's Hell."Negro American Literature Forum* 7 (1973), 132-42.

Cooke, Michael G. "The Descent into the Underground and Modern Black Fiction." *The Iowa Review* 5 (1974), 72-90.

Klinkowitz, Jerome. *Literary Disruptions.* Urbana: University of Illinois Press, 1975, pp. 102-11.

Pennington-Jones, Paulette. "From Brother LeRoi Jones Through *The System of Dante's Hell* to Imamu Ameer Baraka." *Journal of Black Studies* 4 (1973), 195-214.

V. POETRY

Breman, Paul. "Poetry into the Sixties," in *The Black American Writer: Vol. II,* ed. C.W.E. Bigsby. Baltimore: Penguin Books, 1971, pp. 99-110.

Major, Clarence. "The Poetry of LeRoi Jones." *Negro Digest* (March 1965), pp. 54-56.

Otten, Charlotte. "LeRoi Jones: Napalm Poet." *Concerning Poetry* 3 (1970), 5-11.

Sollors, Werner. "Does Axel's Castle Have a Street Address, or, What's New? Tendencies in the Poetry of Amiri Baraka (LeRoi Jones)." *Boundary 2* 6 (1978), 387-414.

Wright, Jay. "Love's Emblem Lost: LeRoi Jones' 'Hymn for Lanie Poo.'" *Boundary 2* 6, (1978), 415-34.

VI. DRAMA

Adams, George R. "'My Christ' in *Dutchman.*" *CLA Journal* 15 (1971), 54-58.

Bermel, Albert. "*Dutchman,* or The Black Stranger in America." *Arts in Society* 9 (1972), 423-34.

Brecht, Stefan. "LeRoi Jones' *Slave Ship.*" *The Drama Review* 14 (1970), 212-19.

Brady, Owen E. "Baraka's *Experimental Death Unit No. 1:* Plan for (R)evolution." *Negro American Literature Forum* 9 (1976), 59-61.

Coleman, Mike. "What is Black Theater?: An Interview with Imamu Amiri Baraka." *Black World* (April, 1971), 32-36.

Jeffers, Lance. "Bullins, Baraka, and Elder: The Dawn of Grandeur in Black Drama." *CLA Journal* 16 (1972), 32-48.

Klinkowitz, Jerome. "LeRoi Jones: *Dutchman* as Drama." *Negro American Literature Forum* 7 (1974), 123-26.

Lederer, Richard. "The Language of LeRoi Jones' *The Slave.*" *Studies in Black Literature* 4 (1973), 14-16.

Miller, Jeanne Marie A. "The Plays of LeRoi Jones," *CLA Journal* 14 (1971), 33-39.

Mootry, Maria K. "Themes and Symbols in Two Plays by LeRoi Jones." *Negro Digest* (April, 1969), 42-47.

Nelson, Hugh. "LeRoi Jones' *Dutchman:* A Brief Ride on a Doomed Ship." *Educational Theatre Journal* 20 (1968), 53-59.

Phillips, Louis. "LeRoi Jones and Contemporary Black Drama," in *The Black American Writer: Vol. II,* ed. C.W.E. Bigsby. Baltimore: Penguin Books, 1971, pp. 204-19.

Reck, Tom S. "Archetypes in LeRoi Jones' *Dutchman.*" *Studies in Black Literature* 1 (1970), 66-68.

Reed. Daphne S. "LeRoi Jones: High Priest of the Black Arts Movement." *Educational Theatre Journal* 22 (1970), 53-59.

Taylor, Willene P. "The Fall of Man in Imamu Amiri Baraka's *Dutchman.*" *Negro American Literature Forum* 7 (1974), 127-31.

Witherington, Paul. "Exorcism and Baptism in LeRoi Jones' *The Toilet.*" *Modern Drama* 15 (1972), 159-63.